P9-DXZ-560

ALSO BY BRUCE PANDOLFINI

The ABCs of Chess

Beginning Chess

Bobby Fischer's Outrageous Chess Moves

The Chess Doctor

Chess Openings: Traps and Zaps

Chess Target Practice

Chess Thinking

Kasparov and Deep Blue

More Chess Openings: Traps and Zaps 2

More Chessercizes: Checkmate!

Pandolfini's Chess Complete

Pandolfini's Endgame Course

Power Mates

Square One

Weapons of Chess

The Winning Way

PANDOLFINI'S ULTIMATE
GUIDE TO CHESS

BRUCE PANDOLFINI

A FIRESIDE BOOK
Published by Simon & Schuster
New York London Toronto Sydney

FIRESIDE
Rockefeller Center
1230 Avenue of the Americas
New York, NY 10020

Copyright © 2003 by Bruce Pandolfini
All rights reserved,
including the right of reproduction
in whole or in part in any form.

FIRESIDE and colophon are registered trademarks
of Simon & Schuster, Inc.

Designed by Katy Riegel

For information regarding special discounts for bulk purchases,
please contact Simon & Schuster Special Sales
at 1-800-456-6798 or
business@simonandschuster.com

Manufactured in the United States of America

20 19 18 17 16 15 14 13 12

Library of Congress Cataloging-in-Publication Data

Pandolfini, Bruce.
    Pandolfini's ultimate guide to chess / by Bruce Pandolfini.
        p.   cm.
    "A Fireside book."
    Includes bibliographical references and index.
    1. Chess.   I. Title: Ultimate guide to chess.   II. Title.

GV1445.P25793 2003
794.1—dc21   2003054221

ISBN 0-7432-2617-8

For my daughter Sarah, for every moment I live and beyond

CONTENTS

PROLOGUE

Chess, The Universal Game

Somewhere back in time, human beings invented chess. Ever since, men and women have tried to explain their fascination for, attraction to, even obsession with a checkered board and its symbolic figures. A struggle of will, a contest of intellects, the vicissitudes and intrigue of power relationships, childhood delight, and just plain fun—chess can stand for it all.

Chess reflects the real world in miniature. Endeavor, struggle, success, and defeat—they are part of each game ever played. Thomas Huxley, the scientist who helped Darwin write the theory of evolution into nineteenth-century philosophy, said: "The rules of the game are what we call the laws of nature. The chessboard is the world" and "The pieces are the phenomena of the universe."

Ben Franklin, possibly the best American chessplayer of his time, also believed that the chessboard constituted a microcosm of the real world. Studying chess had practical value, he argued. Understanding the moves, rules, and structure of the game encouraged the development and training of essential intellectual skills such as inductive and deductive reasoning, long-term planning, and creative problem-solving. Plenty of present-day educators who have studied the effects of chessplaying on other disciplines have added their approval to Franklin's words. Once again Old Ben was on to something ahead of the pack.

Chess is more than a game. It's a universal tale of interlocking relationships, layered thinking, analytical drive, and an intuitive sense of how things work. It's mathematical yet musical, logical but theoretical. It can be art or sport, contest or dream, fantasy or reality. Whatever the game's ultimate significance, perhaps you've picked up this book hoping to go beyond the moves and rules to exploring some of the game's aura and seductive mystery.

What better way to learn the universal game than through a universal learning process? Almost as soon as a child begins to talk, it starts asking questions, many unanswerable. In this book, a teacher uses Socratic methods to reveal the fundamentals of chess interactively, in give-and-take conversations with a rather challenging student. We learn through their question-and-answer sessions. Their debates over chessic possibilities make up the chapters. And each chapter constitutes an actual chess lesson—on the game's moves and rules; on opening, middlegame, and endgame structure; on principles, tactics, and strategy; and on anything else germane to the improvement of chess skill that might come up.

Since we learn best by doing, the teacher in this book illustrates chess essentials by using an instructionally created but perfectly natural game. White and Black, teacher and student, discuss their choices and reasoning just as players would if they were going over a real game—by considering options, variations, and possibilities throughout.

What makes their game different is that it doesn't emphasize the state-of-the-art moves grandmasters play and seldom bother to explain. Rather, it includes a normal mixture of good, reasonable, and even bad moves that inexperienced players are likely to consider. Furthermore, the moves and their respective variations, though shown in clear diagrams that everyone can understand, are also expressed conversationally, in asides and as thoughts seem pertinent. That's just the way players converse about chess in any country of the world. To avoid confusion from the real game's moves and their analytic alternates, boldface is used for actual moves, and ordinary type for moves that are possible but not played.

Most introductory chess books offer lofty principles, presenting them as if they're inviolable absolutes in a grand narrative. But those learning the game naturally have many questions about the other side of things, when particular principles don't apply and the story takes unexpected twists and turns.

Pandolfini's Ultimate Guide to Chess offers an abundance of principles, but it also devotes time to their exceptions and subtle colors—the very things that make the game and those who play it distinctive. Furthermore, because we're dealing directly with principles and their exceptions, our teacher and student may take a second or even a third look at an idea throughout the course of the game. No lesson is wholly and completely digested in one try anyway, and the flow of the book's discourse reproduces this reality. Repetition is a crucial part of typical learning, and this text aims to capture the natural feel of the learning process. To this end, the dialogue includes the constant use of instructional reinforcement, as well as the sort of typical banter and lighter moments integral to the interactive exchange of question-and-answer learning.

This book partially draws on ideas in my earlier publications. But over time, experience teaches us how to compose more precise formulations and more effective presentations. *Pandolfini's Ultimate Guide to Chess* uses an innovative framework to show you exactly what you need to know in order to understand how chess is played, and how it ought to be played. Reading it should help equip you with the tools required to play and enjoy a challenging game of chess, even if you're starting from a position of knowing relatively nothing about pawns or society's metaphors for them. As you absorb specific chessic knowledge, you'll acquaint yourself with valuable analytic weapons that can be used to sharpen your approach, not only for playing chess, but for any intellectual endeavor whatsoever.

While you're luxuriating in the joy of pure mental stimulation, perhaps even learning how to beat someone you've never quite been able to beat before, you might also pick up on something else: how *not* to beat yourself. How many games can offer all this and be as rewarding as all that?

LESSON 1

In the Beginning

THE MOVES AND RULES

Teacher: Let's not set up the board just yet.

Student: Why not?

Teacher: Because we should start at the beginning.

Student: And where's that?

Teacher: It's hard to say. Maybe wherever myth, stories, and history happen to intersect. Before *Alice in Wonderland* but after *The Book of the Dead*. Inside Samuel Beckett's play *Endgame* or on the screen with Humphrey Bogart in *Casablanca*.

Student: Chess is our culture?

Teacher: East or West. Take the moral of this particular chessic fairy tale as an example. According to the story, the game was created by the philosopher Sissa, a Brahmin. The sage's aim was to teach a rich and despotic king a valuable real-life lesson. In the game, the king learns he can't win without marshaling all his forces. From the game he learns that he can't rule without the support of his subjects.

Student: Is that the only explanation?

Teacher: Not by a long shot. Chess has its own mythology—about the game's origins, its proponents and players, and even its very purpose. But no one really knows who invented chess. Some historians claim the Greeks invented the game; others say the Egyptians should be given the credit. The Chinese, the Persians, the Jews, the Irish, and the Welsh have their champions, too. There are even chess quotes attributed to Heraclitus and Aristotle, but they are clearly the result of some pretty imaginative rewriting of history.

Student: Why?

Teacher: Both men were dead centuries before the game had ever been conceived.

Student: Okay. So when do we think the big chess bang occurred?

Teacher: Most authorities believe chess is a descendant of *chataranga,* a game played in western India, probably sometime between the fifth and sixth century A.D. We're fairly sure the *chataranga* pieces paralleled segments of the Indian army of the time. From the get-go, the figures apparently represented real-world counterparts and imitated them in the way they moved. For example, the *ratha,* or chariot, which, in some cases, was a *roka,* or boat, moved up and down or across and was positioned in the corner at the game's start. It became the rook in chess. The *asva,* or horse, became the knight, with movement exactly like today's knight, remaining unchanged for the past fourteen centuries. And the *padati,* or infantryman, moved one square forward. In chess it became the pawn.

Student: So chess is an Eastern thing?

Teacher: Well, at least an Indus Valley thing. Traveling mainly with itinerant merchants, it didn't really reach Europe until the late Middle Ages, and from there was brought to America a few centuries later. But no one in the New World knew much about it before Benjamin Franklin penned America's first chess book. Here, take a look at it.

Student (*reading*): "The game of chess is not merely idle amusement. Several very valuable qualities of mind, useful in the course of human life, are to be acquired and strengthened by it." Cool. Did Franklin really write this?

Teacher: He certainly did. In any case, we probably won't ever know how and when chess was created for sure. Some aspects of chess probably evolved from earlier games, including the board itself. Playing surfaces with differently colored squares can be traced back to some of the most ancient board games ever found, even to the discoveries at Ur from around 4000 B.C. But some of chess's key concepts may have been generated spontaneously at a much later time. Not necessarily by men, either.

Student: Actually, I've seen medieval paintings of women playing chess.

Teacher: Some observers have claimed that the game's creators could have been women, sitting at home or in the court, taking part in a form of mock war by emulating the fighting going on for real somewhere else. But to date, I'm afraid all this entertaining conjecture about the game's origin has yet to prove anything conclusive.

Student: Is there anything I can accept for sure about chess?

Teacher: Absolutely. For example, the moves and the rules. Now let's take out the board and have a look. Chess is played by two people on a board of sixty-four squares, of which thirty-two are light and thirty-two are dark. There are eight rows of eight squares each. The squares appear in three kinds of rows: (1) files, the vertical rows (diagram 1); (2) ranks, the horizontal rows (diagram 2); and (3) diagonals, the slanted rows of one color (diagram 3).

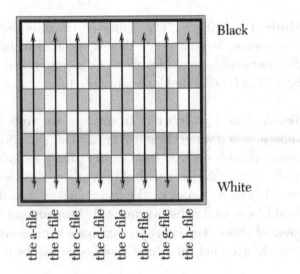

Black

White

the a-file the b-file the c-file the d-file the e-file the f-file the g-file the h-file

Diagram 1. Files.

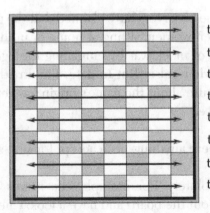

the 8th rank

the 7th rank

the 6th rank

the 5th rank

the 4th rank

the 3rd rank

the 2nd rank

the 1st rank

Diagram 2. Ranks.

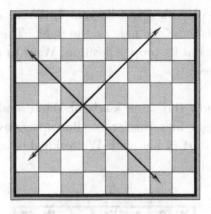

Diagram 3. Diagonals.

Teacher: Files are lettered **a** through **h**, beginning from White's left. Ranks are numbered **1** through **8**, beginning from White's nearest rank. The players sit on opposite sides of the board, next to their forces. Pieces occupy first ranks (diagram 4).

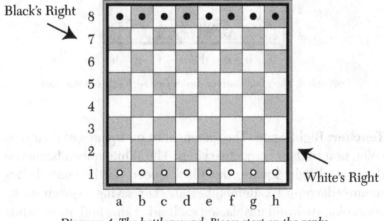

Diagram 4. The battleground: Pieces start on the ranks marked by bullets.

Student: Those are the ranks closest to each player?

Teacher: Right. The pawns occupy second ranks, the next rank in for each player. There should be a light square in the near corner at each player's right (diagram 4). There are a couple of sayings: "light is right" or "light on the right." They will help you place the board in its proper position. Want to guess how the pieces are placed?

Student: I know the same kinds of White and Black pieces begin on the same files. Black rooks line up against White rooks, Black knights start in line with White knights, and so on (diagram 5).

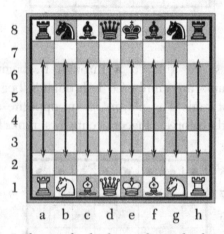

Diagram 5. The same kinds of pieces face each other at the start.

Teacher: Right again. The queens start on squares of their own color, next to their respective kings. The White queen begins on the central light square, the Black queen on the central dark square (diagram 6). Remember another saying, "queen on its own color," to avoid misplacing each side's king and queen when setting up. If the board is placed correctly, with a light square on the right, the queens can be placed correctly and centrally, on their own color.

Teacher: Now let's set up the whole board. Make sure that light squares are on each player's right hand, the queens are on their

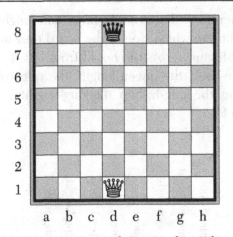

Diagram 6. Queens start on their own colors: White on light,
Black on dark.

own colors, and all White and Black pieces line up directly across
from each other (diagram 7).

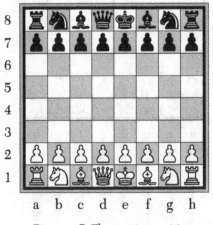

Diagram 7. The starting position.

Student: I've heard players referring to the queenside and
kingside when they talk about chess. What do they mean?

Teacher: In chess parlance, we sometimes want to be able to
refer to pieces and pawns according to their position at the start

of a game. Therefore, the rooks, bishops, and knights are often named according to which side of the board they are on in the initial setup. Moving across the board from left to right, you'll find the queen-rook, the queen-knight, the queen-bishop, the queen, the king, the king-bishop, the king-knight, and the king-rook (diagram 8).

Diagram 8. The descriptive names of the pieces.

Student: What about the names of the pieces? Do they change based on where they go?

Teacher: The name of the piece never varies, no matter where it's moved in the course of a game. The king-rook is always the king-rook, even if it winds up on the queenside of the board.

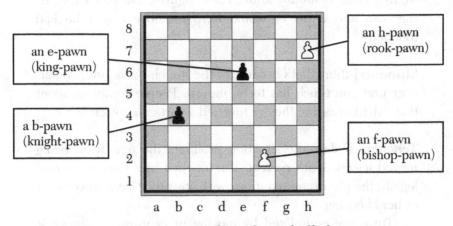

| an e-pawn (king-pawn) |
| an h-pawn (rook-pawn) |
| a b-pawn (knight-pawn) |
| an f-pawn (bishop-pawn) |

Diagram 9. Pawns are named according to the file they are on.

Student: When I watched a game, players took turns moving one piece per turn, in one direction per turn.

Teacher: And White always moved first. All moves must conform to the rules. If a move violates a rule, it's illegal and must be replayed with a legal move, using whatever unit was touched.

Student: Why don't you say, "whatever piece was just touched?" Using the term *unit* makes it sound so military.

Teacher: Chess is a war game. But don't be confused by that. By war game, I don't mean a game revolving around medieval pageantry, with knights dressed in shining armor, going through tournament maneuvers and the like. Nor am I talking about staged battles, where players reenact famous confrontations. Rather, I'm referring to the way certain games are won—by capturing or destroying something in particular. In this sense, chess is a war game, which is won by "capturing" the other side's king. Also, chess parlance differentiates between pieces, which include everything but the pawns, and pawns, which are therefore not pieces. That's why we'll use the word "unit" when we're talking generally about chess figures. Do you know, by the way, why a player would have to move a unit he had touched?

Student: I think that's because of the "touch-move rule." Whatever unit you touch has to be moved. People complain about that, whether or not they've touched a particular piece.

Teacher: Unless the situation prohibits the unit from being moved legally, that's correct. If a touched unit can't be moved legally, the player may continue with any other legal move of his or her choosing.

Turns are completed by moving or capturing. A move is defined by the transfer of a unit from one square to another. A capture is the replacement of an enemy unit by a friendly one. In chess, units are not jumped. A captured unit is taken from the board and can no longer participate. No move or capture is compulsory unless it's the only legal play. Players capture enemy units, not their own. A unit may capture any enemy unit, if it's a legal move. Two units can never occupy the same square. Two units can't be moved on the same turn.

Student: Unless you're castling.

Teacher: True. That's the only time two units move at the same time, but we'll get to that shortly. Let's continue with what we can accept for certain: Two enemy units can never be captured on the same move. In the course of a game, all sixty-four squares can be used for legal moves and captures. Each side starts with a force of sixteen units: eight pieces and eight pawns. The lighter-colored force is called White and the darker Black, regardless of their actual colors. Each unit moves according to prescribed rules. Each side's eight pieces consist of one king, one queen, two rooks, two bishops, and two knights.

Student: You said eight pieces for each side. Don't you mean sixteen?

Teacher: No, eight. As I've said, everyday language allows us to refer to pawns as pieces, the specific terminology of chess doesn't. None of the pawns are counted as pieces, and when chessplayers talk about material, which means the combined or relative value of playing units, they always distinguish between pieces and pawns. So there are sixteen units per side, but only eight pieces per side. Okay, now it's time to explain how each unit moves.

Student: All right. Could we start with the king?

Teacher: It's the royal thing to do. Kings move or capture by going one adjacent square in any direction: horizontally, vertically, diagonally, backward, or forward. In capturing, they simply make their move and replace whatever occupies their destination square.

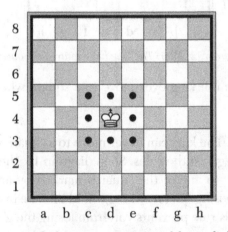

Diagram 10. The king can move to any of the marked squares.

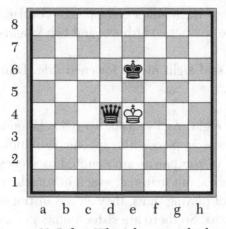

Diagram 11. Before: White's king can take the queen.

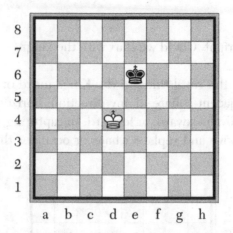

Diagram 12. After: The king has captured the queen.

Student: Can the king ever move to a square where it can be captured?

Teacher: No. The king can never move to a square where it can be taken. It's against the rules. So in diagram 13, the White king couldn't move to any of the squares marked by an X because either the opposing queen or king would then be in a position to capture it. This rule prevents you from losing the game in some foolish ways.

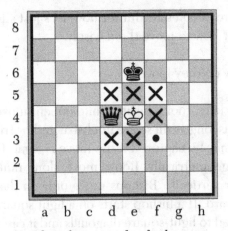

Diagram 13. White's king can only take the queen or move to the square marked by a bullet.

Student: What about the expression I've heard, that "a king can't take a king"? Doesn't this allow me to move my king next to the enemy king with impunity?

Teacher: The expression doesn't come from chess but from people trying to encapsulate chess in convenient rules of thumb that aren't quite right to begin with. It's true that a king can't take a king in a practical sense, because a king isn't ever allowed to move into position to be taken by another king. The actual rule is that you're not permitted to expose your king to capture at any time. Therefore, it's not possible for a king to be moved close enough to the enemy king to be captured by it. That's why a king can't take a king. My advice? Forget that expression altogether.

Student: Is there a similar restriction on other pieces as well? Are they also not allowed to move to squares where they can be taken?

Teacher: No, you can legally move them where they can be taken, though in most cases it doesn't make sense to expose them to capture needlessly. But for now, let's just stick with how they move, not how to move them wisely.

Student: How do they move?

Teacher: The king, rooks, bishops, and queens move along prescribed paths as long as these are unobstructed by friendly units. Enemy units may be captured if the move is legal. Here, it may help to think geometrically. Rooks move along ranks and files, horizontally or vertically. Bishops move only on diagonals, forward or backward. If a bishop starts on a light square, its movement is confined to light-square diagonals and it can never move to or capture on a dark square. The opposite is true for a bishop beginning on a dark square. It can never move to or capture on a light square. The queen possesses the powers of a rook and bishop combined. It moves in any direction in a straight line along as many unblocked squares as desired. If an enemy unit is captured, that always ends a move, no matter which unit makes the capture or is captured.

In diagrams 14–19, the White piece can move to any of the marked squares.

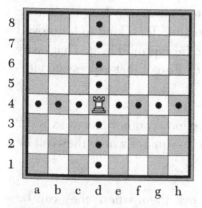

Diagram 14. The rook has fourteen different possible moves from d4.

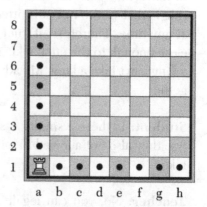

Diagram 15. On an otherwise empty board, the rook always has fourteen different possible moves.

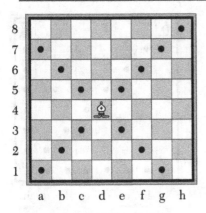

Diagram 16. The bishop has thirteen
different possible moves from d4.

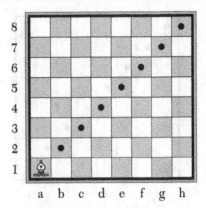

Diagram 17. The bishop has seven
different possible moves from a1.

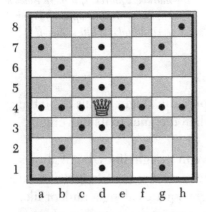

Diagram 18. The queen has 27
different possible moves from d4.

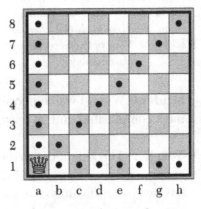

Diagram 19. The queen has 21
different possible moves from a1.

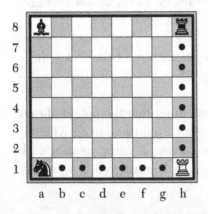

Diagram 20. White's rook may
move to any of the marked squares.
White's rook may also take either
Black's rook or knight. Neither
capture is compulsory. If it were
Black's turn, either the bishop or
the rook could take White's rook,
though neither has to.

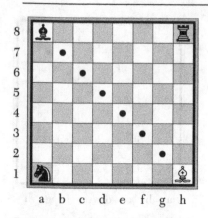

Diagram 21. White's bishop may take Black's bishop or move to any of the marked squares. If it were Black's turn, Black's bishop could take White's bishop, which could also be taken by Black's rook. None of the pieces have to take anything.

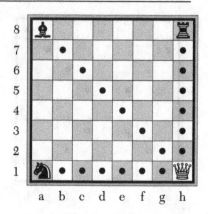

Diagram 22. White's queen may take any of Black's pieces or move to any of the marked squares. If it were Black's turn, either the bishop or the rook could take White's queen.

Student: When I watch people play, the knight seems to be the most complicated unit, at least when it comes to its movement.

Teacher: The knight doesn't move in straight lines, but it always makes a move of the same distance and design. A knight's move has two parts. It can go two straight squares along a rank or file, then move one square at a right angle; or one square along a rank or file, then two straight squares at a right angle. The full move, from start to finish, backward or forward, left or right, looks like the capital letter L.

Student: They're tricky little creatures, aren't they? Anything else I should know about them?

Teacher: It might help if you remember that the knight always lands on a square of a different color from the one on which it started. If it moves from a light square, it must go to a dark square; if it moves from a dark square, it must go to a light one.

Because it's the only piece that can jump over obstacles, the knight can move and capture regardless of intervening friendly or enemy units, as if they didn't exist. Nothing can block a knight.

Student: Does this mean that the knight's unique jumping ability makes it the only piece that can move in the opening position?

Teacher: Yes, because a knight can scale the obstructing pawns. Other pieces can't move until pawns are moved out of the way.

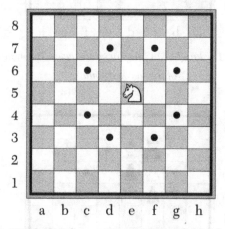

Diagram 23. The knight can move to any of the marked squares.

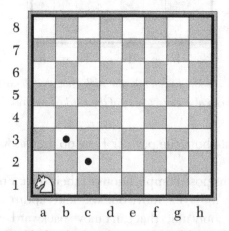

Diagram 24. The knight can move to either of the marked squares.

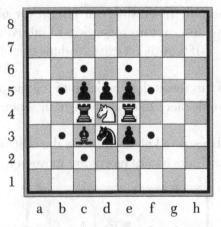

Diagram 25. The knight can jump over obstacles. It can move to any
of the marked squares.

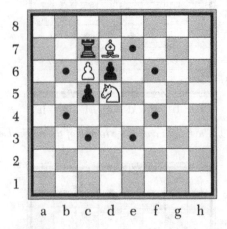

Diagram 26. The knight can take the rook, though it doesn't have to.
It can also move to any of the marked squares.

Student: What about the pawns? How do they move?

Teacher: Pawns pose complications of their own. For one thing,
they're the only units that move one way and capture another way.
They're also the only units that can't move backward or to the side.
They move one square straight ahead, except for a two-square

option on each pawn's first move, but they capture one square *diagonally* ahead. They can't capture straight ahead. Therefore, anything occupying the square immediately in front of a pawn prevents it from moving straight ahead. As I've just indicated, each pawn has an option on its first move: It can move either one or two squares forward. After its first move, however, it can never move two squares again, even if it didn't go two squares initially.

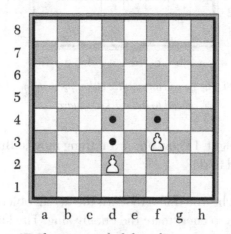

Diagram 27. The pawn on the left, at d2, can move one or two squares. The pawn on the right, at f3, can move just one square.

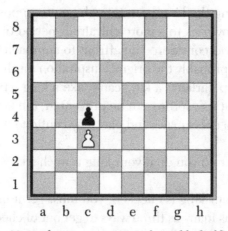

Diagram 28. Neither pawn can move, being blocked by the other.

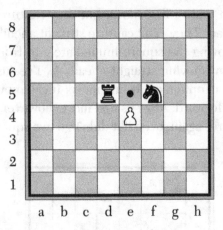

Diagram 29. The pawn can capture either piece or move straight ahead to the marked square.

Student: All right, I know how everything moves. But now what am I supposed to do?

Teacher: Maybe you'd like to learn the actual object of a chess game, which is to checkmate the enemy king. The king is *checkmated* when it's under direct attack, threatened by capture, and its capture on the next move cannot be prevented. The game ends at that point, without the capture actually taking place. This rule—not taking the king even though you're in position to—is probably a throwback to a more chivalrous period of human history, when it was considered an affront to approach the king directly. It's also probably the original inspiration for the expression you brought up earlier: "a king can't take a king." If the king is threatened, but its capture can be prevented, the king is merely *in check*, not in checkmate, and play may continue.

Student: What do you do if your king is in check?

Teacher: If your king is checked, you must get it out of check. There can be as many as three ways to get out of check. You can, if the situation legally allows it, (1) move the king to safety, where it can't be captured; (2) block the check by putting a friendly unit in the way; or (3) capture the checking enemy unit. You can choose any method to end the check, if it's legally available. If there's no way to stop the check, it's checkmate, or simply mate, and the game is over.

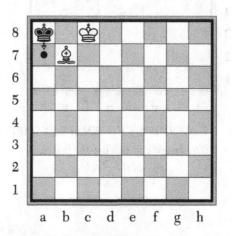

Diagram 30. AVOIDING CHECKMATE BY MOVING: The Black king can get out of check by moving to the marked square, a7.

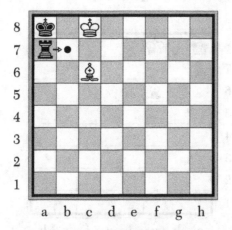

Diagram 31. AVOIDING CHECKMATE BY BLOCKING: The rook can block the check by moving between the Black king and the White bishop to the marked square, b7.

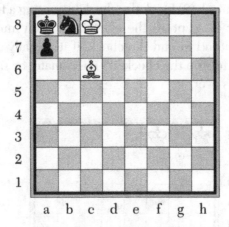

Diagram 32. AVOIDING CHECKMATE BY CAPTURE:
The knight can capture the bishop
to end the check.

Three Examples of Checkmate:

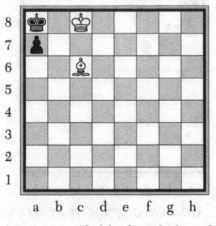

Diagram 33. Black has been checkmated.

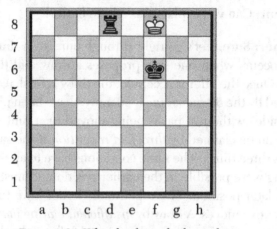

Diagram 34. White has been checkmated.

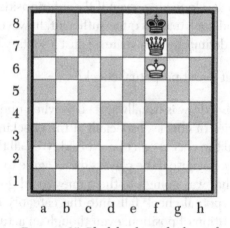

Diagram 35. Black has been checkmated.

Student: Does someone always have to win? Does the game ever end in a tie?

Teacher: Yes, but we don't call it a tie. We call it a *draw*. There are six ways a game can end in a draw: (1) agreement; (2) the 50-move rule; (3) threefold repetition; (4) insufficient mating material; (5) perpetual check; or (6) stalemate.

Student: Can you explain this a little better?

Teacher: Sure. Let's go right through our list. A draw by *agreement* occurs when one side proposes a draw and the other accepts. Once the offer is accepted, the draw is final. A draw can be claimed by the *50-move rule* if 50 moves have been played (50 for each side) without a pawn being moved or a unit captured. A draw can be claimed by *threefold repetition* if the same position occurs three times. The same conditions have to apply—that is, if castling were possible in the earlier position, it must be possible in the later position. The repetitions do not have to happen on consecutive moves. A draw by *insufficient mating material* occurs if neither player has enough material left to checkmate, even with the other side's cooperation. For example, a king and a bishop can't beat a lone king, even if the inferior side is trying to lose. A king-and-rook team is quite sufficient, however. Together, they can most definitely force mate against a solitary king.

Student: What about perpetual check?

Teacher: Such a draw is usually agreed to when one side begins an endless series of checks, especially if the checking side can't force mate and the checks can't be averted. We call this situation *perpetual check* because if the players didn't agree to a draw once it was clear what was going on, the game would go on forever. Ultimately, perpetual check falls into the category of draws by threefold repetition of position, even though an actual threefold repetition doesn't necessarily occur. It's understood that eventually the position would surely be repeated three times without either player getting anywhere, so the players agree to draw because a draw is inevitable. Once it becomes clear a player intends to check perpetually to force a draw, the players generally end the game right there, splitting the point. This means that, in a tournament, each player would get half a point for drawing. A full point would be awarded for a victory, and nothing for a loss.

Student: Any more points to draw on?

Teacher: A draw by *stalemate* occurs if the side to play has no legal move with any unit whatsoever but is not in check. Even if one side has vast material superiority, stalemate can occur if the other side is not in check but doesn't have a legal play. In fact, luring the opponent into an "accidental" stalemate is often a losing side's last hope.

Student: I better make note of that, just in case.

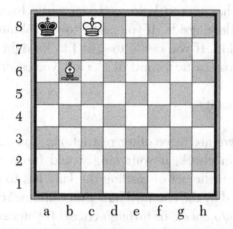

Diagram 36. If it's Black's move, the game is drawn.
Black has been stalemated.

Teacher: Let's review distinctions: You are in check if your king is under direct attack but there's a way or ways to get out of check. You're checkmated if your king is under direct attack—in check—and there's no way to get it out of check. You're stalemated if you're not in check but don't have a legal move.

Student: I've heard that castling is a way to try avoiding checkmate. How so?

Teacher: The time has come to explain a very special rule. *Castling* is also an integral part of strategy, which we'll discuss later. For now, let's just concern ourselves with the rules. Castling is the only situation in which you can move two pieces on the same turn. Start by assuming that the king and at least one of your two rooks have not left their original squares. Now, if nothing occupies the squares between your king and that rook, you may castle. It doesn't matter which rook, as long as your king and that particular rook haven't yet moved. The move of castling has two parts. You castle by: (1) moving your king two squares along the rank toward the rook; and then (2) moving the rook in question next to the king on its other side. You can castle using either rook, provided nothing is in the way and neither the king nor the castling rook has moved before. If you castle toward White's right, you castle kingside. If you castle toward White's left, you castle queenside. If you castle toward Black's right, you castle queenside. If you castle toward Black's left, you castle kingside.

Student: Is that it?

Teacher: There are three other restrictions. You can't castle if your king is in check, if your king would be in check after castling, or if in the act of castling the king has to pass over a square attacked by the enemy. Think prepositions: You can't castle *in* check, *into* check, or *through* check. If you can get out of check without moving the king or the rook, and that means either capturing the checking piece or blocking the check with your other forces, you may still castle on future moves, assuming the move is then legal.

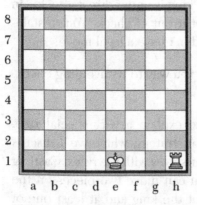

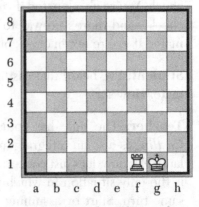

Diagram 37. *Before White castles*   Diagram 38. *After White castles*
            kingside.   *kingside.*

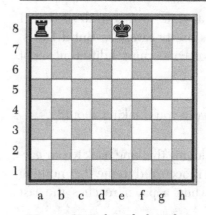

Diagram 39. Before Black castles queenside.

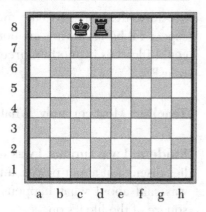

Diagram 40. After castling queenside.

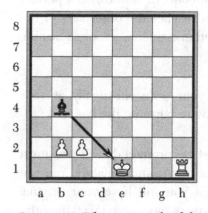

Diagram 41. White can't castle while in check.

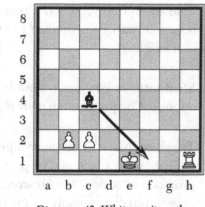

Diagram 42. White can't castle through check.

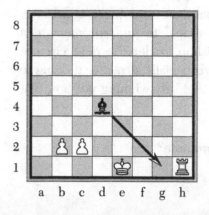

Diagram 43. White can't castle into check.

Student: It's going to take me a while to digest all of that. I expect I'll be reviewing my notes pretty carefully. But if I may, could I lead us in another direction concerning a different set of rules?

Teacher: Most certainly. What were you thinking about?

Student: I was curious. I was suddenly thinking back to our earlier discussion about pawns, and it occurred to me that nothing was said about what happens when a pawn reaches the last square of the file it's on.

Teacher: That's a very important concern, and this is a perfect time to explore it. When a pawn reaches the other side of the board, it must be *promoted* to either a queen, a rook, a bishop, or a knight.

Student: So you can't thumb your nose chessically at your opponent by just leaving your pawn a pawn on the last rank?

Teacher: Nope. The pawn must be promoted, and you must indicate what piece you're promoting to immediately. You can promote to a new queen even if you still have your original queen. You can promote to any type of piece, even if all the original pieces are still on the board. This way, you can have two, three, or more queens, rooks, bishops, or knights, in any combination. The choice is yours. Usually, an extra queen is decisive. But sometimes it might be desirable to *underpromote* to a knight, or even to a rook or bishop, under the right circumstances. Promoting to a knight is especially attractive if doing so gives immediate checkmate, or a clearly winning position that leads inevitably to checkmate.

Student: How do you actually promote?

Teacher: After you advance the pawn to the final square on the pawn's file, you replace the pawn with something else. Either you take the new piece from one of the previously captured pieces, or lay the promoted pawn on its side and stipulate what it is to become by saying it aloud. To distinguish it thereafter, assuming you can't find a replacement piece of some kind, you might try any of several other things. You could, for instance, wrap a rubber band around the promoted pawn. You could put tape on it. Or you could even tie a piece of string to it.

Student: I've seen people use upside-down rooks.

Teacher: That's another way to go. Players often use a previously captured rook to represent a new queen by simply turning it upside down. You may even be able to borrow a piece from another chess set, but remember to return it at the game's end. Most of the time, though, pawns promote during the final stages of the contest, when previously captured pieces are readily available, so what you're looking for can possibly be found in your opponent's stash of captured pieces.

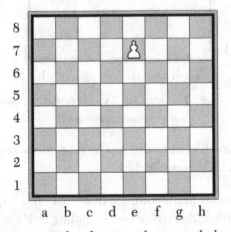

Diagram 44. Before the pawn advances to the last rank.

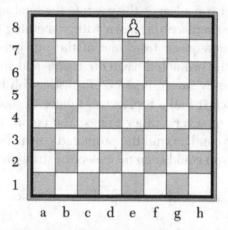

Diagram 45. The pawn has just advanced to the last rank.
The move isn't completed yet.

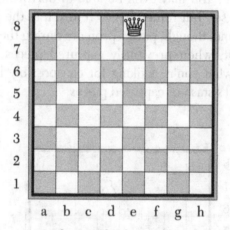

Diagram 46. The pawn has been promoted to a queen,
and the move is completed.

Student: I think it's beginning to dawn on me why pawn movement can be a little complicated.

Teacher: It's even more complex than that. You'll get a greater sense of the difficulties we've been alluding to if we turn our attention to another distinctive rule, also applying only to pawns. I'm referring to *en passant*, which is a special kind of capture that

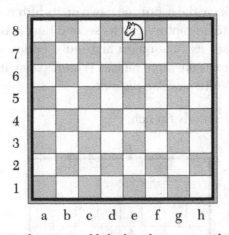

Diagram 47. The pawn could also have been promoted to a knight, a
rook, or a bishop. Here it has been promoted to a knight.

involves just pawns, one White and one Black. The pawns must occupy adjacent files. One pawn captures and the other is captured. The pawn that captures must be on its fifth rank counting from its side of the board. The pawn to be captured must start on its second rank, counting from its side of the board.

Student: Okay, what happens?

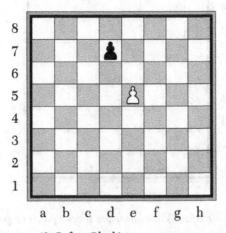

Diagram 48. Before Black's pawn moves two squares.

Teacher: Let's say the capturing pawn on its fifth rank is White's and the pawn to be captured on its second rank is Black's. If the Black pawn uses its two-square first-move option so that after moving it occupies the same rank as White's pawn, it can be captured by the White pawn *en passant*.

Student: That sounds French.

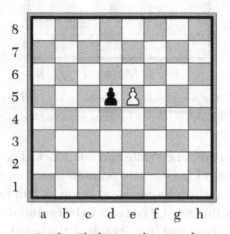

Diagram 49. After Black's pawn has moved two squares.

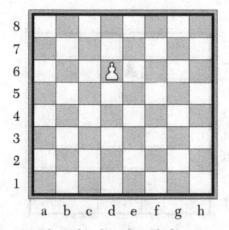

Diagram 50. After White has taken Black's pawn en passant.

Teacher: It's French, and it means "in passing." The White pawn takes the Black pawn as the Black pawn tries to pass the White, capturing the Black pawn as if it had moved only one square, not two. There's a further and important requirement: *En passant* captures must be exercised on the first opportunity or the option is forfeited.

Student: I think this is another section I'll be reviewing later on. Let me change direction again, if I may. Many players seem to write their moves down.

Teacher: And that's important. Chessplayers record their moves using a system of letters and numbers that name each square on the board. There are two popular systems: the descriptive, used in many older chess books; and the algebraic, used in most chess books published since the mid-1970s. We'll use the latter here. In fact, we already began doing so a while back.

Student: I've noticed those symbols here and there and wondered. Is learning algebraic notation going to be as problematical as understanding pawn moves?

Teacher: Actually, it's easy once you get the hang of it. In the algebraic system, the board is viewed as an eight-by-eight grid. Every square has a unique name based on the intersection of a file and a rank. You remember, I'm sure, that files, the vertical rows of squares, are lettered *a* through *h*, beginning from White's left. Ranks, the horizontal rows of squares, are numbered *1* through *8*, beginning from White's nearest rank. Squares are named by combining letters and numbers, the letter being lowercase and written first. So in the starting position, White's king occupies e1 and Black's king occupies e8. All squares in the algebraic system are named from White's standpoint.

8	a8	b8	c8	d8	e8	f8	g8	h8
7	a7	b7	c7	d7	e7	f7	g7	h7
6	a6	b6	c6	d6	e6	f6	g6	h6
5	a5	b5	c5	d5	e5	f5	g5	h5
4	a4	b4	c4	d4	e4	f4	g4	h4
3	a3	b3	c3	d3	e3	f3	g3	h3
2	a2	b2	c2	d2	e2	f2	g2	h2
1	a1	b1	c1	d1	e1	f1	g1	h1
	a	b	c	d	e	f	g	h

Diagram 51. The algebraic grid. Every square has a unique name.

Student: Besides letters and numbers, there are other symbols, too, right?

Teacher: In addition to the letters and numbers that identify each square on the board, chess notation uses symbols to represent each unit as well as specific chess operations, like capturing enemy units or checkmating the king. The names of pieces are often abbreviated using capital letters: *K* for king; *Q* for queen; *R* for rook; *B* for bishop; and, to avoid confusion with the symbol for king, *N* for knight. Some books still use the older *Kt*.

Student: And for the pawns, do you use a *P*?

Teacher: Pawns are another matter. No letter is necessarily used to designate a pawn in recording unless there's a practical reason to use *P* or *p*, usually either for instruction or in order to delineate a position. If a move is given without a capital letter, say d3, the reader should assume that a pawn is doing the moving. By the way, you might want to copy these symbols onto an index card, which you can also use as a bookmark.

OTHER USEFUL SYMBOLS

K	king
Q	queen
R	rook
B	bishop
N	knight
-	moves to
x	captures
+	check
#	checkmate
0-0	castles kingside
0-0-0	castles queenside
e.p.	*en passant*

Student: Could you show specifically how to write down a move?

Teacher: Let's say, at the very beginning of a chess game, that White moves his kingside knight from g1 to f3. Both players would write on their score sheets 1. Nf3. The *1.* introduces White's first move; *N* stands for the knight, the moving piece; and *f3* is the name of the arrival square. Note there's a period and space between the *1* and the *N*, by the way.

Student: Suppose White's fourth move is the capture of a black pawn on d4 with a knight from f3?

Teacher: In the full version of move recording, this move would be written 4. Nf3xd4. The *4.* indicates it's White's fourth move; *N* means a knight does the moving; *f3* is the square of departure; *x* means it's a capture; and *d4* is the name of the arrival square, the square on which the capture takes place.

Student: I'm not sure everybody writes all that stuff. Some seem to write less.

Teacher: Most veteran chessplayers tend to abbreviate their notation by dropping the departure square, so that 4. Nf3xd4 could be written as 4. Nxd4. Others abbreviate even further, to 4. Nd4. In their more experienced minds the capture on d4 is implied and need not be symbolized.

Student: Probably I should use the longer version of recording until I feel comfortable enough to shift to the shorter methods of writing down moves. But I'm still a little mixed up about using or not using the *P* to indicate pawn captures.

Teacher: Generally, no indication need be given that a pawn is captured, or that it does the capturing, even if you use the form of recording that signifies what's being captured. If an *x* is used to indicate a capture, readers infer that some unit has been captured, and this notation will provide enough information for the reader to correctly play the move on the board. You can see what's being captured merely by going to the correctly indicated square. Most people aren't going to read chess moves in their heads. Instead, they're going to play them on the board. As a result, they will see exactly what has occurred. If, for example, White captures a black pawn on d5 with his e4-pawn, that move could be written e4xd5.

Student: I'm getting the idea. No letter has to be used to designate a pawn, if the sense of the move is totally clear.

Teacher: Quite so. Many players even use personalized symbols for some of these transactions. That's usually okay as long as they remain consistent and if others, such as tournament directors, can follow the score once it's been explained to them. After all, recording is just another mode of communication. Chess games, by the way, are not just recorded by writing down moves made by White or Black, but also by commentary. Some of this commentary comes in words, but a lot of it takes the form of more symbols. Below are some of the most common symbols for analytical assessments and statements about the game.

SOME SYMBOLS FOR COMMENTARY

!	good move
!!	very good move
!?	probably a good move
?!	probably a bad move
?	questionable move
??	blunder
1.	White's first move
1 . . .	Black's first move (when appearing independently of White's)
(1-0)	White wins
(0-1)	Black wins

Student: I feel a bit tired just thinking about all this.

Teacher: Learning how to read and record a chess game may seem a daunting task, but it's as helpful to assimilating chess as understanding how to conjugate verbs is to mastering a language. Chessplayers record their moves for various reasons, especially in tournament play.

Student: What are some of those reasons?

Teacher: Chessplayers notate to (1) pace themselves and monitor their rate of play during a tournament or clock game; (2) make sure they don't forfeit on time; (3) reduce blundering by writing moves down before they are played to check for potential mistakes and observe their opponent's reactions; (4) enable others to learn and benefit so that the game itself can evolve, which pertains especially to strong masters; (5) look back on one's personal playing history; (6) become conversant with reading chess moves, in order to study and improve; (7) show the games to someone—mainly a teacher—to learn from one's errors; and (8) settle disputes.

Student: How about playing a quick game?

Teacher: Rather than playing a quick game, why don't I show you one—in fact, the shortest game possible. It's only two moves: two for White and two for Black.

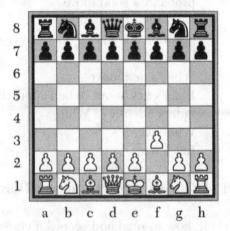

Diagram 52. 1. f2-f3 (White's first move). White moves the pawn from f2 to f3.

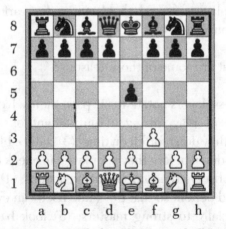

Diagram 53. 1 . . . e7-e5 (Black's first move). Black moves the pawn from e7 to e5.

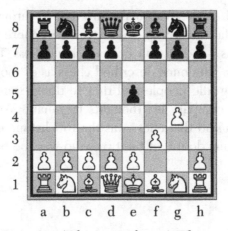

Diagram 54. 2. g2-g4 (White's second move). White moves the pawn from g2 to g4.

Diagram 55. 2 . . . Qd8-h4# (Black's second move). Black moves the queen from d8 to h4. This is checkmate.

Student: That was fast. I suppose you could beat me that quickly.

Teacher: Actually, I probably couldn't, especially now that I've shown you what not to do. But you'd be surprised. Good players don't always win so quickly. Sometimes they take longer than expected, so they can make sure not to throw away their advantage or fall for a trap. Funny thing is, there are a lot of misconceptions—and misconceivers—about chess. Take George Bernard Shaw, who once described chess as a "foolish expedient for making idle people feel they're doing something very clever." Then compare his thoughts to Johann Wolfgang von Goethe's, who said that chess was the touchstone of the intellect. Is there any doubt, of the two, who was the better chessplayer?

LESSON 2

Arming for Attack

NON-MATING TACTICS

Teacher: So those are the moves and rules. Now that you know how to play, you'll want to learn how to play well.

Student: How did you know that?

Teacher: Just a gut feeling. But let's agree to operate on this assumption: Any statement you make about chess is open to question. The game is home to infinite variety, and any rule, principle, or theory is subject to the changes such variety can impose. At one point, a chessic principle may seem to answer a positional problem. At another, it may be of no help whatsoever.

Student: No wonder chessplayers talk like philosophers.

Teacher: The best chessplayers question even the right moves. The greatest philosophers leave no statement unexamined.

Student: It sure takes some concentrated thinking to get good at this game.

Teacher: And you need tools to win—not just the rules of the game, but helpful principles, guidelines, and tactics. Just be prepared. There's only one thing in chess that's beyond any doubt.

Student: Checkmate?

Teacher: That's right. With that said, let's start discovering pathways to the only chess conclusion that can be called a final one. We'll begin with tactics.

Student: And they are?

Teacher: Tactics are winning ideas. They refer mainly to a local opportunity rather than an overarching, long-term goal. They're almost always employed after one side has made a mistake. Once you see an inaccuracy, however slight, you may be able to take advantage of it immediately by using a specific tactical weapon. Other times, you might have to make a few moves to set up your use of a given tactic. Many tactical ideas are designed to gain material advantages, because having greater material is usually the easiest way to win. Other tactics lead directly to checkmate. Tactics gaining material fall into the class of *non-mating tactics.* Those resulting in mate are obviously called *mating tactics.* For the remainder of this discussion we'll focus chiefly on non-mating tactics.

Student: How do I use non-mating tactics?

Teacher: First, get familiar with them. After you've learned some fundamental tactics, you can begin to use them in your own games to win enemy units and get the better of exchanges. In order to perform these tasks, you must be acquainted with the relative value of the pieces. As a rule, whenever considering any transaction of forces, try to give up less than you get back. Take a look at the chart. It lists the chess worth of all units except the king, which is not assigned a numeric value because the rules prevent it from being taken or exchanged at any time.

TABLE OF RELATIVE VALUES

Pawns are worth	1
Knights are worth	3
Bishops are worth	3
Rooks are worth	5
Queens are worth	9

Student: How should I interpret this chart?

Teacher: According to the chart, and aside from even-up trades, you should be willing to surrender a pawn for any piece; a knight or a bishop for a rook or a queen; a rook, a bishop, or a knight for a queen; a bishop and a knight for a queen; a rook and a knight or a rook and a bishop for a queen; or a rook for a bishop and a knight. Using this system as a guide, you can reliably analyze most tactics materially.

Student: Are there many different non-mating tactics to think about?

Teacher: There are many, but we're going to limit our discussion to eleven separate categories of tactics. These eleven cover the game's tactical brass tacks for winning material. We'll start with *en prise.*

Student: That's another one of those French terms.

Teacher: Chess is international. But yes, this specific term is French. It means "for the taking." A unit is *en prise* if it's unguarded and under direct attack so that it can be taken at no cost to the capturer. If a unit is *en prise* we say it's *hanging,* or that it can be taken *for nothing* or *for free.* I should warn you, though. Chessplayers are like anyone else, and they may alter a word's meaning so that it can imply more than the original definition would logically suggest. *En prise* can refer simply to an unguarded and defenseless unit. It can also signify the act of capturing that unit.

Student: Can anything be *en prise*?

Teacher: Any unit can be *en prise* except the king, which can never be captured. If a king is in position to be captured, that's checkmate, and the game ends there.

Student: I see you've set up a position. What is it you want from it?

Teacher: I'd like you to take a look at it. Notice that whoever moves can take the other side's bishop for nothing.

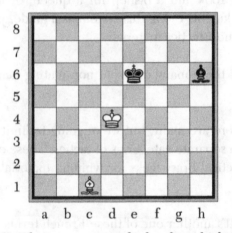

Diagram 56. Whoever moves can take the other side's bishop for free.

Student: I think in this position I'd want it to be my turn. But I have a question about something else. What's a fork?

Teacher: A *fork* is not just silverware. It, too, is a tactic. You give a fork when one of your units attacks two or more enemy units with the same move. Sometimes only one of the enemy units can be saved, sometimes neither of them can. All units can fork. All can be forked. The queen is the best unit for giving forks, since it can strike in all directions. But the pawn gives perhaps the most serious forks. Whatever it attacks, it can capture without loss of material, even if the unit to be captured is already protected, because nothing is less valuable than a pawn.

Student: Is this position a fork?

Teacher: This next diagram shows a knight forking Black's queen and rook. I'm leaving the kings out of the diagram so you can concentrate on the concept.

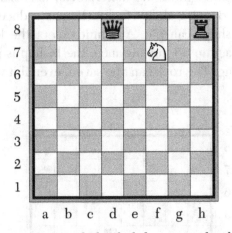

Diagram 57. The knight forks queen and rook.

Student: I see. If one of the two attacked Black pieces moves to safety, my knight is still in position to capture the other. I'll make sure to look for forks in my own games.

Teacher: And while you're looking for forks, you might also start looking for pins. The *pin* is a straight-line tactic that usually involves three units: an attacker and two defenders. All three units occupy the same straight line, which means the same rank, file, or diagonal. In a pin, the attacker threatens an enemy unit that shields a more valuable enemy unit along the line of attack. The unit closest to the attacking unit is pinned to the unit behind it. Either the pinned unit can't be moved off the line of the pin legally, or it can't be moved without incurring disadvantage or actual loss of material.

Student: How do you win with a pin?

Teacher: Sometimes the shielding pinned unit is captured with material gain. In other cases, the pin renders the shielding unit helpless, so that it can be attacked and won by other attacking units. At still other times, no material can necessarily be won, but the pinned unit's ability to function is reduced. Queens, rooks, and bishops can pin. Any unit except the king can be pinned. In diagram 58, for instance, the bishop is pinning the rook to the king. The rook can't be saved, even if it were Black's move.

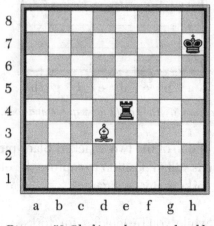

Diagram 58. Black's rook is pinned and lost.

Student: Now that's an obvious but nasty pin.

Teacher: Some pins are more intricate than that, and it can take a few moves to experience their full worth. As I've just said, sometimes you don't capture the pinned unit at all. Rather, you pile up on it with other forces, until it can't be defended adequately. And there are times when the pin doesn't win anything. It's just maintained to limit the other side's options. In diagram 59, Black's knight is pinned to its queen and also attacked by a pawn. The knight is lost in a practical sense. If it moves, Black's queen could be taken by White's rook. Since the knight can't move without even greater loss, the pin gains the knight.

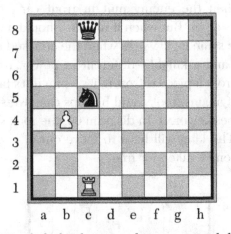

Diagram 59. Black's knight is pinned to its queen and also attacked by a pawn. If the knight moves, the rook can take the queen.

Student: Are there other cool ways to win material besides forks and pins?

Teacher: Well, there's the *skewer,* which is another straight-line tactic. Like a pin, it also involves one attacker and two defenders. But unlike a pin, the shielding defender is not frozen in place. Rather it's attacked and practically chased out of the way, either exposing the defender behind to capture or aiming for use or control of a key square on the same line. In a pin, the attacker is first in line, the less valuable defending unit is second, and the more valuable defending unit is third. In a skewer, the attacker is first, the more valuable defending unit is second, and the less valuable one is third, although for some skewers, the defending units can be the same, such as two knights, or instead can have the same value, such as a bishop and a knight.

Student: Could you distinguish further between pins and skewers?

Teacher: When the enemy unit in front can't or shouldn't move, then it's a pin. But when it must or should move, then it's a skewer. The same logic works when the attacked enemy units are a bishop and a knight—different in power, but similar in value. If the front a piece is frozen, it's a pin; if it's being chased, it's a skewer. Queens, rooks, and bishops can give skewers, and all units can be skewered. In diagram 60, the rook skewers king and bishop. The king will have to move out of check, and the bishop can then be taken for free.

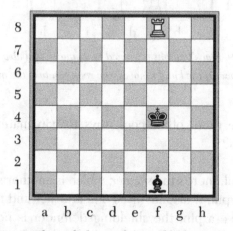

Diagram 60. The rook skewers king and bishop. After the king moves out of check, the bishop can be taken for free.

Student: All these tactics are appealing, but is there one with a little bit more surprise to it?

Teacher: Many players are charmed by the *discovered attack* or *discovery*. That's a third type of straight-line tactic. Unlike pins and skewers, however, the discovered attack involves two attackers and only one defender along the primary line of aggression. One attacker moves, the other stays stationary. The moving unit unveils the stationary unit's attack on a defending unit or to an important square. The stationary unit gives the discovered attack.

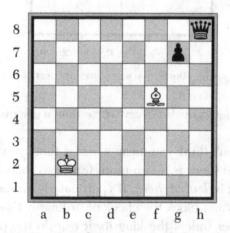

Diagram 61. By moving the pawn to g6, Black attacks the bishop and unveils a discovered attack to the king from the queen, which is also a check.

Student: I've heard people refer to discoveries in slightly different ways. Are there different kinds of discoveries?

Teacher: There are several different kinds. A more deadly form of discovery is *discovered check*, like Black's queen delivers to White's king after the pawn moves in diagram 61. Discovered check occurs when the stationary part of the discovery winds up giving check to the enemy king, once the moving part of the dis-

covery makes any move at all. In diagram 62, a bishop move
undrapes a discovered check from Black's queen.

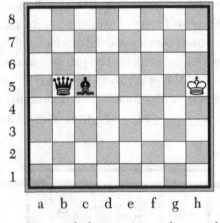

Diagram 62. Any bishop move gives discovered check.

Student: Is there any discovery worse than a discovered check?

Teacher: I don't think you mean worse. I think you mean more
deadly. Indeed there is. Even more ferocious than a single discovered check is *double check*. It's particularly insidious because
the defender can't block the check or ordinarily take one of the
checking pieces unless the king itself can do the taking on an
adjacent square. Usually the defender's only legal recourse is
to move his own king out of check, which may include taking
one of the two checking enemy units if possible. Double check
can often lead to significant material gain or even checkmate.
Although the main thrust of this section is the gain of material through non-mating tactics, discoveries can lead to some
remarkable mating positions, as you can see in diagram 63. By
moving the bishop to b5, White dispenses double check and
mate.

Student: Could you go over which pieces can do what in a discovery?

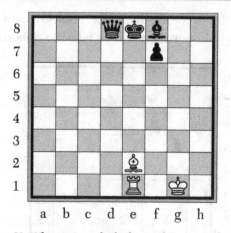

*Diagram 63. White moves the bishop to b5, giving double check
and mate!*

Teacher: Queens, rooks, and bishops can be the stationary components in a discovery. Every unit except the queen can function as the moving attacker.

Student: Why is it that the queen can never be the moving part of a discovery?

Teacher: Because if there were an attacking queen in front to start with, it would already be giving a direct attack or posing an immediate threat. No line-piece behind the queen could reveal a power the queen doesn't already possess and therefore issue.

Student: Is there a piece that's impervious to discoveries?

Teacher: No, there isn't. Every unit is capable of being exploited by a discovery, either by the stationary attacker, the moving attacker, or both. Let's look at another position. In diagram 64, the bishop can take the pawn at b5, attacking the queen. The same bishop move produces a discovery from the white rook to the black king. Since this is discovered check, Black doesn't have time to save his queen because he must first save his king. First comes first. After Black moves his king to safety, White's bishop will be able to take the queen for free.

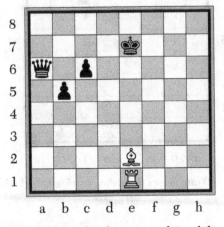

Diagram 64. The bishop takes the pawn on b5 and the rook simultaneously gives discovered check.

Student: That would be a royal disaster.

Teacher: Enough about discoveries. Here's another way to make life hard for your opponent. It's called *undermining*. A unit is undermined when its protection is captured, driven away, or immobilized. Then it can often be captured for free. When a unit's protection is captured, let's say by an even exchange, the tactic is also known as *removing the defender* or *removing the guard*. Any unit can undermine an enemy unit. All units except the king can be undermined. In diagram 65, the defense of Black's knight is undermined when White's rook takes Black's. After the pawn takes back the rook, White's bishop then takes the knight for free.

Student: Whew. I'm beginning to feel like a tactical wizard.

Teacher: Try conjuring up this tactical concept: the *overload*. A unit is overloaded if it can't fulfill all its defensive commitments. A typical instance is when a unit tries to guard two friendly units simultaneously. If one of the threatened units is taken, the defending unit may be pulled out of position when it recaptures.

Diagram 65. White undermines the knight by first exchanging rook for rook.

This might leave the other friendly unit unguarded, so that it could be taken for free, or inadequately supported, so that it can be exploited in some way. All units can become overloaded. Every unit can be lost by an overload tactic, except the king.

Student: Could you give an example?

Teacher: Diagram 66 below shows a pawn guarding a bishop and a knight, which are both, in turn, attacked by the White

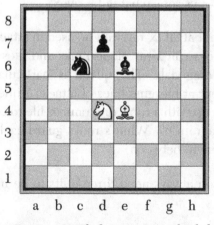

Diagram 66. Black's pawn is overloaded.

knight. The pawn is overloaded. White can gain a piece in either of two ways, both involving the overloaded Black pawn. If Black's knight on c6 is taken by White's bishop on e4, and the pawn on d7 takes back, the bishop on e6 is left unguarded and can be captured for free by the knight on d4. Or, instead, if the Black bishop on e6 is first captured by the White knight on d4, and the Black pawn then takes back on e6, White's bishop on e4 would be able to capture the Black knight on c6 for free. Through either variation, White gains a minor piece.

Student: It may be an overload, but I'm close to overdose.

Teacher: We're almost done with our introduction to the tactical life. I'd like you to learn about the *x-ray*, or *x-ray attack*, which some people call a *hurdle*. The basic kind of x-ray, though not the only kind, involves two units of one color and one of the other, all three occupying and having the ability to move along the same line. A typical lineup would be, for example, (1) a White unit; (2) a Black unit; and (3) a White unit, in that order. If either White unit is captured by the Black unit, the other White unit could take back. Thus unit (1) defends unit (3), and unit (3) defends unit (1), even though unit (2) is in the middle. Units (1) and (3) provide x-ray support, by protecting each other right through the Black unit.

Student: Are x-rays somewhat defensive?

Teacher: No, not at all. X-rays can be used in attack or defense. Queens and rooks can x-ray along ranks and files; queens and bishops along diagonals. The queen is particularly effective because it's adept at merging lines of attack. A queen can use a diagonal to join up with a rook, or a rank or file to converge with a bishop. In diagram 67, White's rooks guard each other, even with a Black rook in between.

Student: Do you always need three units to be involved in an x-ray?

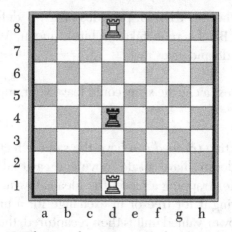

Diagram 67. White's rooks protect each other through Black's rook.

Teacher: Sometimes the x-ray doesn't concern three units on the same straight line, but two units and a key square on the line in question. In this instance, the x-ray might consist of (1) a White unit; (2) a Black unit; and (3) a key square the White unit guards and/or influences through the Black unit. I'm going to give you an example of a mating attack instead of a non-mating one in order to demonstrate the idea more clearly. In diagram 68, White can force checkmate by checking with his queen on

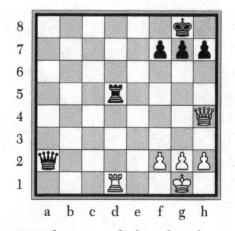

Diagram 68. White's queen checks on d8, with x-ray support
from the rook at d1.

d8, knowing that his d1-rook provides an x-ray defense of the queen. After Black's rook takes White's queen, White's rook takes back on d8 and gives mate.

Student: I guess a chessic x-ray could leave your opponent a little exposed.

Teacher: Getting *trapped* can have the same effect. A piece is trapped if it doesn't have a safe move and can't adequately be protected. After trapping a piece, the idea is to win it by direct attack, capturing it for free or in exchange for a unit of lower value. If the lower-valued unit is then recaptured, the attacker—the trapper—still comes out ahead.

Student: What should a trapped thing do?

Teacher: Often the only remedy left to the trapped unit is to sell its life as dearly as possible, taking the most valuable unit in sight, even if that's only a pawn. Even a pawn is something, and that's generally better than nothing. Every unit can be trapped

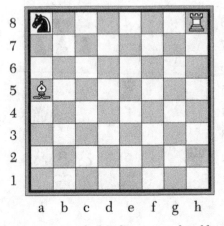

Diagram 69. The knight is trapped and lost.

and won. When it happens to the king, the game is over by checkmate. In diagram 69, the knight is trapped by the bishop and attacked by the rook. The knight is lost.

Student: You said "even a pawn." But what about promotion, when a pawn can grow up to become a more imposing piece? In addition to being a rule, could promotion also be considered a tactic?

Teacher: You're right. The pawn's ability to advance and promote upon reaching the last row can be a vital tactical weapon. Like most tactics, the ability to execute this particular one usually depends on some or several mistakes by your opponent. You probably wouldn't enjoy seeing an enemy pawn make it to your own side of the board.

Student: I guess not. Does promotion always win?

Teacher: No, not automatically, though promotion generally decides a game unless the dynamics of the situation are quite extraordinary or the other side promotes immediately afterward. But even in such cases where both sides promote, the side promoting first usually wins. Of course, let me also point out that promotion tactics can be non-mating or mating. Here we're not so interested in promoting to give checkmate as we are to gain material.

Student: You've just said that promoting usually wins. But at the end of the movie *Searching for Bobby Fischer,* I recall that the boy who promoted first actually lost the game.

Teacher: Learning chess is like learning a language. There are the rules, and then there are the exceptions. Here's another illustration with a surprising twist. Most of the time, players promote a pawn to a new queen because an extra queen is almost always decisive. But there are times, as we've already adumbrated, when less force is better and it's more effective to underpromote to a rook, a bishop, or a knight.

Student: I get it. Less can be more.

Teacher: Believe it or not, there can be possible drawbacks to making a new queen. In a situation in which you are clearly winning, you shouldn't promote to a queen if doing so draws the game by stalemating your opponent, or even by giving him the mere opportunity to stalemate. Why take unnecessary chances? In such cases, when you need to promote to a piece that still enables you to win while avoiding a stalemate, it may be better to delay promotion or to underpromote to a rook.

Student: An extra rook should win, right?

Teacher: Are you kidding? You should almost always win with an extra rook—that is, if you're playing chess and know how to play it. But there are times when promoting to a rook might not be prudent either—for example, if doing so gives stalemate or misses out on an opportunity that only a knight could provide. Bear in mind that a knight can do what a queen or a rook can't: it can give a forking knight check or a knight checkmate. Clearly there are instances when it's preferable to underpromote to a knight—when less is most definitely more.

Student: Okay, when should I start thinking that more could be less?

Teacher: As is practically always the case in chess, it all depends. Most of the time, direct promotion to a queen will win. But clearly, as our discussion has shown, sometimes it's better to choose something other than the queen.

Student: Could you just show a typical promotion, without a fancy underpromoting theme?

Teacher: Be glad to. In diagrams 70–72, White's pawn advances to the last rank and promotes to a queen, giving checkmate.

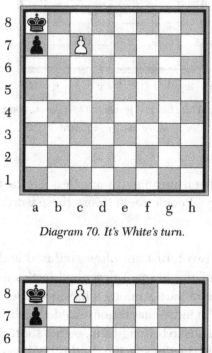

Diagram 70. It's White's turn.

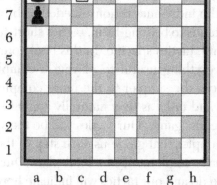

Diagram 71. White has just advanced the pawn to the last rank,
but has not completed the move.

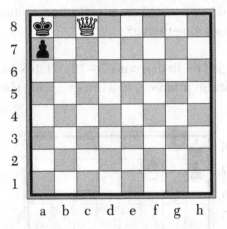

Diagram 72. White has just promoted to a queen, completing the move and giving mate.

Student: I've been meaning to ask this: Are tactics the same thing as strategy? People seem to use these words to mean the same thing.

Teacher: The two terms are often confused and misused. At the beginning of the lesson I described tactics as local operations. For the most part, strategy refers to an overall plan, while tactics signify the individual actions needed to bring about that plan. Strategy tends to be long-term, tactics short-term. Strategy is usually general, tactics specific. In this book, our strategy will be to cover everything useful to playing a complete game of chess, going from the simpler to the more complex, examining specific tactics and tasks as they naturally apply to the developing stages of a chess game. Our tactics will be the specific explanations and examples that guide us each step of the way, so that we can eventually implement our total plan. Our strategy will show us what to do and our tactics will indicate how to do it. But that's enough for now. A Bobby Fischer can't be created in one lesson. Sometimes it takes three, four, or even more.

MATING PATTERNS

Teacher: What is the real goal of a chess game?

Student: To win, which means giving checkmate. Most of the time, it's the only goal.

Teacher: Vince Lombardi once said winning was the only thing. While checkmate is the obvious goal, there are others, such as learning how to think with discipline and with enthusiasm. Practically speaking, your tactics and strategy should work toward checkmate. Intellectually, your goal should be a better brain.

Student: So chess combines the sportical with the cortical?

Teacher: There's a thought. Now back to this one, all right? We've just spent some time discussing individual non-mating tactics that can be used throughout the game to gain material. We can do the same kind of thing with *mating tactics,* also known as *mating patterns* or *mating nets.*

Student: How?

Teacher: Let's start with the basics. Usually, a few chess units are needed to give mate. One unit checks the enemy king, while others keep it from escaping. Sometimes only one unit is needed to give the mate, and on occasion the opponent's own forces obstruct escape and are part of the arrangement. However it comes about, the result is called a mating pattern. A successful chessplayer has a stockpile of mating patterns.

Student: How many are there?

Teacher: At least hundreds, in all their variations. But we don't need to know that many in order to proceed or play a worthwhile game of chess. Let's take a look at a few examples in order to get the hang of it. In diagram 73, you'll find a mating pattern involving the queen and bishop, sometimes called a *crisscross mate*. Examine the position carefully and make sure that the Black king can't avoid being captured on the next move, remembering that the king is never allowed to move into check. Then explain to me why this position constitutes checkmate.

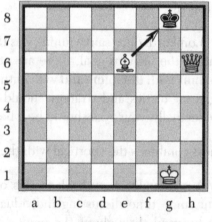

Diagram 73. A crisscross mate.

Student: It's mate because the White bishop checks the Black king, the White bishop can't be blocked or captured, the Black king has no safe escape square, and the Black king would be captured on White's next move—if the rules of the game didn't require the game to end right now by checkmate, without another move being played.

Teacher: Very good. Can you see how White can mate Black in one move in the next diagram? Here's a hint: In all problems of this kind, start by looking for moves that check the enemy king.

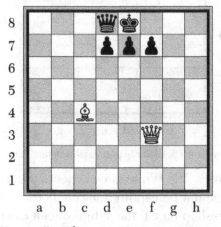

Diagram 74. White can give a support mate at f7.

Student: I don't think it's right to take on f7 with the bishop, even though it's protected by the queen, because the king could get out of check by moving to f8. No, the right answer must be Qxf7#.

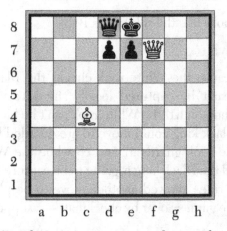

Diagram 75. White gives a support mate, the queen being protected by the bishop.

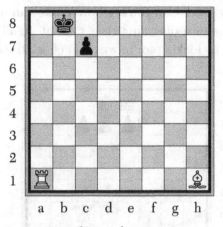

Diagram 76. White to play, mates in one move.

Teacher: Correct. The White queen checks the Black king, the White queen cannot be captured legally because it's protected by the White bishop on c4, the White queen can't be blocked, there are no escape squares for the Black king, and the Black king would be captured on the next move if the game didn't stop here—which it does. Since the White queen is supported in its invasion by the bishop at c4, this type of mate falls into the support mate category. Now in diagram 76, White can mate Black in one move. How does White do that?

Student: It looks like the solution is Ra8#.

Teacher: Why?

Student: Because the White rook checks the Black king, the White rook can't be captured legally since it's protected by the White bishop on h1, the White rook can't be blocked, all the squares the Black king could move to are guarded by White, in that the White rook guards a7 and c8 while the White bishop guards b7, and the Black king is going to be captured on the next move—if the rules allowed another move to be played, which they don't. The game is over by checkmate—a support mate.

Teacher: Great. You're ready for a test. Let's see if you can figure out twenty common mating patterns. Cover the answer dia-

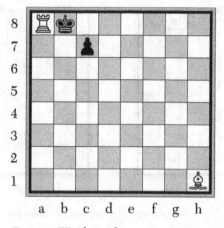

Diagram 77. The rook gives a support mate.

gram on the right and figure out which piece can be moved in the diagram on the left to mate the Black king in one move. Study the diagrams closely—they show how units work together to give mate. Notice that units not directly involved in the mating patterns are not shown, which is why the White king is sometimes absent. Let me know how you scored when you're finished, all right?

Student: Actually, *you'll* have to let me know how I've done.

Teacher: Actually, I think there's a good chance you'll know before I say anything.

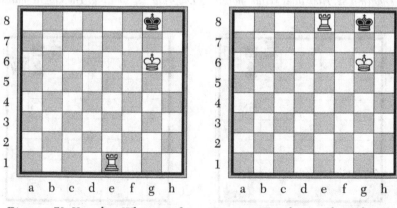

Diagram 78. How does White mate?   *Diagram 79. Solution: The rook mates.*

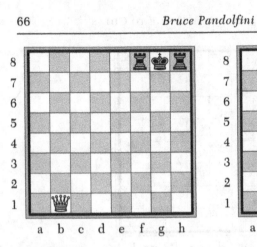

Diagram 80. *How does White mate?*

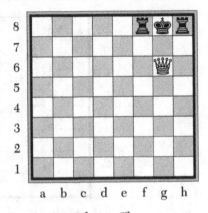

Diagram 81. *Solution: The queen mates.*

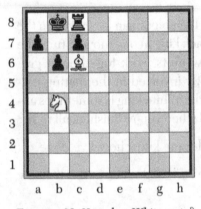

Diagram 82. *How does White mate?*

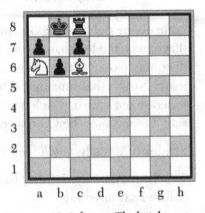

Diagram 83. *Solution: The knight mates.*

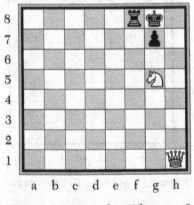

Diagram 84. *How does White mate?*

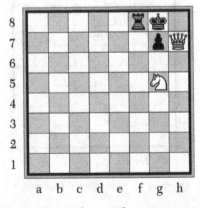

Diagram 85. *Solution: The queen mates.*

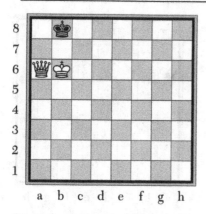

Diagram 86. How does White mate?

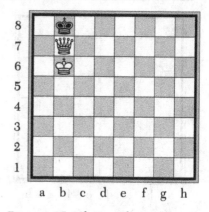

Diagram 87. Solution: The queen mates.

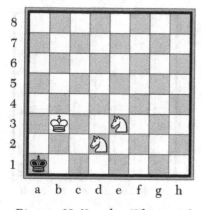

Diagram 88. How does White mate?

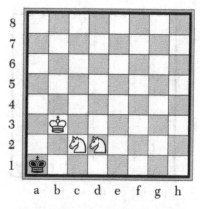

Diagram 89. Solution: The knight on c2 mates.

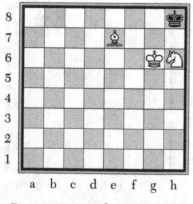

Diagram 90. How does White mate?

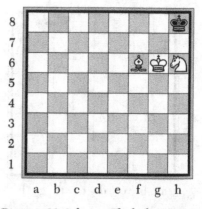

Diagram 91. Solution: The bishop mates.

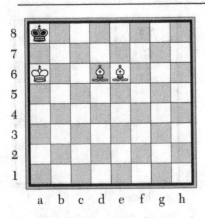

Diagram 92. *How does White mate?*

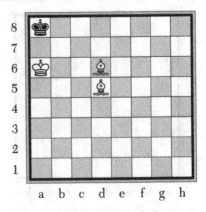

Diagram 93. *Solution: The light-square bishop mates.*

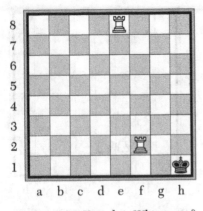

Diagram 94. *How does White mate?*

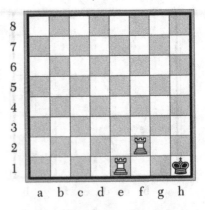

Diagram 95. *Solution: The rook on e1 mates.*

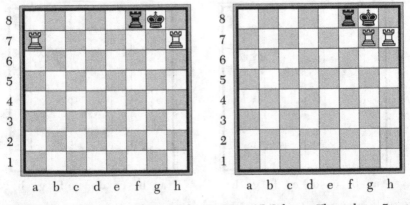

Diagram 96. *How does White mate?*   Diagram 97. *Solution: The rook on g7 mates.*

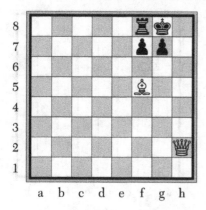

Diagram 98. How does White mate?

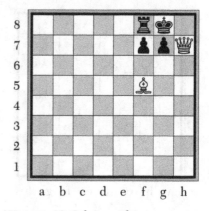

Diagram 99. Solution: The queen mates.

Diagram 100. How does White mate?

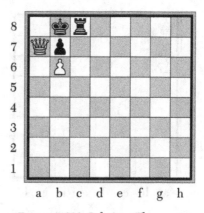

Diagram 101. Solution: The queen mates.

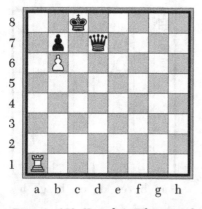

Diagram 102. How does White mate?

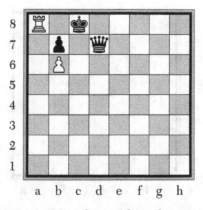

Diagram 103. Solution: The rook mates.

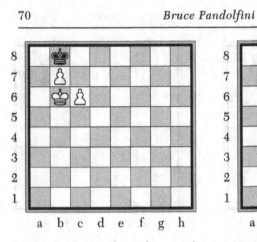

Diagram 104. How does White mate?

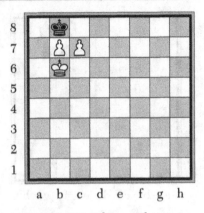

Diagram 105. Solution: The pawn on c7 mates.

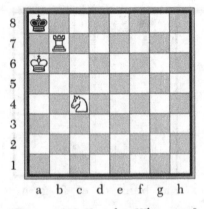

Diagram 106. How does White mate?

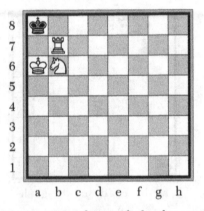

Diagram 107. Solution: The knight mates.

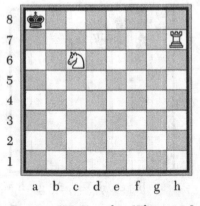

Diagram 108. How does White mate?

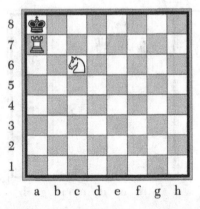

Diagram 109. Solution: The rook mates.

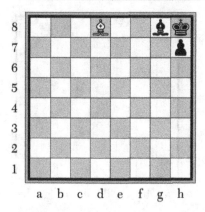

Diagram 110. How does White mate?

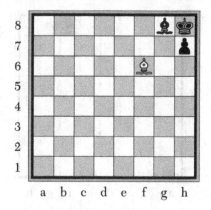

Diagram 111. Solution: The bishop mates.

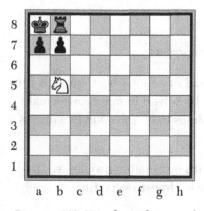

Diagram 112. How does White mate?

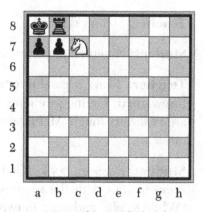

Diagram 113. Solution: The knight mates.

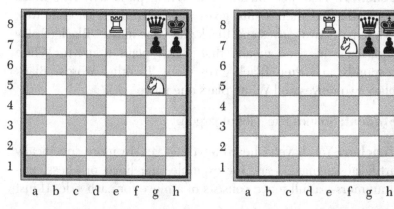

Diagram 114. How does White mate?   *Diagram 115. Solution: The knight mates.*

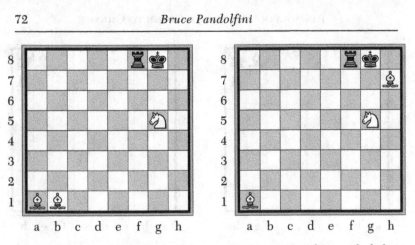

Diagram 116. How does White mate?   *Diagram 117. Solution: The light-square bishop mates.*

Teacher: So how'd it go?

Student: Nineteen out of twenty correct.

Teacher: That's a passing grade. Let's move on then, but be forewarned. Mating problems to be solved in one move usually aren't so very tough. Mating problems to be solved in two moves often are.

Student: I've seen books filled with just mating problems. They seem to start with the same words almost every time, namely "White to play and mate in two."

Teacher: That just means that White plays a move, Black responds, and then White gives mate. To put it another way, White plays two moves and Black plays one move. "Black to play and mate in two" means that Black plays a move, White responds, and then Black gives mate. In other words, Black plays two moves and White plays one move.

Student: Sounds like a lot of jargon.

Teacher: You haven't heard anything yet. In more specifically artificial language—say, for example, the lingo of chess programmers—a full move consists of a move for each side. If just one side plays a move it's thought to be half a move, often expressed as *one ply*. The full move, with both sides responding, is described as being *two ply*, but most chessplayers don't usually refer to their moves in this fashion.

Student: Fortunately, I don't have to think or talk like a chess programmer. Thinking like a beginner, and fearlessly expressing myself as such, why are some chess problems apparently more difficult to solve than others?

Teacher: The difficulty of a chess problem depends on all kinds of factors, but for the newcomer it often has to do with the number of possible enemy responses. The more enemy responses, the more difficult the problem tends to be. The easiest problems to solve usually are those that force the enemy to respond with a particular move.

Student: Which kinds of moves can force particular responses?

Teacher: The most compelling moves tend to be threats to capture units, because if they're not answered the attacker will execute his threat and indeed capture the unit. Real threats should be answered. Apparent threats, those that contain no true menace or bite, can often be ignored or even exploited. The most serious threats tend to involve checks, since by the rules of the game they must be answered. So when considering a mating problem, try to find moves such as checks that force precise responses. This limits your opponent's options and makes it easier to look ahead, because then you have some sense what to anticipate. If you can't control your opponent's responses you can't really see into the game's future, which means you're not playing chess.

Student: Okay. Give me another problem, no matter what it is I'm playing.

Teacher: The next problem allows the defender only one possible response to the correct first move. Remember my earlier advice?

Student: I should look for a check.

Teacher: Right. Diagram 118 illustrates a position where White can play and mate Black in two moves. Try to solve the problem, but don't be alarmed if you have difficulty. The ability to look ahead comes with experience.

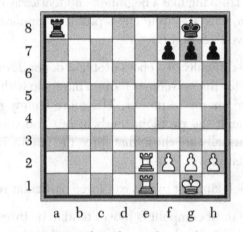

Diagram 118. White plays and mates in two moves.

Teacher: Any ideas?

Student: I suspect that White's correct first move is Re8+.

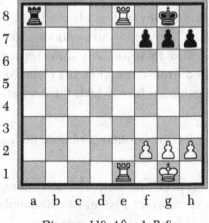

Diagram 119. After 1. Re8+.

Teacher: That's correct. Black's only possible response is to capture the White rook with his rook: 1 . . . Rxe8. So he must do that. But how should White then continue on his second move?

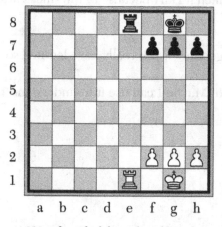

Diagram 120. After Black has taken the rook, 1 . . . Rxe8.

Student: For his second move, White continues by capturing the Black rook, which gives mate simultaneously: 2. Rxe8#.

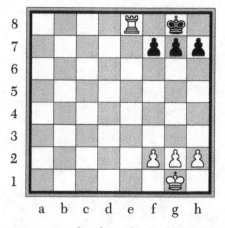

Diagram 121. After the rook takes back, 2. Rxe8#.

Teacher: Just to make sure, let's review why this is mate.

Student: It's mate because the White rook checks the Black king, the White rook cannot be captured or blocked, the Black king cannot escape and get out of check, and the Black king would be captured on the next move, if only the game were to go that far—which it can't because of the rules ending the game right now.

Teacher: My goodness, you really have learned something.

Student: Good. Maybe I can use it to understand Lesson 4.

LESSON 4

Terms of Engagement

THE ELEMENTS

Student: I'm curious about something. I know we'd planned to start talking about how to start a chess game. Wouldn't it have made more sense to discuss that earlier, before getting into tactics and mating patterns? Then we could have dealt with those topics after learning some good beginning moves.

Teacher: I understand your point. But chess is an unusual discipline. It can be studied backward or forward with equal profit, though the methods of presentation would necessarily have to be different. But I had my reasons for showing you some essential tactics and mating patterns before we got started. Chess is goal-oriented. It's easier to reach for something if you know what you're reaching for. Furthermore, the game is complex enough without initially having to focus on all the forces at once. By breaking the process up into smaller bits, we arm ourselves with some weapons before tackling the entire edifice. But enough about the theory of chess teaching. Let's get on with our game.

Student: How long do you think it will take to play?

Teacher: Some games are over in a few moves, and some seem to go on forever.

Student: I'm not sure I'm for either extreme. I guess I could hope for a happy medium, right?

Teacher: You can relax. Typical chess games last between 30–50 moves and have three phases: *opening, middlegame,* and *endgame.*

Student: Okay, I can figure out when the game starts, and I can see when it actually ends, but how do you know when you're in the thick of things—that is, when you're in a middlegame?

Teacher: You don't have to be in a middlegame to be in the thick of things. You're always capable of being enmeshed in complications, no matter what part of the game you're in. The position can be simple or complex, whether you face opening, middlegame, or endgame.

Student: Let me rephrase the question. What are some of the key differences between phases, and how do you know when one phase ends and another begins?

Teacher: There are no hard-and-fast boundary lines between phases. Moreover, the transitions between phases can be subtle, even difficult to perceive and appreciate. During the *opening,* which usually lasts from ten to fifteen moves, players gather their forces and prepare for action. In some cases, if one side neglects king safety and normal build-up, the other can deliver checkmate before the opening is over.

Student: So what is the *middlegame* mainly concerned with?

Teacher: Practically everything. Planning and strategy are certainly important there, but so are everyday tactical operations. To achieve the opening's objectives, pieces are often maneuvered and repositioned throughout the middle stage in hopes of luring the opponent into exploitable situations. In some cases the middlegame seems like an extension of the opening, with no definite break to distinguish the two phases.

Student: Where does this leave the *endgame*?

Teacher: At the end, but let me be clear here. A game can end without there ever having been an endgame. The two-move Fool's Mate we went over at the conclusion of Lesson 1 didn't even have an opening. It was over before it got started.

Student: Long before a chess game is over, no matter which phase they're in, players seem to know who has the advantage and who's in trouble. How do they determine which side has the upper hand?

Teacher: By considering the *elements*, and this doesn't mean checking the weather outside. There are five main elements that interact and overlap throughout a chess game. They are *time, space, material, pawn structure,* and *king safety.* Each component affects the others. Each is related. Their relationships are dynamic, and they can change on virtually every move.

Student: Can't practically everything in chess change?

Teacher: That's a rhetorical question, right?

Student: What do you mean by time?

Teacher: *Time* is not limited to the minutes on a chess clock. Generally, it refers to this chessic rule of thumb: Try to gain time, and try to avoid losing it. If you make your opponent move a piece to a poor square, or back to where it came from, without making any concessions yourself, you gain time. If you force your opponent to stop his plans and start responding to yours, you gain time. If your pieces are better developed than your opponent's, you're probably ahead in time. If you have freedom and can do whatever you want, you most likely have the edge in time. But if you must wait to see what your opponent is going to do before doing what you'd like, and then can't do what you'd like anyway, you're probably behind in time.

Student: I often hear the words *initiative* and *time* used interchangeably.

Teacher: You also have a time advantage if you can attack and your opponent must defend. Having such superiority—being able to attack, not having to defend—is known as *having the initiative.*

Student: Can you make time last?

Teacher: Mostly, time flies. And in chess, time advantages tend to be temporary. If you don't take advantage of them now, the other side is likely to catch up and your ephemeral time advantage will disappear. For example, if you have more pieces out than your opponent does, you should gain something tangible as a result soon. Otherwise, the other side will eventually get the rest of his pieces out and your superiority will dissipate.

Student: If time is temporary, which elements tend to be more long-lasting?

Teacher: Material and pawn structure are more tangible and therefore more permanent. If you're ahead by a pawn, you're likely to remain a pawn ahead unless something radical happens. If, however, you're ahead by merely a unit of time, which is called a *tempo,* you should use it or lose it.

Student: I'm thinking I read something about a space-time continuum once.

Teacher: I hope so, because I was beginning to fear a space-time warp. But let's just stay with the concept of chess space and the final frontier. Do one player's pieces have more options and more mobility? Do they influence and control more squares on the board? If so, that player probably has an advantage in *space*. You can also have an advantage in space if your opponent is particularly constricted by feebly placed pawns, which hinder their own pieces from moving freely.

Student: It's fairly easy to see who's ahead in material. I guess you just have to count and compare to what the other player has. Can you also count up differences in time and space?

Teacher: Not exactly. But you can usually tell who's ahead in time by seeing who has more pieces out and whether they are positioned meaningfully. You can try to count your opponent's wasted moves, assuming you haven't wasted any yourself. And as far as space goes, you can usually sense who possesses more territory by seeing which side has farther-advanced center pawns. These sight indicators are not absolute, but they tend to be trustworthy.

Student: You've explained time, space, and material. What about pawn structure and king safety?

Teacher: Pawn structure and king safety include some specific positional issues. Take *pawn structure* first. In judging which side has stronger and more elastic pawns, you'll want to determine if your pawns can guard key squares easily enough, and without repercussions; if they can defend each other satisfactorily; if they can move flexibly and with support; if they are subject to harassment; and finally, whether they provide sufficient shelter to shield their own king.

Student: How does pawn structure relate to king safety?

Teacher: The two are aligned in a very intimately defined way. In comparing your position to your opponent's, you'll want to figure out which king is more exposed. You'll also have to hope your own king isn't exposed at all; how easy it might be to get at your king in the future; if you still must waste time to get your king to safety, or if it has ways to get out of potential trouble; which part of the board is safest for your king—whether king-side, queenside, or center; and whether your king's need to be secure reduces your options significantly. The degree to which a king is safe from attack is a major aspect to chess, and it's largely determined by the strength and flexibility of sheltering pawns. You can have the greatest game going, but if your king has no shielding pawn refuge and is suddenly menaced, a mountain of advantages can collapse under the weight of royal vulnerability.

Student: Let me change direction a bit. How come White always gets to go first?

Teacher: That's just a convention. In fact, before the rules were set in writing, game circumstances varied. Many people played with Black going first. And as far as why the pieces are called White and Black instead of Yellow and Blue, that too is a convention. It probably stems from the fact that white and black are natural colors, readily part of the substances used to make early chess pieces. It was simply easier to find light and dark materials and call them White and Black. Moreover, by insuring that the pieces were of two distinct colors, it became easier to distinguish them, regardless of playing conditions. Nothing was otherwise ever implied by the colors or their respective names. Anyhow, no matter the actual colors of the pieces, the lighter-colored army is always called White and the darker Black. Moreover, White always goes first. This balances out because the players usually alternate colors from game to game.

Student: Is it an advantage to go first?

Teacher: At the start of a game it's advantageous to go first, because choosing the opening move defines ensuing options for both players. The first move offers the ability to start attacking. It tends to be much harder to defend than to attack, particularly because the attacker gets to act while the defender must be prepared to react. Moreover, the consequences of a letdown are usually much greater for the defender than for the attacker.

Student: So White can attack first?

Teacher: By virtue of going first, White starts the game with a slight but expected initiative. A chessplayer has the initiative when he or she can force the action and direct the flow of play. Having the initiative confers an advantage in time, as I've already mentioned. Strategically, White tries to maintain this opening advantage, looking for every opportunity to increase it and eventually convert it into something concrete by gaining positional dominance, winning material, or forcing checkmate.

Student: I don't suppose Black just creeps off into some chessic sunset?

Teacher: Black initially is the defender. Still, that shouldn't stop him from making every attempt to squelch opposing onslaughts. Naturally, when warding off enemy assaults, every effort should be made to seize the initiative with a timely counterattack. So White needs to watch it, as does Black. To err is human, but it can cost you, especially if you overextend yourself trying to win. True, the attacker has a built-in advantage, inasmuch as he or she can often make a mistake and still not lose because the defender may be mentally unprepared to launch a counteroffensive on a moment's notice. Defenders naturally focus on responding to an attack rather than a mistake, so they sometimes allow their opponents to play erroneously with impunity. A mistake by the defender, on the other hand, is more likely to be fatal, since attackers are usually more attuned to the possibility of such lapses, having already factored them into their plans. Attackers generally have some sense what they aim to do ahead of time, whereas defenders aren't quite as sure what may hit until it happens.

Student: I guess you're right.

Teacher: A player who ignores the initiative is like a boxer who allows his opponent a free swing. Humorist Artemus Ward once rewrote Shakespeare to make the same point: "Thrice is he armed that hath his quarrel just—And four times he who gets his fist in fust." Using the initiative, White should strive to achieve two fundamental aims during the opening stages of the game: to develop friendly forces and to play for the center.

Student: Can I conclude that Black should try to do exactly the same thing?

Teacher: Unless Black enjoys watching his chess sun go down in ignominious defeat, that's right. What's good for the goose's development is good for the gander's.

Student: What does development actually mean?

Teacher: Let's develop our ideas further. A fundamental aim of the opening is mobilization of your forces for action. You should *develop* them, which means increase their scope and power. You do this by moving a few pawns out of the way and then transferring the pieces on the back rank from their original squares to more useful ones, especially toward the center. Remember, chess terminology distinguishes between pawns—the units occupying each player's second rank at the start—and pieces— kings, queens, rooks, bishops, and knights.

Student: I know. Every kind of chess figure is called a piece except for the pawn.

Teacher: You have a better chance of accomplishing your aims if you attack with all your pieces, not just one or two. A rule of thumb is to develop a different piece on each turn so that you can try to assemble a mounting assault with numerous forces. Intelligently developed pieces work together, attacking and defending simultaneously and harmoniously, building the foundation for a concerted and effective offensive. So don't attack aimlessly with the same pieces, particularly your queen. Such unfocused and sporadic flurries are likely to be repulsed by a careful opponent's coordinated efforts, and it gets worse if your opponent actually looks at your moves.

Student: It almost sounds as if you shouldn't attack before you've started developing your game. Is that true?

Teacher: It's largely true, but not absolutely so, as is the case with so much of chess advice. If your plan is to attack by developing your queenside forces, and your opponent blunders on the kingside, allowing you to win in one move, I think you'll forget about the queenside plan and go with the mate. But as a rule, once you're mobilized or developed, you can advance into enemy territory with greater authority. On the other hand, you have to be careful not to develop pointlessly, merely for development's sake. Aim to develop and threaten at the same time. Try to limit your opponent's freedom of action, hindering efforts to bring his forces to their ideal squares, where they might attack or threaten you.

Student: Could you clarify something for me? Aren't attacks and threats the same thing?

Teacher: Not really. You're attacking something if you're in position to capture it, even if it's not desirable to do so. You're threatening something if you're in position to capture or exploit it to your explicit advantage. Indeed, a *threat* is an attempt to gain advantage, generally by inflicting some immediate harm on the enemy position. Most commonly, a threat is designed to win material, either by capturing for nothing or by surrendering less force than you gain. So an attack can be good, but not all the time. A threat is always good, unless it's a false threat that enables the opponent to respond in a way that improves his situation.

Student: Like giving up a pawn to capture a knight, which is worth three pawns?

Teacher: Yes, but there can be more serious threats, and these usually involve danger to the king. Less important threats may hinge on dominating certain squares or creating weaknesses in your opponent's camp. As a rule, you shouldn't ignore threats. Whenever it seems you're being threatened, you should determine if the threat is real. If it is, you should always do something about it. You should aim to defend against it, produce a more immediate or serious threat of your own, or respond with a simultaneous defense and attack. The last is usually most prudent, as it affords an opportunity to seize the initiative while taking care of chessic business.

Student: To me, it always seems that the best players act as if they have White all the time, actively pursuing their opponent right from the start. How does this happen?

Teacher: Some experienced competitors generally handle the Black side of the opening phase by playing precisely but aggressively, so that every move is fraught with threat and tension. Usually, from turn to turn, such contentious contestants seek the move that causes their opponents the greatest problems, sometimes even at risk to their own game. This has led some grandmasters to subject opening moves to extremely profound analysis, hoping to find the minutest advantage and the single saving move, which has enriched the theory of the game immeasurably.

Student: It's also resulted in some of the most massive tomes ever seen.

Teacher: Generally I try to keep my own books under five hundred pages, so that students have the illusion they can get through them quickly and easily. But even in the thinnest ones I usually say something about the center.

Student: The center: Is there that much to be said about it?

Teacher: To be centered is where it's at. The most important squares on the chessboard are in the middle.

Student: What do you mean by the center?

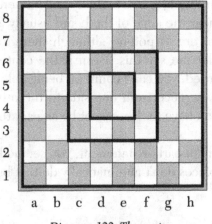

Diagram 122. The center.

Teacher: The *center* is the portion of the board consisting of the squares d4, d5, e4, and e5, as outlined in diagram 122. In many discussions, the central region is augmented to include the squares immediately surrounding the center: c3, c4, c5, c6, d6, e6, f6, f5, f4, f3, e3, and d3. This expanded area is known as the *enlarged* or *big center* and is also represented in the diagram. Pieces sitting on these squares generally enjoy greater *mobility,* which means they tend to have more possible moves and greater flexibility. This busy central district is habitually the key to the shifting fortunes of battle.

Student: Why is that?

Teacher: A piece stationed there, on a relatively unimpeded board, can usually move in any direction with little trouble. Such a piece has greater mobility and options, meaning it has potential access to more squares, which also implies it can be a real pain for the other side.

Student: What about pieces placed on the edge?

Teacher: Pieces positioned away from the center generally, though not entirely, enjoy less mobility and influence less space. Pieces placed near the edge of the board usually aren't as flexible, and seldom are as potent, although there are exceptions here too. But let me say this: Even if the center isn't totally blocked or guarded, you can't count on being able to maneuver an out-of-the-way piece from one side to the other when you suddenly find you have to. It may not be an easy thing to do.

Student: But in an earlier statement, you seemed to be implying that some pieces don't automatically do that badly when off to the side.

Teacher: Obviously, all the line-pieces can effectively strike from far away. But in the main, only the rook can be as mobile on the wing as in the center—that is, on an otherwise empty board. On a board with no piece or pawn impediments, a rook can move to any of fourteen different squares no matter where it's placed. Every other piece, including the king, attacks more squares from the center than from anywhere else. For this reason, it becomes less necessary to place a rook in the center. In fact, positioned in the actual center, a rook may be easier to harass than if it were far away on an unblocked file that leads straight to the enemy heartland.

Student: Could you show more certainly how pieces fare in the center compared to elsewhere?

Teacher: Take a look at the raw numbers. Let's place each piece in turn on various squares in the center and on the wings of an otherwise empty chessboard and see what possibilities there are. As the following chart illustrates, the center is the place to be.

Squares a Piece Can Move to When On . . .

Piece	e4	f6	b2	h1	Total Mobility
Queen	27	25	23	21	1456
Rook	14	14	14	14	896
Bishop	13	11	9	7	560
Knight	8	8	4	2	336
King	8	8	8	3	420

Total Mobility = total number of squares a piece can move to from all the squares on the board added together.

Student: So I guess it's a wise thing to try to control the center?

Teacher: Most certainly. By controlling the center you might be able to drive a wedge into the enemy's position, splitting the opposing army in two. You thereby prevent and/or discourage your opponent from coordinating or pulling together his forces effectively. Lack of free and easy movement and its resulting diminished options should cause your adversary plenty of problems. If you can do so fruitfully, you want to control the center, occupy it, and influence it in any meaningful way you can.

Student: When do I get my chance to play for the center?

Teacher: As soon as you're ready for the next lesson. I'll even give you the White pieces.

LESSON 5

Staking out Territory

OPENING PRINCIPLES AND THE FIRST MOVE

Teacher: Every move, like every lesson, should have a purpose. During this next session you'll learn some essential opening principles. Keep in mind that all principles are subject to change. Every move creates a new world on the board. Nevertheless, with each move in the opening, you should try to do one or more of the following: (1) develop a new piece or clear lines for future development; (2) fight for the center by occupying, attacking, or influencing it; (3) gain space and increase overall mobility; (4) strengthen your position while avoiding weaknesses; (5) pose at least one threat, if not multiple ones; and (6) meet all enemy threats. If you can more or less follow this program, you should be in good shape. At least you're not likely to get mated in four moves.

Student: Whew! That's a heavy intellectual regime. But what do I do for a first move?

Teacher: Your first move is to think about setting up two boards side by side. As we proceed with our actual game, it's inevitable that we'll find ourselves exploring variations, options, and choices we might make, but don't in the end. So why don't we use one chess set and board for playing the actual moves, and another set and board for considering possible moves? That way, we'll always be able to get back to where we were before we go on to what may be.

Student: Seems like a little extra work, but it makes sense.

Teacher: I've got lots of diagrams here to help make the process easier. Now, back to your question. I recommend that most newcomers begin with **1. e4.**

Student: Why?

Teacher: There are a number of reasons for this opening move. For one, it places a pawn right in the center, immediately staking White's claim to the sector. In addition to the key central square d5, White zeroes in on and snatches control of another salient point, f5. A knight positioned here later on can often inflict great damage if Black is castled kingside. The thrust **1. e4** is an assertive start. It contributes powerfully to rapid development, because White can now bring out his queen and light-square bishop. Advancing the e-pawn has opened diagonals for both of these pieces.

Student: Doesn't moving the e-pawn one square also work?

Teacher: Very true. For the same two pieces—the queen and king-bishop—you can also open up diagonals for development with 1. e3, a push of only one square. But this move doesn't gain as much space as advancing the e-pawn two squares, to e4, nor does it seriously pressure the center. Too, by going only one square, White places another obstacle before his own dark-square bishop, making it harder to develop it along the c1-h6 diagonal. Generally, moving a central pawn only one square on the first move for White is unnecessarily timid. Of course, one can play such a move with purpose and intelligence. But if it's done for lack of know-how, a seasoned opponent might detect that fact and exploit this information to play aggressively—even rashly—without fear of retribution.

Student: So moving two squares gives me more area.

Teacher: Quite right. Moving two squares instead of one seizes more space. Usually, the more advanced your pawns, the more space or room you have behind the lines. When we get further into our lesson, you'll see that the placement of pawns is paramount to the nature and course of the game. Another reason I recommend the king-pawn opening of **1. e4** is that it tends to produce positions that are more open and direct. The less complicated the situation, the easier it is to find a good plan. Blocked positions, on the other hand, especially those with interlocked central pawns, are ordinarily more subtle than open positions, and determining a reasonable course of action in such situations can be significantly more difficult for the apprentice. But we'll have to discuss that some other time.

Student: Isn't moving the queen's pawn just as good to start the game?

Teacher: Yes, but before I respond to your question more concretely, I'd like to address something else. In chess parlance, we tend to drop many of the possessives of ordinary conversation. So instead of saying queen's pawn, we'll say queen-pawn. This is especially helpful, because a series of chess terms could otherwise be loaded with several cumbersome possessives. Just imagine spitting out the phrase "king's bishop's pawn's."

Student: How about if I just repeat my question about moving the queen-pawn first? Or is it the d-pawn?

Teacher: Queen-pawn, d-pawn—it's all the same thing. You'll get the hang of it, I promise. Now, let's address your question. It's perfectly plausible for White to start the game this way, though moving the d-pawn two squares on the first move tends to lead to slightly more sophisticated positions that require greater experience to be played well. It's true that the advance 1. d4 attacks e5 and occupies d4, both central squares. It also enables the queen to enter the fray; not via the d1-h5 diagonal, as with **1. e4,** but frontally along the file. Although the dark-square bishop has the c1-h6 diagonal on which to move after the opener 1. d4, the queen must escape up along the d-file, to either d2 or d3, neither of which tends to be that promising. So after 1. d4, the queen usually waits for other, later opportunities to get activated. But the queen's placement does offer the d-pawn what the king's placement doesn't offer the e-pawn: ready-made support for an advance.

Student: I hadn't thought about that. Having protection for a possible advance might be important.

Teacher: That's right. And because the king-pawn doesn't start with a natural backup, it's harder, at a later point, to play the king-pawn two squares than it is to play the queen-pawn two squares. This means that central exchanges are slightly less likely to take place in queen-pawn openings than they are in king-pawn openings. The move 1. d4, instead of **1. e4,** lends itself to producing a somewhat slower, obstacle-ridden game that can manufacture real problems for a novice trying to find his way. Therefore, though **1. e4** and 1. d4 are equally attractive opening moves for veteran players, it makes more sense for newcomers to begin with the slightly less labyrinthine king-pawn opener, at least until they've learned how to be more comfortable over a chessboard.

Student: Are there any other good first moves for White?

Teacher: There are several levelheaded first moves for White in addition to moving either center pawn two squares. They include 1. Nf3, 1. g3, 1. c4, and 1. b3. But to play them purposefully, and to understand how they can be used winningly, requires a much more informed approach than most newcomers have. Such moves as 1. a3, 1. b4, 1. f4, and 1. Nc3 have also been essayed successfully. Even a risky "spike" such as 1. g4 can't be ignored. Yet none of these moves, either reasonable or unreasonable, offer as much for the novice as **1. e4** or 1. d4. The latter two achieve essential goals more quickly and efficiently than the others, controlling the center and paving the road for the rapid development of pieces in ways that beginning players can grasp quickly and practically.

Student: Still, it's nice to know I have options.

Teacher: You most certainly do, but let me ask you a question. Suppose, after playing **1. e4,** you were allowed to play another move, so that you actually get two moves before Black gets to play any. What would you play?

Student: But no one ever gets get two moves to start a game. Why should I even bother to think about it?

Teacher: Suppose after your first move of **1. e4** your opponent were to play a totally irrelevant and innocuous move that did practically nothing, that ignored your first move altogether? Wouldn't it then be as if your opponent gave you two free moves to start the game? Wouldn't you then have carte blanche to do what you wanted on your second move, as if it, too, were another first move?

Student: I think I see your point. In addition to trying to anticipate my opponent's responses, I should be prepared to play for my ideal circumstances, just in case my opponent doesn't reply intelligently.

Teacher: Right. In that case you can get what you want without a fight. You should know what's a good extra second move just in case your opponent plays illogically. You shouldn't depend on your opponent's mistakes, but you'd like to be prepared to capitalize on them if they should happen.

Student: So what moves would be great extra moves for White?

Teacher: A number would be useful here. The one that makes the most sense, however, is 2. d4, since we've already indicated it would be just as good as the actual move you've chosen, **1. e4.** Imagine how wonderful it would be to play the two strongest moves before your opponent has made a meaningful move of any kind. After moving both center pawns two squares ahead, White occupies d4 and e4, two of the four center squares, and controls d5 and e5, the other two. The queen's scope would also increase and the dark-square bishop could be developed. This formation, with two pawns so aligned in the middle, is called a *classical center* or an *ideal pawn center.*

Student: Why is it called classical?

Teacher: For a number of reasons, but primarily because the concept goes back to the earliest generations of strong masters, to those who laid down the bedrock of chess fundamentals. Think about it. The old automobiles of my childhood have turned into collector's items—classic cars, they call them now. Meanwhile, the radio music of my teenage years has turned into "classic" rock. Practically anything that gets old enough can become classic.

Student: Does that include chess teachers?

Teacher: Thanks a lot.

Student: Sorry. Another question: Why should I be ecstatic if I manage to possess a classical center early on?

Teacher: Once you've established a classical center, especially in the beginning stage of the game, you can undertake many reasonable courses of action. Such a center would give White a commanding space edge and make it difficult for Black to fight back adequately in the central region. Against such poised front lines, Black might wind up falling behind in development, because he'd have far fewer squares he could move to safely. White's menacing center would have the capacity to drive back Black's pieces before they could secure themselves on particular posts.

Student: Wouldn't it be equally good for Black to have such a center?

Teacher: Certainly, if the conditions were truly the same. But since Black starts second, he is much less likely to be able to set up such a center logically. Illogically, of course, anything could happen. White might wind up playing so irrelevantly that in effect Black gets the White pieces.

Student: I can see how such a center might help White's development, since it makes it easy to move the queen and the bishops freely. Could you go over some of the possible deployments once the classical center is created, and would these include moving any other White pawns?

Teacher: Actually, White's pieces are now ready to be developed without having to move any other pawn whatsoever! In fact, White needs only eight moves at most to mobilize his forces from here, once the classical pawn center has been formed. For example, the knights could be moved to f3 and c3, the bishops to c4 and f4, and the queen to d3. White could castle kingside (0-0), and finally move the rooks to the central files by putting the king-rook on e1 and the queen-rook on d1, as in diagram 123.

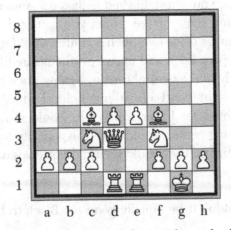

Diagram 123. An opening scheme: White is developed, ready for action.

Student: Would you mind going over the moves leading to the above position?

Teacher: Not at all, but let me warn you: I'm going to leave Black's pieces off the board for the next few diagrams in order to make my point clearly. To create the position in diagram 123, White would have to play 1. e4 2. d4, in either order; 3. Nf3 4. Nc3 5. Bc4 6. Bf4, in any order; 7. Qd3 8. 0-0, in either order; and then 9. Rfe1 10. Rad1, in either order. These ten moves together form an *opening scheme*. Opening schemes are defined by the placement of the pieces around a particular pawn structure. Diagram 124 shows an alternative scheme from the same pawn advances.

Student: How did you get to this other position?

Teacher: To get to the position of diagram 124, White played 1. e4 2. d4 3. Nf3 4. Bd3 5. 0-0 6. Bg5 7. Nbd2 8. Qe2 9. Rfe1

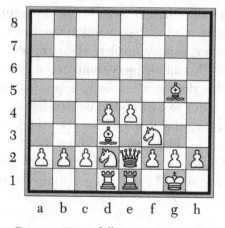

Diagram 124. A different opening scheme.

10. Rad1. Of course, the same position could have been arrived at through different coherent orders. There are also other ways to develop the pieces around a classical pawn center. These are just representative schemes, where Black hasn't had an opportunity to respond to White's moves. In a real game, White would have to reply to Black's moves, so every idea and plan would have to be based on the actual course of the game, rather than on a fixed set of moves set in plaster. Therefore, in real play, the ideal might not happen at all.

Student: It's interesting that the king should be considered developed on g1. Why is that?

Teacher: For the purpose of these exercises, as well as in actual chess games, the king is said to be developed when it's safely castled and the rooks are mobilized so they can stand sentinel over the central files from the squares e1 and d1. It's not so much that you're developing the king; it's that you're getting the king out of the way so that the other pieces, such as the rooks, can move along the home rank more freely.

Student: So development usually entails moving pieces to better places.

Teacher: Generally, though not always. Sometimes you can develop a piece by moving a pawn out of the way. Development of pieces, however, usually involves their transfer to more effective squares. The minor pieces must be moved off the first rank, though this doesn't necessarily apply to the queen and the rooks. The latter two can often be developed effectively by shifting them along the first rank to open files, and if not to open files, then to files that may soon become open once obstructing friendly pawns are moved out of the way. How do you think you might be able to get your own pawns out of your way?

Student: If my pawn advances and subsequently captures an enemy pawn or piece, that will move it diagonally to a different file.

Teacher: Very good. An obstructing friendly pawn may also be removed in another way, when enemy forces capture it. In turn, the opposing unit that captures your pawn may be recaptured by another of your pieces, instead of another potentially barricading pawn. This would keep the line essentially open, for you could probably move your own piece off the line whenever desirable. That's not something you could do as easily with a pawn, which can't move off its file without capturing something. Here's another challenge for you. Practically speaking, can the position of the pieces in diagram 124 be achieved with essentially one less move?

Student: I think I have an idea. I think you could save a move in effect if White castles queenside instead of kingside. The king would wind up a different square (c1 instead of g1), but everything else would be the same if, say on move eight, you castled queenside, 8. 0-0-0, and on move nine played the king-rook from h1 to e1.

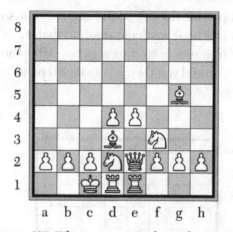

Diagram 125. White saves a move by castling queenside.

Teacher: Really nice. So you see you can achieve this same essential setup in one move. It may only be a single move, but chess is most definitely a game where little things matter.

Student: No wonder so much attention can be paid to whether or not the king-rook moves only once instead of twice. But let me ask you something. Is castling queenside preferable to castling kingside?

Teacher: No, not really, though everything depends on the circumstances you're presented with in an actual game. Kingside castling occurs more often mainly because it can happen sooner, since there are fewer pieces to get out of the way. To castle queenside, one must also move the queen off the castling side's first rank. In a real game, of course, circumstances may make it desirable to position the king on a particular side, so it might be wise to castle in that direction. This suggests the following advice, which works for virtually every aspect of your play: Don't ignore your opponent's moves. Everything you do can be influenced by what the other player does.

Student: I hope this doesn't sound absurd, but suppose your opponent plays without any logic at all, so that it's as if you were granted three free moves to start a game. After the two moves 1. e4 and 2. d4, should you then move a third pawn on your third turn?

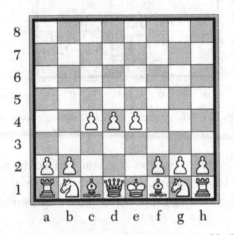

Diagram 126. Moving the c-pawn to c4 is reasonable, but it's not necessary to furthering development.

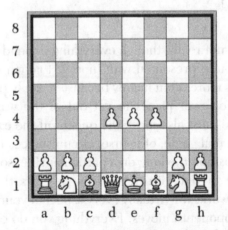

Diagram 127. Moving the f-pawn to f4 is also good, but it's also not necessary for future development.

Teacher: Not at all. Surely you could play 3. c4 or 3. f4 as the next two diagrams show, with an overwhelming position, but there's no reason you couldn't start to develop your knights, for instance, which have to be gotten out anyway.

Student: So I shouldn't move a third pawn in this situation?

Teacher: You could move a third pawn advantageously, but such an advance doesn't contribute significantly to future development to make it essential. To complete your development, it's sufficient to begin the process by moving only the two center pawns. After that, it's easy to develop all your pieces, and no other pawn necessarily has to be moved to complete development, assuming your opponent doesn't respond meaningfully, in a way that would dissuade you.

Student: Obviously, real opponents may try to deter me in every way they can.

Teacher: That's right, so you should be as economical as possible in deploying your forces. Rather than move a third pawn, for the newcomer it's more prudent to commence the mobilization of the pieces on the back rank. You've laid down the front lines with the e-pawn and the d-pawn. Now bring up the support troops behind them and get going.

Student: It still seems a little weird, thinking about the impossible.

Teacher: It's actually not that weird, and it's not that impossible. I know it seems odd to consider what you would do if you could make three unanswered moves in a row. But you'd be surprised how often opponents may play totally unresponsive moves that have little bearing on what's really happening. If your opponent happens to be that foolish, you'll be able to develop as if he is playing no moves at all. Then you'll want to proceed optimally, aiming for the ideal setup. Imagine a game where your opponent plays moves like 1 ... a5, 2 ... Na6, and 3 ... Rb8 (diagram 128). You could more or less do whatever you want. What you should want is to maintain control, so that you can win as expeditiously as possible. In chess, it's all about control. You want to control the game. You aim to control your opponent's responses.

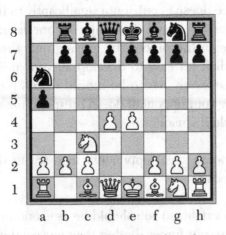

Diagram 128. White has played three logical moves; Black, three illogical ones.

Student: Does thinking about what you'd like to do help you get it done?

Teacher: Yes, because it keeps key things in mind, just in case opportunities should arise. Being mindful of future possibilities and designs always adds a dimension to your play. This is why, as a training procedure, some teachers have their students play as many unanswered moves from the start as they wish until they've achieved what they consider to be the perfect position. If the teacher relies on this approach, he usually insists on one restriction: nothing can be moved beyond one's own fourth rank so that the entire action stays in the realm of build-up, not execution. This exercise helps students think in terms of schemes, plans, and goals. The point is, it's easier to look ahead if you have some idea what to look for. In real games, the other player will probably try to stop you, of course—from doing good things and even from seeing them.

Student: But I should always aim for the best.

Teacher: While being prepared to ward off the worst. Would you like to summarize?

Student: Since White would try to move both center pawns two squares each under ideal conditions, the player handling the White side should try to do exactly that in actual play.

Teacher: But, as we have clearly pointed out, real adversaries will not sit back and let their opponent proceed without contention. Whoever handles Black will naturally try to make White's plans difficult or downright undesirable. Former world champion Emanuel Lasker (1868–1941) wrote a philosophical treatise entitled *Struggle,* which drew analogies between chess and other disciplines. Lasker described the game as a simple battle where the players inevitably tussle for control.

Student: Since they start the game with exactly the same position, do White and Black start with the same plans?

Teacher: Yes and no. Black would like to be able to do what White can, but as you know, he begins a move behind. So I'd put it this way: White tries to convert his first-move advantage into a win, and Black tries to offset that advantage and steal the initiative, essentially so that he can act as if he has the White pieces. In chess, players begin at the beginning with about equal chances. The one who is most likely to gain true control at some point in the game is likely to be the one who takes his idea and follows it up most consistently. Winners don't necessarily make

the first move, just the best or most opportunistic ones at the
right times.

Student: I seem to recall a line about how the winner is the one
who makes the next to last mistake.

Teacher: Are you sure you've never played this game before?

Student: I hope this doesn't get us off track, because I know
we've mainly been focused on pieces and their development.
Still, I'd like to ask another question about pawns. I see some
things about how pawn moves can be good when they attack or
defend soundly. But what are the consequences of bad pawn
moves?

Teacher: Any kind of bad move is bad by definition, so I suspect you're really talking about *unnecessary* pawn moves. Even
if such moves don't lead to serious weaknesses, they simply
waste time that could be put to better use developing pieces.
Especially in the opening, every move, every *tempo*—which, as
in music, constitutes a unit of time—is critical and should be uti-
lized for the mobilization of the forces.

Student: Could you go into more detail on that?

Teacher: You bet. Once pawns advance beyond a point, they
can never again guard the squares they've passed. Unlike pieces,
pawns can't move backward. Their consequences are irre-
versible. If you make a bad pawn move, you're stuck with it.
With pieces, on the other hand, you sometimes get an opportunity to retract errors at the cost of a wasted move, though that
can mean trouble too.

Student: Are pawns good defenders, or are they simply too
weak to be relied on?

Teacher: Pawns can be great defenders, especially because they're not valuable. This makes them more expendable than other units. Every enemy piece must respect a square guarded by a pawn, for if the piece lands on that square, it may be captured without fear of losing material, even if the pawn that takes the piece is then taken back. Who wants to lose a piece for a pawn?

Student: Supposedly, you shouldn't move the pawns around your king without a good reason.

Teacher: You shouldn't do anything without a good reason, but as a rule it's especially wise not to move the pawns in front of your king unless truly desirable or necessary. Pawns are particularly good defenders for the king, where their intact arrangement around a castled king's position tends to ward off most enemy invaders. Move those pawns and you might expose your king to a rash of invasive forces.

Student: I've heard this may be especially true for the f-pawn.

Teacher: Quite so. Deadly consequences, for example, may result from pushing the king-bishop pawn, otherwise known as the f-pawn, because moving it greatly weakens an uncastled king's setup. Of course, pushing the f-pawn tends to be a far less serious offense after the king is already castled kingside. Moving the f-pawn then can even be a good thing, because your own king-rook might be able to capitalize on the opening of the f-file. But if you do move your f-pawn after castling kingside, you'll want to make sure the suddenly opened diagonal running from queen-rook-7 to king-knight-1 can't be exploited by your opponent.

Student: Many inexperienced players move up their rook-pawns to keep enemy knights and bishops from invading. Is that a good idea?

Teacher: Not really. In fact, it can be weakening and a waste of time. Unless you have a good reason for doing otherwise, and really understand the implications, try not to move your rook-pawns in the early part of the opening. It does nothing for development. It also reduces the ability to control certain squares on the adjacent knight file, and it's even possible for the rook-pawn in question to become a target itself.

Student: Okay, I'll try not to move my rook-pawns unnecessarily.

Teacher: Moving any pawns unnecessarily in the opening is generally not a good idea, and some of the shortest games in chess history have resulted from ill-considered premature pawn thrusts. Remember the game we examined at the end of our first lesson? That game, nicknamed the Fool's Mate, provides perfect proof of the pernicious consequences of unnecessary pawn moves. Similar losses can occur even when masters are playing, no matter how masterfully they think they play. Take a look at this game, played between two French masters in the 1920s.

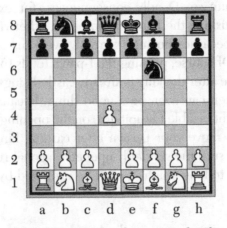

Diagram 129. After the moves 1. d4 Nf6.

Teacher: Black's first move prevents White from building a classical pawn center by moving the e-pawn two squares, for now it would be captured for free. The move Nf6 also develops a piece toward the center.

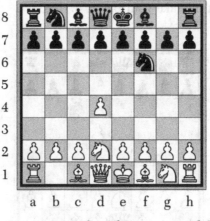

Diagram 130. After White's move 2. Nd2?.

Student: That's a developing move.

Teacher: Yes, but not a productive one, since it at least temporarily blocks in the queen and the dark-square bishop.

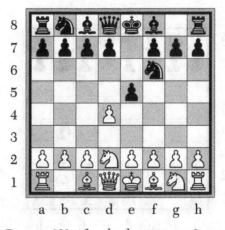

Diagram 131. After the sharp counter 2 . . . e5.

Student: What an audacious-looking move.

Teacher: It's an attempt to hijack the initiative by a temporary pawn sacrifice.

Student: So let me take your pawn, 3. dxe5.

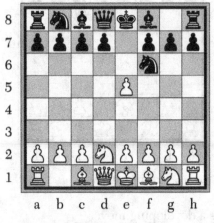

Diagram 132. After taking Black's pawn, 3. dxe5.

Teacher: And allow me to move my knight to safety, 3 . . . Ng4.

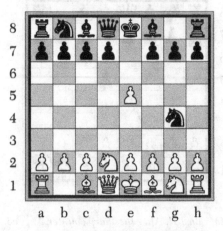

Diagram 133. After Black's knight invades, 3 . . . Ng4.

Student: I have this tremendous urge to drive away your knight with 4. h3.

Diagram 134. After White blunders with 4. h3??.

Teacher: That's what White actually did play, and Black refuted it by 4 . . . Ne3!!

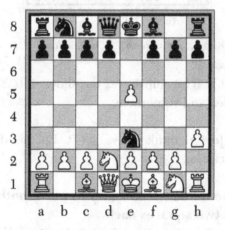

Diagram 135. After Black threatens White's queen by 4 . . . Ne3!!

Student: What? That makes no sense. I can take your knight for free.

Teacher: For free, but not without repercussions, which is why in the real game White resigned here. He realized that he had to either allow his queen to be taken by the knight or capture the knight, exposing his king to a deadly check from Black's queen at h4. Thus, if 5. fxe3, White is bereft of pawn protection for the square g3, so that 5 . . . Qh4+ mates next move. For example, if 6. g3, then 6 . . . Qxg3# is a version of the Fool's Mate, which, as you no doubt recall, we went over at the end of Lesson 1.

Diagram 136. After 6 . . . Qxg3, a Fool's Mate.

Student: I get it. The culprit was the shove 4. h3??, which left g3 less defended and vulnerable.

Teacher: By Jove, I think you've got it. Let me drive home a couple of principles:

1. **If it can be done safely, try to move both center pawns two squares each.**
2. **Don't move too many pawns, especially in the first part of the opening.**

After the principles comes the summary advice. The most effective way to control the center usually is to occupy it with center pawns and to back them up with appropriate piece support. White has a better chance to seize the center initially because of the first-move advantage, which is something like a chessic adaptation of squatter's rights. Unless circumstances lead you elsewhere, try to maintain at least one pawn in the center without having to make significant concessions.

Student: That's fine, because I don't like making concessions anyway.

Teacher: While you're playing chess, that's a good thing. Moving the central pawns opens up space for rapid development. Moving too many pawns will slow down development and weaken your position. Only move pawns when it's clearly helpful or required by the position.

Student: Some pawns can't seem to get any respect.

Teacher: Of course, pawns may appear to be mere bagatelles, so why is it necessary to place so much emphasis on the apparently insignificant? Because in this game of grandiose minds and grand scheming, little things actually matter.

Student: So I should respect little pawns, I guess.

Teacher: I'd advise it. After all, the two of us might only be pawns in someone else's larger game.

LESSON 6

Establishing the Neutral Zone

Teacher: Let's begin by reviewing some opening principles, since White and Black have a similar aim.

Student: To win.

Teacher: You guessed it. Every move should have a purpose. Each *opening* move should help develop your pieces or free lines for future development, establish or lay claim to control of the center, garner space and improve mobility, pose one or more threats, answer any significant threats made by your opponent, and even ward off the possibility of certain threats being made against you in the future.

Student: I have a question about opening goals. The starting setup is the same for both sides, so I could see how their goals might be similar. Clearly, as we've already discussed, White has the small advantage of the first move. But does the fact that White has the first move mean that it's a lot easier for him to secure his goals? Or does it merely mean that Black has to go about achieving his plans differently because he can't make his first move until after White makes his?

Teacher: Of course, doing most things is easier for the player going first. So going second does mean that Black will probably have to be a little craftier, though he can reach chessic nirvana too.

Student: Suppose Black does the same thing as White. That is, after White opens up by moving his king-pawn two squares (1. e4), is it a good idea for Black to follow suit and move his king-pawn two squares as well (**1 . . . e5**)?

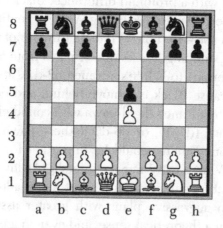

Diagram 137. A double king-pawn opening.

Teacher: It's not a bad idea at all. For a newcomer, it's probably the most practical approach, especially because it tends to be more direct and easy to understand. There are other plausible things that Black can do, but however he replies, his moves should take into account White's moves and likely follow-ups. Nothing should be played in a vacuum.

Student: What specifically does **1 . . . e5** do?

Teacher: A number of things. Three of the more significant reasons for countering with a double king-pawn defense (**1 . . . e5**) are to: (1) get a fair share of the center; (2) clear lines for development; and (3) discourage White from moving his d-pawn to d4.

Student: Could you expand on this double king-pawn stuff please?

Teacher: After **1. e4 e5,** the opening falls into the double king-pawn variety, meaning that both sides have advanced their king-pawns two squares each. Black does so for reasons similar to White's, but with a profound difference. Black's thrust is additionally concerned with dissuading White's eventual d4. Black is thinking defense—for now. White, in turn, is not really thinking so much of stopping Black's queen-pawn from moving to d5 (Black's counterpart to White's advance d2-d4), at least, not at this point, because Black is a move behind and doesn't really have the time to advance the d-pawn with confidence yet. Still, such an advance (d7-d5, or d6-d5 if the d-pawn has already been moved one square) could be important for Black down the road. So White's extra move confers a playing edge in this symmetrical setup, at least to the extent that it allows White to pursue certain aggressive plans with greater assurance than Black could. In a theoretical sense, and even in a practical one, White is playing for a win and Black for a draw—with the same move!

Student: In general, is it wise for Black to copy White's play?

Teacher: Not really, but let's think this through. For practical reasons it's inevitably impracticable to copy for very long anyway. If one side gives a check, for example, the opponent must first get out of check before being able to ape the other side. Moreover, it may be impossible to restore the same setup as the first player after the check is given, even if you had the time to try. The position may not allow it. And suppose the first player gives checkmate? That can't be copied, no matter what, for there's no last licks in chess—the game is simply over. And there's even a psychological consideration. If one player copies the other, it's as if he's saying I'm content to draw. That's a very dangerous situation to be in once the other player senses it, because it enables him to take chances he might not otherwise take, realizing that the defender is not likely to want to get his hands dirty.

Student: So that's why we don't see more copying, because it tends to be impossible, difficult, or even deleterious to the copier's own game?

Teacher: That's right, not just because it's hard to do, but also because it's often undesirable, even when it doesn't immediately lose. We see this in many examples of symmetrical play—even fairly early in the attempt at symmetry, the second player gets the worst of it. The Petrov Defense, 1. e4 e5 2. Nf3 Nf6, provides a clear instance.

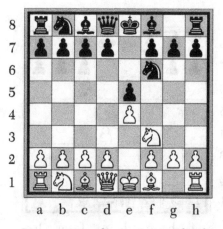

Diagram 138. After 1. e4 e5 2. Nf3 Nf6.

Student: What happens if White takes Black's king-pawn now, 3. Nxe5?

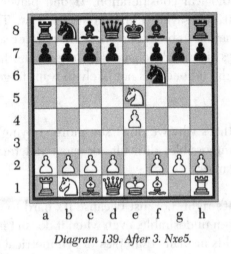

Diagram 139. After 3. Nxe5.

Teacher: If White were to capture the e-pawn, 3. Nxe5, it would be a mistake for Black to continue in like vein, 3 . . . Nxe4. Instead of taking back on e4 right away, which we'll soon look at, the right decision is to delay taking in favor of first driving away White's knight from e5, specifically by 3 . . . d6.

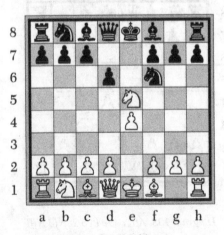

Diagram 140. After the possible response 3 . . . d6.

Student: Suppose White then retreats his attacked knight, 4. Nf3?

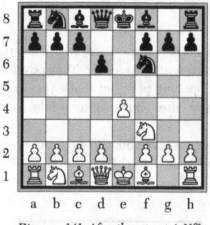

Diagram 141. After the retreat 4. Nf3.

Teacher: After the knight retreats, then it's okay to take the White king-pawn, 4 . . . Nxe4, and Black can cope with the pinning 5. Qe2 by the unpinning 5 . . . Qe7.

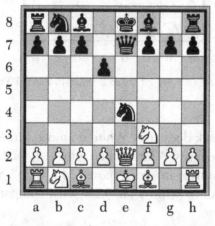

Diagram 142. After 4 . . . Nxe4 5. Qe2 Qe7.

Student: It's interesting. If White were now to play 6. d3, and if Black were to retreat his knight, 6 . . . Nf6, the position would once again be symmetrical, although White would still have the extra move. How did they get symmetry without copying exactly?

Teacher: By a kind of *transposition*, where a certain position is arrived at by a different move order. Transpositions can be cardinal to serious opening play, but that's a concept best left for your chessic future, after you've mastered the essentials.

Student: Can you show me how White should continue if Black takes the king-pawn, 3 . . . Nxe4?

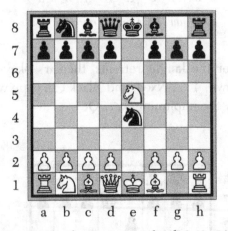

Diagram 143. After 1. e4 e5 2. Nf3 Nf6 3. Nxe5 Nxe4.

Teacher: If Black does copy White on move three, 3 . . . Nxe4, he runs into the nasty White queen attack, 4. Qe2, a move earlier, when his mirror-image response, 4 . . . Qe7, would fail to 5. Qxe4, defending White's knight against comparable capture by Black's queen.

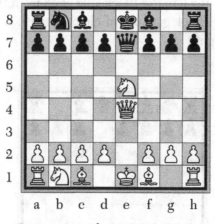

Diagram 144. After 4. Qe2 Qe7 5. Qxe4.

Student: But after 4. Qe2, couldn't Black simply retreat his knight, say 4 . . . Nf6?

Diagram 145. After 4. Qe2 Nf6.

Teacher: That doesn't help, for White can answer with 5. Nc6+, freely attacking Black's queen at d8 and delivering a mesmerizing discovered attack to the Black king at e8 from White's queen at e2. However Black gets out of check, he winds up losing his queen for a knight.

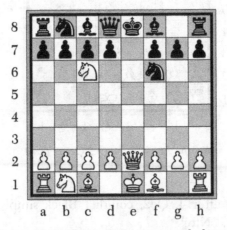

Diagram 146. After 5. Nc6+, winning Black's queen.

Student: Okay, this example of mimicry didn't work out. But it seems as if even serious competitors occasionally respond with the same or similar-looking moves.

Teacher: But they generally do so for at least slightly different reasons. Furthermore, they try to remain vigilant for possibilities to break the symmetry favorably, increasing or pilfering the initiative in the process. Bobby Fischer, in particular, was a genius at finding meaningful small differences in apparently symmetrical games.

Student: So it's unwise to copy your opponent without good cause. But let me ask you this. One reason you said Black plays **1 . . . e5** was to discourage White from moving his d-pawn two squares. How does this actually stop White from opening up in the center? And does Black have other ways to deter White's 2. d4?

Teacher: Let me play around with the second question first. Black has several alternatives to **1 . . . e5** that discourage White from playing a favorable 2. d4. For one, Black can play the Sicilian Defense, 1 . . . c5, which, like the double king-pawn response **1 . . . e5,** immediately guards the square d4. In both cases, after either 1 . . . c5 or **1 . . . e5,** White's advance 2. d4 could then be answered by a pawn capture, when White doesn't really want to take back on d4 with his queen, exposing it to early attack.

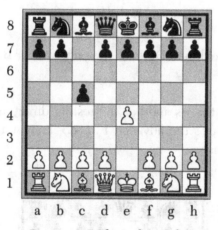

Diagram 147. The Sicilian Defense.

Student: Is there an alternative approach for Black, such as not guarding against 2. d4 at all?

Teacher: Yes, there is. For instance, you could challenge the White e-pawn instead. Thus, after 1 . . . Nf6, Alekhine's Defense, White's own king-pawn would be menaced, requiring some immediate attention.

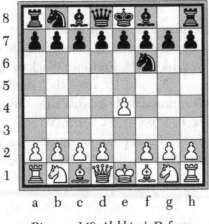

Diagram 148. Alekhine's Defense.

Student: Is Alekhine's Defense the only way for Black to attack e4 directly?

Teacher: No, there's another interesting direct assault on the e-pawn, and that's the advance 1 . . . d5, known as the Center Counter Defense.

Diagram 149. Center Counter Defense.

Student: But doesn't that lead to the early development of Black's queen after 2. exd5, when 2 . . . Qxd5 3. Nc3 gains a tempo for White?

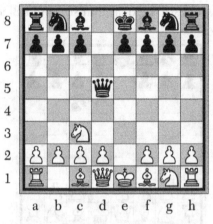

Diagram 150. After 2. exd5 Qxd5 3. Nc3.

Teacher: Very observant of you. And you're right, bringing out the queen too soon is a chessic no-no. But this is a case where Black is actually doing fine. Potentially (among other responses), he could move his queen to a5 (diagram 151) and continue satisfactorily. Furthermore, you haven't considered the possibility that Black doesn't bring his queen out immediately

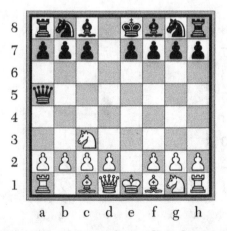

Diagram 151. After 1. e4 d5 2. exd5 Qxd5 3. Nc3 Qa5.

on move two, that instead he delays queenly development by first playing 2 . . . Nf6 (diagram 152), attacking the d5-pawn for a second time. But let's not get into all that here. Suffice it to say that Black could indeed counter with 1 . . . d5 if he were so inclined. White would still be okay, but so would Black.

Diagram 152. After 1. e4 d5 2. exd5 Nf6.

Student: There really are a lot of possibilities here.

Teacher: Of course, there are options. All these moves (c7-c5, Ng8-f6, and d7-d5) are possible for Black, as well as several others, but they require a more developed comprehension of chess

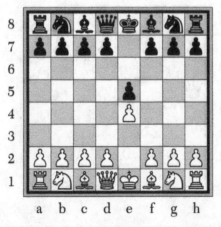

Diagram 153. The Double King-Pawn Defense.

to play correctly. For a beginner, though, **1 . . . e5** is the most direct way to cope with the potential of 2. d4.

Student: But what about my first question? Does **1 . . . e5** essentially stop White from playing 2. d4?

Diagram 154. After 2. d4.

Teacher: Not really. White certainly can play 2. d4 without losing material. If, for example, Black captures the queen-pawn, 2 . . . exd4, White can recoup the pawn by 3. Qxd4. So 2. d4 doesn't lose a pawn; rather it trades d-pawn for e-pawn. Trading is not losing.

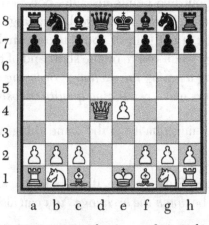

Diagram 155. After 2 . . . exd4 3. Qxd4.

Student: Wait a second. Could you differentiate between trading and losing?

Teacher: Absolutely. You win material if you get more than you give up. You lose material if you get less than you give up. And you trade material if you get the same in value as you give up.

Student: So winning material is generally good, losing material is generally bad, and trading material is not necessarily either one, but dependent on the circumstances of a given position?

Teacher: That's right. In fact, everything in chess is dependent on circumstances, not just the desirability of trading. If trading material turns out to be a bad transaction, it will be for non-material reasons. Naturally, if a trade is desirable for one player, it tends to be disagreeable for the other.

Student: I hear the word *exchange* used a lot. Is that the same as a trade?

Teacher: Yes, and no. It's true that chessplayers also refer to trades as exchanges. But the word exchange has another meaning too. *To exchange,* the verb, which means to trade, should not be confused with *the exchange,* the noun. By the same token, the phrase *the exchange* has a specific meaning. It refers to the difference of about two points in value, between a rook and a minor piece. You *win the exchange* by trading a bishop or a knight for a rook, a net gain of about two pawns in value. You *lose the exchange* when you're on the short end of the same deal. Instead of saying *winning the exchange* or *losing the exchange,* some chessplayers may say *winning quality* or *losing quality.*

Student: So gaining quality is the same thing as gaining the exchange.

Teacher: Correct. Furthermore, if you're *up the exchange,* your opponent must be *down the exchange.* You can also *sacrifice the* *exchange,* often shortened to *sac the exchange,* which means you voluntarily give up a rook for a minor piece. Such a transaction can be offered for either tactically immediate or strategically long-term considerations.

Student: So is it good for White to move his d-pawn two squares ahead here, on his second move, or not?

Teacher: It's not that simple. White can play d4 without losing material, for 2 . . . exd4 can be answered by 3. Qxd4, bringing out the White queen (diagram 156). Of course, White could delay capturing on d4 until other units are in place so that the queen doesn't have to come out unfavorably. The problem is when White's queen does take back immediately on d4. That's when Black can start to attack it by developing his own forces usefully, namely his queen-knight to c6. This gains time at White's expense, for White will then have to waste a move shifting the queen to safety.

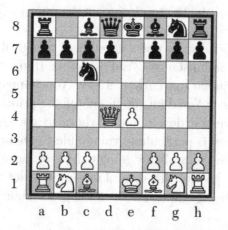

Diagram 156. After 3 . . . Nc6, forcing White's queen to move.

Student: You've just told me that Black is okay after 1. e4 d5 2. exd5 Qxd5 3. Nc3 (diagram 150). So why isn't White okay after 1. e4 e5 2. d4 exd4 3. Qxd4 Nc6 (diagram 156)? Aren't they virtually comparable?

Teacher: Not entirely, because White has an extra move, which he has used to advance his e-pawn two squares. In some cases, that decision could turn out to be detrimental, since White's king-pawn might soon serve as a target, thus requiring White to invest time and resources in its protection. Still, White's position in diagram 156 is not unreasonable. He simply has better ways to insure long-term pressure on Black. White doesn't need to take such early chances, bringing the queen out this way.

Student: And the earlier position, the one we saw in diagram 150?

Teacher: There, Black is fighting to establish a kind of dynamic equality, so bringing his queen out early is more in tune with his aims to bring "a gun to a knife fight." In chess, the smallest differences can lead to important ones.

Student: So how bad is it to bring out the queen early?

Teacher: Generally, it's not a good idea, though it very much depends on circumstances. You wouldn't think twice about bringing the queen out early if it gave you immediate checkmate, would you? You'd just do it and tell the principle advising against early queen development where to go. On the other hand, the queen is particularly vulnerable to enemy threats. If it's menaced, you're probably going to have to move your queen away to safety, possibly for several moves, in order to prevent it from either being captured or finding its abilities severely impaired.

Student: You know what I hate? Losing queen for queen.

Teacher: No one likes to lose his queen, but trading queens is an entirely different matter. Wouldn't you be willing to trade queens if doing so enabled you to win the game for sure on the next move?

Student: I guess.

Teacher: You guess? Of course you would. But by the same token, if you'd be willing to trade queens because you know you'd win for sure on the next move, perhaps you could understand why strong players, with all their experience and know-how, might be willing to trade queens for the tiniest of meaningful reasons. They know that such small advantages almost always win in the end too.

Student: I get it: Small advantages, in the right hands, win just as easily as big advantages in smaller hands.

Teacher: Well put. Now back to the point. Bringing the queen out early isn't always a bad idea, but it can easily lead to a loss of time, and losing time can be critical in the opening.

Student: So moving the queen early on tends to fritter time away, but not always?

Teacher: That's about right. Sometimes you can waste a turn to save your queen and still maintain an advantage in time, especially if you can move the queen to safety while issuing a counter-threat in turn. But if you have to move your queen over a series of unnecessary moves, this can add up to a serious loss of time that might even cost you the game. Think what can happen by playing four pointless moves. Imagine being reduced to four moves with the lone queen, while your opponent uses the same time to put four different pieces into the field. It could result in chessic disaster for the side with the hapless queen.

Student: So if I wanted to bring out the queen early, I would have to have a very good reason for doing so.

Teacher: Right. Rather than bringing out the queen so early, it makes practical sense to first bring out other friendly forces. As a rule, try to attack in number, using all your pieces, especially the bishops and knights, which are your minor pieces. Don't attack impetuously with lean forces. Prepare the queen's entrance by bringing out the support troops first. Eventually, the queen will be ready for action, and then it can become a real menace to weak points in the enemy's camp because of its wide range and striking power. Since it's able to attack in all directions, it's capable of delivering multiple threats with the same move. The ability to issue several threats at once is vital weaponry when grappling for material advantages.

Student: But isn't it easy to see how beginners would want to win quickly with superior and overwhelming force?

Teacher: It's easy to see how even strong players would want to do that, but they tend to know better, particularly when it comes to the ways in which early deployment of the queen can backfire. Newcomers naturally overuse the queen because they are impressed by its great strength, without considering the possible ramifications of such misuse. It's funny, but we're not really sure how the queen got to be so powerful in the first place. Originally, the queen was a weak piece known as the advisor, sitting next to the king. It moved only one diagonal square at a time, like an inferior bishop. Apparently, its powers reflected political belief at the time. In the real world it was thought that true power rested with the monarch, not his advisors. We see how different our own world has become. Somewhere around the 13th century, the advisor became the queen. Perhaps its rising importance paralleled the expanding role of ruling queens in Western history.

Student: So not only was the game possibly invented by woman, its most powerful piece is symbolically feminine. Is that why so many beginners avoid queen trades altogether?

Teacher: Probably this is not the chief reason for most beginners. I suspect it has more to do with fascination over the queen's value, which leads novices to avoid early queen exchanges. They tend to feel that without the queen they either can't play at all or that the game is less interesting. This is easy to understand, because the queen's clout is so appealing. But what could be more attractive than winning itself? If trading queens brings this about, that's the way to go. You have to aim for the ultimate good, however it's achieved.

Student: Okay, here's an idea for you: I think I understand the queen's power and abilities better than I do the other pieces. That's why I don't want to trade it so much, because for me the queen is easier to grasp, and by keeping my queen, I can play better.

Teacher: From the way you've just put it, keeping your queen implies that you'll play worse. I can, however, see what you're trying to say. Certainly each particular piece demands particular attention, methods, and techniques. But before you can master the queen, it makes greater sense to try to understand to some degree the rook and the bishop, the two pieces that compose the queen's power. The whole is certainly greater than the sum of its parts, but it doesn't follow that the whole is necessarily easier to understand. That's why we analyze in chess, to break moves down into their conceptual constituents. Players should learn how to use all the pieces, not just the queen, especially if they want to play the game astutely. That can be hard to do if they unreasonably cling to indefensible principles.

Student: But can't you violate principles against weaker opponents, especially if you're a very strong player?

Teacher: Base your decisions on the board, not your opponent's strength. Analyze all positions objectively, and then select a course of action. Never play a move you know to be bad or against the spirit of the game, because even a weak player might exploit it if given the opportunity. Good players don't take unnecessary chances. They try to win by risking virtually nothing. As a rule:

1. **Never violate a principle without a good reason.**
2. **Play the board, not the opponent.**

Student: After 1. e4 e5 2. d4 exd4, you've implied that White doesn't have to take back on d4 right away. Instead of 3. Qxd4, what else could he profitably do?

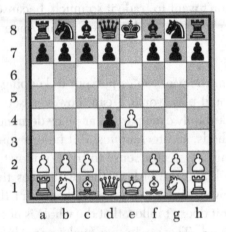

Diagram 157. After 1. e4 e5 2. d4 exd4.

Teacher: White instead could offer a pawn sacrifice, not aiming to take back on d4 right away, in order to gain time for development. Two alternatives are 3. c3 (diagram 158) and 3. Nf3 (diagram 159), but exploring these possibilities in detail can be left for another time. For now, suffice it to say that if White were to offer such a sacrifice it would be with the hope of building an attack by going ahead in development. Furthermore, by playing 3. Nf3, White isn't necessarily sacrificing a pawn. In some cases he may simply be delaying capture for a move or two, using the time to increase his development, as Black does in the line 1. e4 d5 2. exd5 Nf6 (see diagram 152).

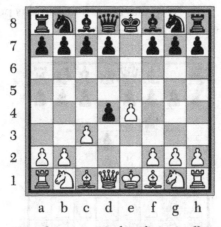

Diagram 158. After 1. e4 e5 2. d4 exd4 3. c3, offering a gambit.

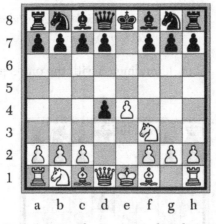

Diagram 159. After 1. e4 e5 2. d4 exd4 3. Nf3.

Student: I'm curious. After 1. e4 e5 2. d4, should Black let White's pawn be and defend his own instead?

Teacher: The correct move for Black here is to take White's pawn. Unless White is mentally prepared to play differently, he will have to expend a move to take the pawn back. At least temporarily, this gives Black the initiative and the next free move. This doesn't mean that Black couldn't defend his e-pawn satisfactorily, say by 2 . . . Nc6 (diagram 160). But this position is not so easy for a newcomer to understand.

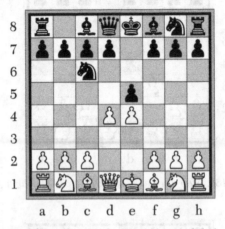

*Diagram 160. Reasonable for Black, but slightly harder for
a beginner to play.*

Student: How about defending e5 with the one-square advance 2 . . . d6?

Diagram 161. Too passive for Black.

Teacher: One thing Black shouldn't do is defend e5 by playing to 2 . . . d6. That would lead to an unfavorable trade of queens for Black, and a desirable exchange for White, after 3. dxe5 dxe5 4. Qxd8+ Kxd8 (diagram 162). Black has lost the ability to castle and his king remains in the center, where it's more vulnerable to White's forces because the center is open.

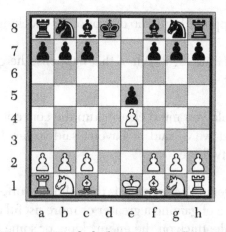

Diagram 162. Black's king is potentially exposed.

Student: Is it always bad to lose the right to castle?

Teacher: Sometimes losing the right to castle doesn't lead to chessic suicide, especially when players are moving toward the endgame. At that point, the king may actually be better placed in the center. But in most cases involving the opening, losing the right to castle usually means that the defender will have to be very careful, hoping to get his king to safety before enemy pieces can start sniping at it. It's no fun to find your king the mark for target practice.

Student: Obviously, it's clear the trade of queens may be desirable for non-material reasons. But what about sacrificing the queen, giving it up for less material? Is that ever a good idea?

Teacher: You can only do this if you know for sure that your sacrifice is going to work. Otherwise, giving the queen up at a loss would be foolish. There's an exception, of course.

Student: Isn't there always?

Teacher: Yes, although there are exceptions to that, too.

Student: I suppose there's no exception to checkmate.

Teacher: Not if it's legal. When that happens, the game is most definitely over.

Student: Would you mind clearing up the concept of sacrifice? Based on what we've said or haven't said so far, I feel there's some ambiguity there.

Teacher: In general, a *sacrifice* is the voluntary offer of material for the purpose of gaining a greater or more useful advantage in either material, attack on the enemy king, or some other factor. Often the sacrifice is made in conjunction with a number of moves in a combination. Rudolph Spielmann, in his *Art of Sacrifice in Chess*, said: "The beauty of a game of chess is usually appraised, and with good reason, according to the sacrifices it contains. . . . The glowing power of the sacrifice is irresistible: enthusiasm for sacrifice lies in man's nature."

Student: Is a gambit a sacrifice?

Teacher: Yes, it is. A *gambit* is a voluntary offer, usually of a pawn in the opening, in an attempt to gain another kind of advantage, especially in time. The gambiteer hopes to garner several tempi for the pawn and build a winning attack. Give any opponent three extra moves and see what happens. Time advantages in the opening can affect the whole game. Obviously, if you use your time edge to force checkmate right away, there's no middlegame or endgame, and you can forget about who has the better pawn structure or more material. If particular sacrifices or gambits seem to bring you closer to winning, then you should seriously consider offering them. If they don't seem to be too promising, however, then don't play them. It's that simple.

Student: Can you give me some specific examples of gambits or opening sacrifices?

Teacher: How about the double-edged King's Gambit? It's possibly the most celebrated opening sacrifice of all. It's brought about by the moves 1. e4 e5 2. f4. Although it can give White a powerful initiative, it can also lead to a breach in the protective wall around his own king.

Diagram 163. The King's Gambit.

Teacher: Another gambit can be found in E. M. Forster's *Abinger Harvest*. There the writer conveys a fascination for the Evans Gambit, which occurs after the moves 1. e4 e5 2. Nf3 Nc6 3. Bc4 Bc5 4. b4. It was first played in the 1820s by a Welsh sea captain, William Evans. White sacrifices the b-pawn for open lines and central activity. Forster liked this aggressive game, but it's come to my attention that he lacked the knowledge needed to conduct the offensive.

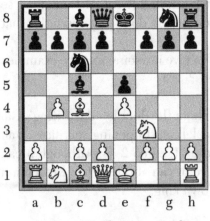

Diagram 164. The Evans Gambit.

Student: Are there other advantages to be found in gambits?

Teacher: Yes. They include gaining an attack, increasing or seizing the initiative, or improving and adding to development. All are nice goals at any point, but they are especially so during the opening, when the most handy weapon is often the asset of an extra move. But gambits are small sacrifices. It's quite another matter to sacrifice your queen. Before doing that, you'd better know what you're doing. Of course, if you know what you're doing, and you can see your way to victory, sacrificing the queen may not be a sacrifice at all. It's no sacrifice on my part.

Determining Priorities

DEVELOPMENT AND THE CENTER

Teacher: Can you summarize what you've learned about the importance of time in the opening?

Student: Since gaining time is vital during the opening stages of a game, both players should avoid moves that waste it. Players squander time by bringing the queen out too early and making unnecessary pawn moves.

Teacher: Right on the money.

Student: Maybe I should start betting on my games. But not before I figure out the more subtle differences between pawns and pieces during the initial stages of the opening. How should these various things be used?

Teacher: In the early part of the opening, pawns should be used to stake out territory and clear lines for developing pieces.

Student: We've already talked about that. But I'm sure there are more intricate issues involved.

Teacher: Pawns are excellent for warding off invaders. They are generally more efficient defenders than the heavy pieces, the queens and rooks. Tying down a pawn to a protective chore is more economical than squandering a queen or a rook for that purpose. Bishops and knights, the minor pieces, fit neatly between heavy pieces and pawns. They can be decent attackers, able to strike across distances, and they are more expendable than either queens or rooks, which explains why it's imperative to activate them expeditiously in the opening. They should lay claim to the center of the board and arrive ready for potential invasions into the enemy camp.

Student: I used to love camp.

Teacher: Let's consider a few more subtleties. Compare, for example, the unit values of a rook and a pawn vs. two minor pieces. They seem to be even, at six points for each side. In actuality, they're not really equivalent. True, a rook and a pawn are worth about six, but a bishop and a knight together are worth about seven, not six. Call it the new chess math. Three and three add up to something like seven, where the whole is greater than the sum of its parts. But the evaluation of different combinations always has something to do with circumstances and the accompanying phase of the game.

Student: I think I'm finally beginning to understand that everything is always dependent on everything else.

Teacher: And not only on a chessboard, either. Still, in terms of sheer worth, two minor pieces are usually preferable to a rook and a pawn in the opening and the middlegame, though the balance of power can sometimes shift in the endgame. The bishops and knights begin to pull their weight almost from the moment they leave their home rank, often threatening trouble in tandem, making them particularly valuable in the early stages of a game, when opponents could easily be caught unprepared. Bishops and knights can become effective immediately for both attack and defense, and they can reach good squares without much trouble. Rooks and pawns, on the other hand, aren't as readily deployed early on. The pawn, in particular, is usually confined more or less to the file it originally occupies, and even a capture only takes it to an adjacent file.

Student: So rooks tend to have little impact in the opening?

Teacher: That's not always true, just for the most part. Even after castling they're often half asleep. Usually, rooks are at their best in the late middlegame and approaching the endgame. By then, files are open and the board is sufficiently clear for the rook to strut its stuff. Unobstructed lines into the enemy camp practically invite a rook's intrusion. In fact, in many endgames, a lone rook is just as strong as a knight and a bishop combined. But in the opening, it often takes a rook and two pawns to equal the unified force of bishop and knight. That's chess synergy at work.

Student: And the pawn?

Teacher: As for the plodding pawn, its mobility can be practically nil in comparison to the other units. Move a pawn too precipitously in the beginning and it might become overextended and hard to defend. In the opening a pawn is often, though not exclusively, respected as a defensive unit. To some extent, it's best left on its original square until much later on, unless its movement contributes to control of the center, development, or some definite chessic purpose.

Student: When visions of promotion can aspire it to greatness. Speaking of which, I have to decide on my second move. Should I play 2. d4?

Teacher: After **1. e4 e5,** I don't recommend playing 2. d4, which is too risky and too forcing. Instead, I suggest the steadier **2. Nf3.**

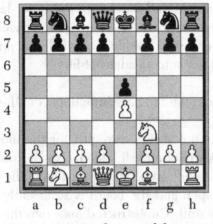

Diagram 165. Developing and threatening.

Student: What's so great about **2. Nf3**?

Teacher: This move actually has at least four patent advantages. It prepares for playing d2-d4 later, at a sounder time; it develops the king-knight toward the center; it threatens the Black e-pawn; and it controls, to some extent, Black's response. He can't afford to lose a pawn for nothing, at least not without a gimmick. He's either got to defend the e5-pawn or play a suitable counterattack.

Student: All right. I accept the worth of **2. Nf3,** especially with all it does. It seems as if you prefer moves that do several things at once.

Teacher: Whenever you can make moves with multiple positive outcomes, some of which are hidden or difficult for the opponent to perceive, you're playing chess as it should be played. If you can get away with disguising your intentions so effectively that you play moves achieving your goals without making any significant concessions, you may call yourself either a master or a master of disguise.

Student: I will attempt to camouflage my thoughts masterfully.

Teacher: But not just here and now.

Student: In that case, I'd like to ask you this. What if Black answers my second move not by guarding his threatened king-pawn, but by a counterattacking knight move of his own, 2 . . . Nf6, hitting my king-pawn? I know we looked at this a little earlier, but it wasn't clear that you thought it was all right to play it.

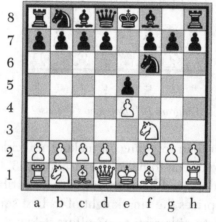

Diagram 166. Petrov's Defense.

Teacher: It's perfectly okay to play. You're talking about Petrov's Defense (1. e4 e5 2. Nf3 Nf6), also known as the Russian Game. It leads to a satisfactory position when handled correctly, but is not suited to players who prefer more active play, mainly because of the static nature of the defense when played imprecisely. The Petrov has been weaponized by such great players as former world champions Anatoly Karpov (1975–85) and Tigran Petrosian (1963–69), as well as perennial world-class challenger Viktor Korchnoi. But these stalwarts probably have a deeper understanding of chess than the guys who play in the park for quarters.

Student: So maybe it would be better for Black to defend his king-pawn rather than counterattacking mine. How is guarding the pawn directly by 2 . . . f6?

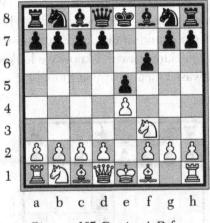

Diagram 167. Damiano's Defense.

Teacher: Other than resigning, or making a suicidal decision to move either the queen to h4 or the bishop to a3, this is practically the worst defense Black has. It doesn't contribute to development and deprives the king-knight of its best square. Moving the king-knight to either h6 or e7 offers it fewer options than going to f6. Moreover, putting the f-pawn on f6 weakens the h5-e8 diagonal as well as the a2-g8 diagonal.

Student: I think I see. A bishop posted on the a2-g8 diagonal, say at c4, would prevent Black from castling kingside, because his king would wind up in check and that's illegal.

Teacher: Move that f-pawn this way and Black can end up with a hideous game. It's not a particularly good idea to make a move incurring several problems with no tangibly favorable outcomes. The rule of thumb is simple: Avoid unnecessary and weakening pawn moves in the opening, especially if they have nothing else going for them.

Student: Just curious, but does this defense, as poor as it is, have a name?

Teacher: The move 2 . . . f6 is actually called Damiano's Defense, named after the Portuguese-Italian master Damiano of the sixteenth century. Although he correctly analyzed 2 . . . f6 as being inferior, someone with a vendetta named the defense after him, and it stuck. Damiano, who deserved better, was one of the first players to advocate a classical pawn center. Among his maxims for good play are "With an advantage make equal exchanges" and "If you see a good move, look for a better one."

Student: Okay, so pawn to f6 on the second move isn't very good. What about 2 . . . Bd6?

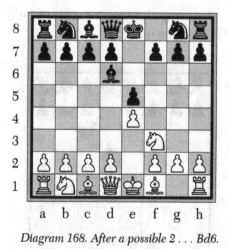

Diagram 168. After a possible 2 . . . Bd6.

Teacher: This move develops a minor piece toward the center, while protecting the e-pawn, but it leads to a crisis of coordination. The bishop now blocks the Black d-pawn, preventing its forward movement. If the d-pawn can't move, the bishop at c8 can't move along the c8-h3 diagonal. As a result, Black would have to develop this light-square piece unnaturally, at least for double king-pawn openings, by moving the b-pawn when it's not especially convenient or desirable to move it. Black might thereafter have to find additional defenses to the e5-pawn to help remedy the situation. This might free the d6-bishop for subsequent movement, but it would cost time, the lifeblood of chess. At d6 the bishop itself might even become an object of attack. It's pretty clear that 2 . . . Bd6 is undesirable.

Student: But it does work, at least for now.

Teacher: Yes, but you can't just play chess for the now. You have to look into the future to insure that there'll be one—at least for you. Good development is harmonious development. No piece should be developed without a scheme for developing the other pieces—plain and simple.

Student: How about the defense 2 . . . Qf6? That defends the king-pawn and develops a piece.

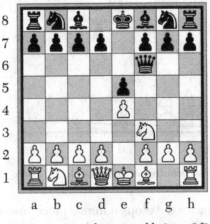

Diagram 169. After a possible 2 . . . Qf6.

Teacher: True, it does both, but neither one desirably. In addition to usurping Black's best square for his king-knight (f6), this move unnecessarily and prematurely develops the queen in violation of principle. After 3. Nc3, for example, White will be threatening further harassment to her ladyship by 4. Nd5. Besides, this defense (2 . . . Qf6) is overkill. Why have the general do what can be done by the private?

Student: I suppose putting the queen on e7 instead of f6 isn't much better.

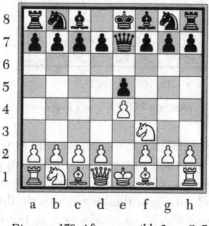

Diagram 170. After a possible 2 . . . Qe7.

Teacher: No, 2 . . . Qe7 isn't really any better than 2 . . . Qf6. While putting the queen on e7 doesn't derail Black's king-knight from going to f6, it certainly impedes Black's king-bishop, which suddenly has no move at all. As a rule, develop your pieces amicably, making sure that they don't step on each other's toes. They should be working in concert, not against each other. And, of course, you shouldn't misuse the queen. It's only a chess piece, after all. Keep it in readiness for circumstances that call for unleashing its extraordinary abilities. Since nothing is unusual here, either queen move (2 . . . Qf6 or 2 . . . Qe7) is premature.

Student: I refuse to give up figuring out Black's best second move. What about 2 . . . d6?

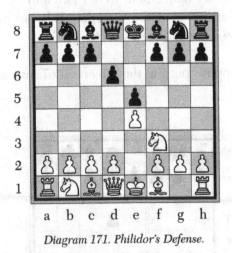

Diagram 171. Philidor's Defense.

Teacher: You're thinking just as chessically as you should. In fact, it's a good approach to seek out at least two possible solutions to a problem, so that you can compare them to see which you prefer. Much of chess thinking is exactly this: comparing possibilities to see which one works best in the given circumstances. Of course, sometimes you know the right move right away.

Student: Especially if you get to say "checkmate" after you've made it.

Teacher: You bet. Here, for Black's second move, we've been looking at a number of reasonable defenses to the king-pawn. This one, 2 . . . d6, is clearly the best so far. The counterattacking Russian Game, 2 . . . Nf6 (diagram 166), is also satisfactory. The move d7-d6 protects the e-pawn solidly, with another pawn, and pawn defenses are often the most reliable. It also clears the way for the queen-bishop to enter the fray, along the c8-h3 diagonal. Now it slightly obstructs the development of the king-bishop by limiting its immediate prospects to the square e7, but that's a small price to pay for solidity. Thus, with 2 . . . d6, Black derives a partially cramped but soundly playable game.

Student: So the problem with d7-d6 is that it blocks in the f8-bishop?

Teacher: No, that's not the only drawback. The move 2 . . . d6 can produce another difficulty. It may result in a wasted tempo if Black should later play for a d5-advance, a key equalizing thrust for Black in many defenses. Such an advance often results in an exchange of Black's d-pawn for White's e-pawn, dissolving at least a portion of the center and leading to a more or less equal game. If White has already exchanged his d-pawn for Black's e-pawn, neither side will have a pawn in the center at all, and accordingly both players should have freedom of action for their pieces.

Student: It seems to me that, in many defenses, advancing the queen-pawn to d5 is a key move for Black. Can you say anything about that?

Teacher: When it comes to many e-pawn openings, a White leitmotif—and that's not French, by the way, but German—is to restrain Black's d-pawn so that it isn't able to advance to d5. As long as White can hold back the Black d-pawn to no further ahead than d6, Black will either be slightly behind in development or have less space or both. Once the pawn moves satisfactorily to d5, however, Black usually has no trouble equalizing.

Student: Can you show me an example of one side having more pawns in the center?

Teacher: One case where Black has two center pawns to White's one is the Sicilian Defense (1. e4 c5 2. Nf3 d6 3. d4 cxd4 4. Nxd4). You might notice that a future exchange of Black's d-pawn for White's e-pawn would actually result in Black having the only pawn remaining in the center. That situation usually gives Black equality and an excellent chance to control the center of the board.

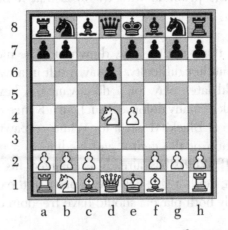

Diagram 172. Black has more pawns on the central files.

Student: You've already told me about Damiano's Defense (diagram 167). Do the moves 1. e4 e5 2. Nf3 d6 have a name?

Teacher: They're called Philidor's Defense, named after the great French player François-André Danican Philidor (1726–95).

Student: This leads me to another question. After 1. e4 e5 2. Nf3, is there a better defense for the king-pawn than 2 . . . d6?

Teacher: There's a better way to protect Black's king-pawn, and that's **2 . . . Nc6.**

Student: What's so good about that move?

Teacher: It does a lot of things, without causing too much trouble. The move **2 . . . Nc6** (1) protects the e5-pawn; (2) doesn't block anything except the Black c-pawn, which doesn't need

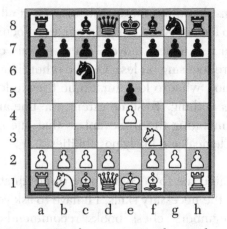

Diagram 173. After 2 . . . Nc6 in the actual game.

to be moved here; (3) develops a new piece toward the center; (4) assails the square d4; (5) avoids all of the liabilities raised by the alternative defenses; and (6) doesn't weaken anything.

Student: Those sound like terrific advantages. Black doesn't really do anything toxic to his game in playing **2 . . . Nc6**. It must be a good move! It's amazing. We're only two moves into a game, and it's obvious that some choices turn out to be far better than others.

Teacher: Each move in chess establishes integral relationships or hinders them. Each move can lay claim to an advantage, either in time, space, material, pawn structure, or king safety. Your job is to play moves that strive to better your position while conceding as little as possible. I think what you've said about some choices being significantly better than others points out something important: how good players can look far ahead.

Student: What do you mean?

Teacher: Besides having good visualization skills, experienced players realize that most moves are not really relevant, and don't have to be considered too thoroughly or even at all. Good players don't try to look at everything. Rather, they focus their attention on only a few logical moves. These players can do more because they're focusing on less. On the other hand, the beginner doesn't know what to look for. So he tries to look at everything and sees nothing. To some extent, the fine art of analysis consists in eliminating the irrelevant so that one can spotlight only the most logical and likely possibilities.

Student: Remind me to become more discriminating. But before I acquire the necessary skills, I'll have to ask you this question. Most beginners' chess books recommend moving the center-pawns two squares each. Why, then, do so many strong players use flank openings? They don't necessarily move their center pawns at all, at least initially.

Teacher: *Flank openings*, where you generally place the king-bishop on the side, directing its power toward the center instead of using it directly to occupy the center, can be effective if you understand how to develop them. When you play a flank opening, you might seem to be abandoning the center, but what seems to be is not always so. A flank opening doesn't ignore the center. It just fights for it in a different way.

Student: I don't get it. How does putting a bishop on the flank affect the center?

Teacher: You can play for the center not just by occupying it, but also by attacking it. A flanked, or *fianchettoed,* bishop aims at the center from either g2 or b2 for White, and either g7 or b7 for Black. The idea is part of a grander strategy: to avoid immediate occupation of the center in favor of first controlling it from the flanks and/or from just off the center. At a later time, when you've gotten a grip on the central squares and feel more secure there, you'll want to place your pieces in the center according to plan.

Student: Assuming I indeed have a plan.

Teacher: Of course you have a plan: to play for the center by attacking from the flank. But you have to face the difficulties first. Initially, you're giving your opponent free rein in the middle when playing a flank opening. If you don't proceed intelligently, you may not be able to come back and undermine his centrally based fortifications. Those who like flank openings think they can. Those who dislike them think they can't.

Student: As a beginner, should I consider playing flank openings?

Teacher: As a teacher, I'd be happy if you just consider playing. Flank openings are not recommended for the beginning student because they're harder to grasp and manage. To comprehend them more fully, it's wise to start playing chess by grappling with more traditional approaches to the center. After assimilating those ideas and playing hundreds of games, you'll probably be better equipped to experiment with flank openings and put them to work. Understanding them better, you'll play them better. At least that's the theory.

Student: I think it's time for another summary. Some of the opening *do's* are becoming clear, but what are some of the important *don'ts* in the opening?

Teacher: Try these on for size. Don't: make unnecessary pawn moves; bring out the queen too early; move a piece twice in the opening; trade a developed piece for an undeveloped one; exchange without good reason; develop just to bring a piece out and not with a specific purpose; block your center pawns; or impede the development of other friendly pieces.

Student: I think I counted eight don'ts. I hope there aren't any more.

Teacher: It's always possible to find more. We could easily add these to the list. Don't: weaken your king's position or move your uncastled king; move knights to the edge of the board; waste time or moves; indulge in pawn-grabbing; sacrifice without good reason; refuse a sacrifice because your opponent made it quickly and confidently—analyze it, then decide; play without a plan; develop in an uncoordinated way; or change plans from move to move.

Student: Sounds like another nine reasons, which makes seventeen all told, at least for now.

Teacher: We're not finished yet. Let's add a few more. Don't: remain uncastled too long; advance pawns too far too soon; ignore your opponent's moves; give pointless checks; capriciously avoid making natural captures or recaptures; take your opponent too lightly or too seriously; play a set order of moves without regard to your opponent's responses; or open the center with your king still uncastled.

Student: Okay, that's at least a total of twenty-five things to remember about the opening. Where do we go from here?

Teacher: To a place where we once again learn not to follow any piece of advice too religiously, namely Lesson 8.

Opening "Don'ts"

1. **Don't make unnecessary pawn moves.**
2. **Don't bring out the queen too early.**
3. **Don't move a piece twice in the opening.**
4. **Don't trade a developed piece for an undeveloped one.**
5. **Don't exchange without good reason.**
6. **Don't develop just to bring a piece out and not with a specific purpose.**

7. Don't block your center pawns.
8. Don't impede the development of other friendly pieces.
9. Don't weaken your king's position or move your uncastled king.
10. Don't move knights to the edge of the board.
11. Don't waste time or moves.
12. Don't indulge in pawn-grabbing.
13. Don't sacrifice without good reason.
14. Don't refuse a sacrifice because your opponent made it quickly and confidently. Analyze it, then decide.
15. Don't play without a plan.
16. Don't develop in an uncoordinated way.
17. Don't change plans from move to move.
18. Don't remain uncastled too long.
19. Don't advance pawns too far too soon.
20. Don't ignore your opponent's moves.
21. Don't give pointless checks.
22. Don't capriciously avoid making natural captures or recaptures.
23. Don't take your opponent too lightly or too seriously.
24. Don't play a set order of moves without regard to your opponent's responses.
25. Don't open the center with your king still uncastled.

COMPARING MINOR PIECES

Teacher: Central control and sensible development: these are valuable to any opening. During our game, we both tried to stake a claim to the middle of the board and develop a minor piece in the process. White and Black have both moved the king-pawn and a knight.

Student: Is it a good idea to develop knights early?

Teacher: Generally, yes. This is just as true for bishops. Both bishops and knights should be mobilized fairly soon.

Student: Why is that?

Teacher: It makes sense to bring out the knights and the bishops early because they're the easiest pieces to activate. The knights can be developed without having to move a pawn. Once the king-pawn has been advanced, the king-bishop is ready for action. And if the queen-pawn is pushed, the queen-bishop can sweep into position. In addition, by bringing out these lighter forces early, advanced posts can be established, making it safer to develop the queen and the rooks later on.

Student: I've figured out that the queen can become dangerously exposed when developed too early, and it may take a while to discover the best stations for the rooks. But which should you develop first, knights or bishops?

Teacher: It depends. Neither, necessarily. It can be easier to develop knights than bishops because of the former's jumping ability. Since no pawn has to be moved to develop any knight, it's natural to see at least one knight enter the fray before any bishop. But it doesn't have to be that way. Just because you can develop both knights without moving any pawns at all doesn't mean you should move both knights, or even one, before developing a bishop. Development, like anything else in chess, depends on circumstances.

Student: Where should knights go when they first move into the game?

Teacher: At the risk of sounding repetitive, it depends.

Student: I should have known. Silly me.

Teacher: If you're free to do anything you'd like, it's usually best to move the knights toward the center, to the bishop-three squares. The White king-knight, for example, almost always stands well on the square f3, observing eight different squares concurrently, thus reaching its full spatial potential. Placed on f3, White's knight prevents an opposing queen incursion at h4, which can be important to dissuade encroachment in the kingside sector. And from f3 the knight may be able to advance later to even more powerful spots in the center, as well as the opponent's half of the board.

Student: I suppose it's safe to say similar things about a Black knight placed on f6?

Teacher: Most assuredly. But let me get back to the f3-knight in particular. If it can later be anchored by a friendly pawn, and placed in a way that denies an enemy pawn actual or practical chances to drive it away, the f3-knight can be positioned beautifully on the attack-square e5. Notice in the constructed position of diagram 174 how the strong knight on e5 severely restricts Black's bishop.

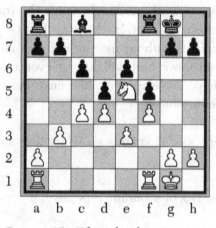

Diagram 174. White's knight is strong on e5.

Student: Why should White have all the fun?

Teacher: Good point, which is why in the imagined situation of diagram 175 you'll find it's Black who has the aggressive knight. Having gone from f6 to g4, the knight assails f2 and h2, the latter in tandem with Black's queen. Fortunately, White can hold the fort by shifting his knight to f1, but it doesn't always work out so conveniently in similar circumstances, and the knightly g4-intrusion can often be more serious.

Student: Could you elaborate on Black's knights?

Teacher: As I've said, Black's king-knight has the same powers from f6 as White's knight on f3. A black knight at f6 is prepared

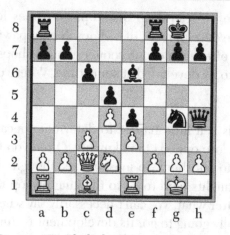

Diagram 175. Black's knight means business on g4.

to move to e4 under ideal conditions, and it's also ready to invade on g4, as we've seen in diagram 175, if the situation is suitably inviting. Queen-knights for both sides can do well from the bishop-3 squares, so it's usually wise to move them there if circumstances support such developments. So both White and Black normally consider the possibility of developing their queen-knights to their respective queen-bishop-3 squares: c3 for White and c6 for Black. But these are not absolute decisions, and circumstances may very easily lead both sides to move queen-knights elsewhere.

Student: I expect it has something to do with the chosen opening—for example, whether White begins with a king-pawn opening or a queen-pawn opening.

Teacher: Very true. It's not unreasonable to say that placing the queen-knight on the bishop-3 square is more likely in king-pawn openings than queen-pawn openings. Even then, the situation may be different for White and Black, since Black is a move behind and may have to make developmental concessions. Let's not get into queen-pawn openings here, though, for this would divert us away from the game at hand.

Student: Fine, we can drop queen-pawn games for now, but what about the development of bishops in king-pawn openings? Knights may often come out sooner than bishops, but bishops still have to be developed at some time. Where do they usually go?

Teacher: This is a little harder to determine because bishops usually have more options than knights. Often you have to wait to see where to put them. In most games, though of course not all, the king-knights tend to go to the king-bishop-three square almost no matter what. We can't necessarily say where the king-bishop is usually going to go. Its development is simply too subservient to attendant conditions.

Student: What about the catchphrase "knights before bishops"?

Teacher: It's a principle with very slight merit. Why does it exist? Well, let's see. It takes a knight at least two moves, even three or four or more, to assume advanced positions. Bishops almost never need that many moves to get into the thick of things, so that's one reason to try to move knights generally before bishops. Another rationale for "knights before bishops" rests on the fact that no pawn has to be pushed in order for a knight to make a move. Therefore, it's easier to develop knights, although I must point out that ease in itself should not necessarily be the linchpin for doing anything. Since bishops do tend to have more options, a knight move involves less immediate commitment and, thus, more opening flexibility. And finally, by developing at least the king-knight first, you secure your position better defensively, in that a knight positioned at king-bishop-3 stops the enemy queen from invading. That is, the White king-knight at f3 keeps Black's queen out of h4, and the Black king-knight at f6 keeps White's queen out of h5.

Student: Sounds like it's almost never good to develop bishops before knights.

Teacher: Never? Like every other principle, this one is open to argument, a never-ending chessic dialectic. In many instances, especially for Black, moving a bishop before moving a knight can be fairly typical and very much in tune with the way the game develops. It can be a wise choice, or even a necessity, to move the bishop first.

Student: If this is so, then why does this principle seem to pop up in so many chess books?

Teacher: Primarily because it was put forth by a number of the classic writers, who often dealt mainly with double king-pawn openings. It turns out that the principle holds slightly more true for games beginning 1. e4 e5, and it tends to be even more reliable for White than for Black. But times have changed, and many vigorous and dynamic opening ideas have worked their way into today's repertory. Today's savvy player will do whatever works, not what he's told will work. Probably I would restate this olden principle this way: "In double king-pawn openings, most of the time, White should develop his king-knight to f3 before developing his king-bishop, unless he prefers to develop the king-bishop first for meaningful reasons." Since this way of putting it has no value to anyone, I offer it as the kind of thing chess writers and teachers say as a matter of course.

Student: I have a modification for you. Does this work? Develop minor pieces before major pieces.

Teacher: Yes, it does. It's a lot more correct. Neither does it stop us so much from thinking on our own—to see what really succeeds, rather than what's supposed to.

Student: Let me ask you this. Since some of these principles seem to get us nowhere, why should we resort to them at all?

Teacher: The better principles have great value. Even imprecise axioms, such as "knights before bishops," can be helpful when you can't seem to find your way. If you need to get your bearings, look for one or two principles in such situations as beacons to guide you to safety. If you can think of a principle or general guideline that seems to relate to the given circumstances, ask some probing questions about it. Try to find out if the principle really does apply and whether it can be used to help you find your way through the forest of variations you face at every turn. If it does, a catchy rule of thumb can function as the foundation for your next move. That's the real value of a principle: to give you a helping hand, to start you thinking.

Student: I guess principles are like the latest weather report. You can never treat them as absolutes, but it makes sense to consult them anyway.

Teacher: Principles are merely guidelines, and subject to exception after exception after exception. In the end, rather than submitting to the iron hand of ruthlessly imposed illogic, we have to determine our own fate if it's to have any poetry, or music, or import at all. But let's get back to our game. It's White's third move. What should he do?

Student: Well, what about opening up with **3. d4**? If you answer me with 3 . . . exd4, I can take back, 4. Nxd4, bringing my knight to a center square.

Teacher: Now you're getting into the spirit of things. You're trying to look three half moves ahead. That is, you're trying to find your move, your opponent's likely response, and your possible answer to that. If you can follow this formula, trying to find your move, his move, and then your move after that, then you're really playing chess.

Student: Since everything seems to have a name, does the move **3. d4** here, at this particular time, signify anything?

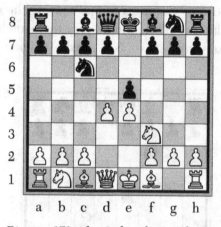

Diagram 176. After 3. d4—the Scotch Game.

Teacher: This opening sequence is known as the Scotch Game. This opening (**1. e4 e5 2. Nf3 Nc6 3. d4**) was first cited in a 1750 book written by the Italian master Ercole del Rio. The Scotch derived its name from several matches played in Edinburgh between 1824 and 1829. According to Joseph Henry Blackburne (1841–1924), the Scotch Game "gives birth to the sort of position that the young player should study." Of course, chess experts often agree to disagree. The German grandmaster Dr. Siegbert Tarrasch (1862–1935) referred to it as "bright and lively but at the cost of solidity." Both men are no longer with us, so we have some leeway here.

Student: That's good to know. Can you tell me anything helpful about the Scotch?

Teacher: On the surface, the Scotch seems to give White movement in the center and quick development. But there are drawbacks. Black has chances for counterplay against the White e-pawn. Moreover, since Black has not had to play the blocking move d7-d6, impeding the f8-bishop, he's not as cramped. Black also has the opportunity to play the freeing advance d7-d5 in one move, instead of wasting a tempo moving the queen-pawn first to d6 and later to d5. If you do play the Scotch, as Black, I am going to take your d-pawn, **3 . . . exd4** (diagram 177).

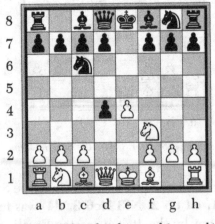

Diagram 177. After the actual 3 . . . exd4.

Student: Since I don't want to lose my queen, I suppose I'm going to take back with my knight, **4. Nxd4** (diagram 178).

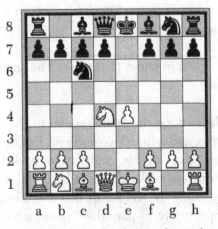

Diagram 178. After the actual 4. Nxd4.

Teacher: You may want to ask yourself this question: should Black force White to expose his queen by 4 . . . Nxd4 5. Qxd4 (diagram 179)?

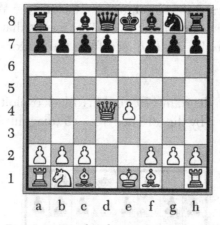

Diagram 179. After the possibility of 5. Qxd4.

Student: That's a good one. It looks like an earlier situation we've considered, namely the position occurring after 1. e4 e5 2. d4 exd4 3. Qxd4 (diagram 155), when Black could start harassing White's queen by 3 . . . Nc6.

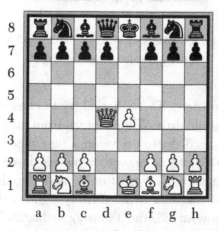

Diagram 180. After 1. e4 e5 2. d4 exd4 3. Qxd4.

Teacher: Actually, it does appear similar. But there's also something quite different about it. In diagram 155 and now diagram 180, Black's queen-knight can develop to c6, assailing White's queen. In diagram 179, Black no longer has his queen-knight. Therefore, he can't develop it to c6, attacking the White queen. You can't move what doesn't exist. This means that Black won't be able to drive the White queen from the center conveniently in diagram 179.

Student: From diagram 179, couldn't Black exploit the position of White's queen by the advance 5 . . . c5 (diagram 181)?

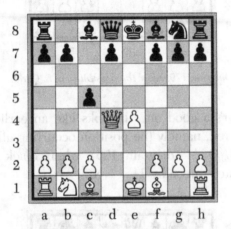

Diagram 181. After the possibility of 1. e4 e5 2. Nf3 Nc6 3. d4
exd4 4. Nxd4 Nxd4 5. Qxd4 c5.

Teacher: You're right. The only real try to chase the queen is 5 . . . c5. That would drive White's queen from the center immediately. But 5 . . . c5 doesn't develop a new piece, nor does it contribute significantly to any other piece's development. The fact that the Black queen thereafter has access to the queenside along the d8-a5 diagonal is not terribly significant. Moreover, with a pawn now at c5, the f8-bishop's diagonal is blocked. Another problem is that this less-than-desirable pawn move severely weakens Black's potential to control d5 and d6. These points can never again be guarded by a Black pawn, and White will have an excellent chance to occupy them, especially d5, which is secured by a White pawn from e4.

Student: So it doesn't matter very much that Black gains a little time by attacking the queen here.

Teacher: That's essentially correct. In trying to take advantage of the White queen's central position by playing c7-c5, Black has to accept a permanent liability—the weak squares along the d-file. A temporary gain in time for an enduring structural weakness is not a fair exchange.

Student: Perhaps money should be offered as well?

Teacher: Funny. But it's interesting to note that this position constitutes yet another exception to a rule—in this case, the one that advises so strenuously against early development of the queen. Once Black has exchanged his queen-knight (1. e4 e5 2. Nf3 Nc6 3. d4 exd4 4. Nxd4 Nxd4 5. Qxd4—diagram 179), it's perfectly satisfactory for White to have his queen out there in the middle of the board. Black has no effective way to attack it. White's queen can sit in the center, striking out in all directions, while Black's queen is unable to assume a comparable position by occupying his own queen-four square, namely d5. But developing the White queen two moves earlier (1. e4 e5 2. d4 exd4 3. Qxd4—diagrams 155 and 180) would have been a different matter altogether, because the queen could then be dislodged effectively at once (by 3 . . . Nc6).

Student: I think the point is clear enough: all ideas in chess are a function of time and place. The same idea, played on a different move, is a different idea.

Teacher: That's right. You have to be there. Astute chessplayers respect minor divergences. A slight change can make all the difference, transforming a bad situation into a good one in a single move.

Student: In this variation, after 5. Qxd4 (diagram 179), it seems that White didn't have to exert himself to bring out his queen.

Teacher: That's a cardinal point. For White to move his queen out would simply be a natural outcome of logical play. Black here causes his own problems by making a bad exchange with 4 . . . Nxd4. You can lose time by exchanging if you exchange a developed piece for an undeveloped one, or your opponent retakes with a developing move. You can even lose something substantial in an exchange if your opponent retakes with an already developed piece while positioning it on a more effective square. So taking the pawn (3 . . . exd4—diagram 177) is one thing, but trading knights (4 . . . Nxd4) is another. Clearly, after exchanging (3 . . . exd4 4. Nxd4—diagram 178) Black should now play a different fourth move.

Student: Could Black now play out his king-bishop, 4 . . . Bc5 (diagram 182), threatening White's knight on d4?

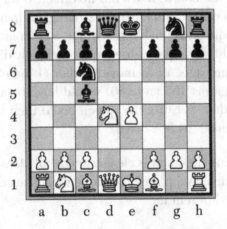

Diagram 182. After the possibility of 4 . . . Bc5.

Teacher: Of course. This is a pragmatic developing move, which indeed menaces the knight at d4. If it's played, White's parry could be 5. Be3 (diagram 183), defending the d4-knight and preparing an unpleasant trap for Black. Can you see what White would then be threatening?

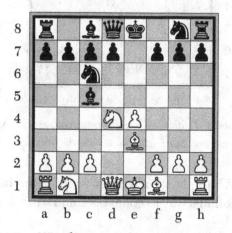

Diagram 183. After 5. Be3, threatening to win a piece.

Student: I'm not sure. The move 5. Be3 seems purely defensive, to guard the knight on d4.

Teacher: It's defensive all right. But the move 5. Be3 also has an aggressive edge to it. This is usually the best way to go in chess: combining offense and defense with the same move. White very definitely has a threat. Given the opportunity, he could capture the queen-knight, 6. Nxc6. After Black recaptures on c6, White would then be able to snatch the bishop on c5 for free, 7. Bxc5, assuming Black's fifth move didn't secure the c5-bishop in some way. A piece up at that point, White would then be able to play for a win by exchanging pieces and avoiding complications where he might potentially lose the position's thread. Keep it simple and under control—that's the way to win when ahead by a piece.

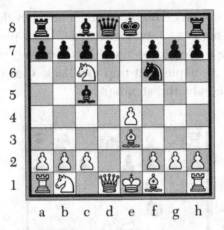

Diagram 184. After the possible continuation 5 . . . Nf6?
6. Nxc6, and Black will lose at least the bishop on c5.

Student: If White plays badly after winning the bishop on c5, couldn't Black find a way to come back and win?

Teacher: Black might be able to come back if he plays doggedly and, more particularly, if White doesn't bother to play at all. But that's the point. White would have to jettison his advantage. If White doesn't blunder, Black will not be in a position to do anything about changing his ultimate fate. White would be in total command, with the ability to force the win no matter how well Black played thereafter, even if Black were Bobby Fischer and Garry Kasparov combined. You can't defy gravity, no matter how light you are.

Student: I don't understand. Shouldn't you consider everything, even the possibility of the other side making mistakes?

Teacher: Remember my earlier point? It's not really necessary to consider everything because most things simply aren't worth it. You have to be careful not to base your strategy on false hopes. When evaluating a chess position, you should only consider the forces and actions that you can control, whether you can see deeply into them or not. In chess, if one side has an extra piece, and the other side has no significant compensation, as is the case here, the side with greater material should be able to win practically for sure by relying on typical simplifying methods and their corresponding principles. After securing the advantage of an extra bishop, correct play will lead to checkmate in 99 out of 100 cases. All other things being equal, the stronger chess army wins. It's ugly, but it's the simple truth.

Student: What is the winning technique with an extra piece?

Teacher: The same as it is in most instances when you're ahead in material: exchange pieces and avoid complications. This emphasizes your advantage because if you trade efficiently, unit for unit, your extra piece is likely to be the only meaningful survivor. Your extra thing will then be able to steal the other guy's remaining things, and you'll be ahead by more and more things until your juggernauting things can force checkmate. Moreover, "trading down" reduces the possibility of counterplay. If the opponent has nothing left, he can't attack. Finally, by keeping it simple, you make it harder for your opponent to trick you into making a turnaround mistake.

Student: I thought chess consisted of things and thoughts, but now I see things are thoughts too, which leads me to an idea. I suspect this is more of an endgame question rather than an opening one. Suppose I'm not up by a piece and ahead by only the exchange. Say, for example, I've won a rook for a minor piece. How should I try to play for a win then?

Teacher: Your thoughts are wandering a little, but let's respond anyway. Being up the exchange means more in some situations than others, but it always refers to cases in which one side has gained a rook for a bishop or a knight. Let's also assume, for the purposes of this discussion, that the other forces on the board balance out for White and Black, the only difference being the rook for the minor piece.

Student: No problem. So how does the side with the exchange up try to win?

Teacher: Generally, to win in such a situation, even if it's early in the game, you should head for the endgame. You should try to trade off pieces, though not necessarily pawns. Ideally, you should be trying to create the pure situation of rook vs. minor piece, with no other pieces on the board. In such an instance, it would be okay if both sides still had a couple of pawns. In the process, you should stay vigilant to ward off enemy counter-play before it develops. Once you find yourself in your desired endgame, position your rook actively, trying to tie down the enemy king and minor piece, forcing them into defensive positions. Meanwhile your own king should take an aggressive stance, moving to key points or attacking positions, if at all feasible.

Student: Okay, suppose I do all that. What's likely to happen?

Teacher: If this approach doesn't bring further material gain, you may be able to surrender the rook for the enemy minor piece, either gaining an extra pawn in the process or enabling your king to penetrate decisively. You might win by promoting an extra pawn or using some pawn as a decoy to gain more pawns elsewhere. Eventually, you win by promoting a pawn to a queen and subsequently forcing checkmate.

Student: Could you give an example?

Teacher: Consider diagram 185. It's Black to move. By giving up the rook for the knight, 1 . . . Rxa2+ 2. Kxa2, Black can clean out White's pawns and eventually make a new queen. The game might then conclude: 2 . . . Kxc2 3. Ka1 Kxc3 4. Kb1 Kd2

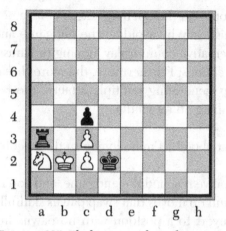

Diagram 185. Black gives up the exchange to win.

(diagram 186), and Black's pawn will advance with protection to become a new queen.

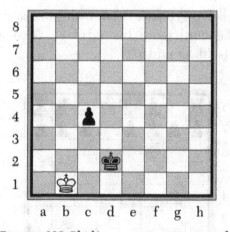

Diagram 186. Black's c-pawn is now unstoppable.

Student: Okay, that's one possible way to win when ahead by the exchange. But what about when behind by the exchange, if one had only a minor piece against a rook? How should I play to increase my drawing chances?

Teacher: If you're in the opening stages of a game, you should play opportunistically by avoiding the endgame and constantly searching for creative counterplay, hoping to harass your opponent into rash actions. Furthermore, the more threats you issue, especially ones generating multiple attacks, the better chance you have of pulling off a swindle.

Student: What about if I'm no longer in the opening?

Teacher: If you've reached the endgame, and you're still losing, you should drum up moves that swap pawns skillfully. You might be able to convert to a position with no pawns in which your lone minor piece confronts the enemy rook, when no further progress can be made. Even though the side with the rook could still win, there are reasonable chances to reach a positional draw. But the draw isn't automatic. Being up the exchange is still a definite advantage.

Student: I'd like to get back to our own game and a possibility for Black on the fourth move. Instead of 4 . . . Bc5, what's wrong with 4 . . . Bb4+ (diagram 187)?

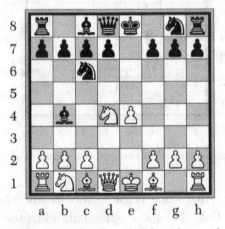

Diagram 187. After the possibility of 4 . . . Bb4+.

Teacher: Plenty. It develops a piece, but not usefully. It gives a check, but not menacingly. White can get out of check pronto with 5. c3 (diagram 188), and the bishop must move again, wasting time. A move that gives check isn't necessarily a good one. A bad check can lose time and, on some occasions, even a game.

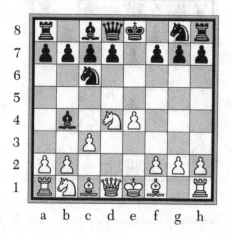

*Diagram 188. After the punishing 5. c3, forcing the b4-bishop
to move again.*

Student: I don't understand. Isn't it a good idea to check the enemy king?

Teacher: Not automatically. Some checking moves can backfire, as in diagram 188, where Black's b4-bishop is forced to move again. But because checking moves appear so forceful, they're irresistible to many players. Be forewarned, however. Perfunctory checks can be deleterious to the giver. Sometimes they lose games. Suppose, for example, one of your units is attacked and, instead of countering that threat, you choose to check the enemy king. If your opponent responds to your check with a move that contains another threat, such as a king move that attacks a second one of your pieces or pawns, you would then need to cope with two threats: the new one and the one you didn't answer to begin with. Chances are you'll solve only one of your problems, not both.

Student: Could you give an illustration?

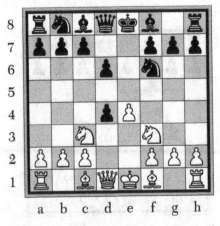

Diagram 189. White should capture the d4-pawn with his f3-knight.

Teacher: Certainly. In diagram 189 it's White's turn to move. White's c3-knight is threatened by Black's d4-pawn. White should capture the pawn and end the threat. But suppose White temporarily ignores the threat to his knight and gives a threat of his own, checking Black's king, 1. Bb5+. If Black were to answer White's check by the block 1 . . . c6, suddenly White would be faced with two threats: the one he never answered to his knight, and now the new one menacing his bishop. However White responds, he must lose a piece, thanks to his ill-considered check.

Student: So, what are you saying?

Teacher: Check only because it's necessary or useful in accomplishing one of your objectives, just as any other move. It's a reasonable rule: Don't give pointless checks.

TRADES, PINS, AND MORE ON MINOR PIECES

Teacher: Let's begin this lesson by first going back. We'll start with our actual game. Can you give the position in algebraic notation, please?

Student: We're here, after the moves **1. e4 e5 2. Nf3 Nc6 3. d4 exd4 4. Nxd4.**

Diagram 190. The actual game, after 4. Nxd4.

Teacher: White appears to have his way in the center, with both a knight on d4 and a pawn on e4. Admittedly, Black has nothing yet in the center, but he's attacking the White knight at d4, which is presently defended. With his next move, he could try to take away some of the initiative by attacking White's e-pawn. So he plays **4 . . . Nf6** (diagram 191).

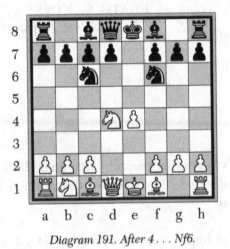

Diagram 191. After 4 . . . Nf6.

Student: So Black has developed a piece toward the center with a gain of time. I see you are threatening to take my e-pawn.

Teacher: Four moves into the game, and the position seems fairly equal. But this can change at any moment, perhaps because of the next move, the move after that, or the move you thought of and forgot to play.

Student: You're right. I'm having trouble remembering the day, let alone the last move.

Teacher: Maybe it'll come back to you. In the meantime, think over this fact: Chess rarely offers players a single choice of moves. On the first turn of a game, twenty moves are actually possible for either side, some better than others. After our game's first four moves, White can consider a number of plausible responses. They include defending the pawn immediately (by either f3, Qd3, or Nc3), or first exchanging knights on c6 and then dealing with the threat to the e-pawn.

Student: What about 5. f3? That guards the e-pawn.

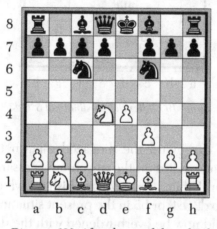

Diagram 192. After the possibility of 5. f3.

Teacher: This move echoes many of the attendant problems of Black's 2 . . . f6, which we explored in diagram 167. Unlike opening pawn moves on the d- and e-files, moving the f-pawn now loses time. White neither develops a piece nor clears a line to allow new pieces to come into play. And 5. f3 also weakens the h4-e1 diagonal leading to the king. Furthermore, if White should now castle, his king becomes potentially vulnerable along the g1-a7 diagonal (say by a Black bishop from c5). The move 5. f3 is just not an effective way to cope with the threat posed by Black's f6-knight. White wants to secure his e-pawn while continuing to build his game. This move, surrendering the initiative, doesn't do it.

Student: Is 5. Qd3 okay?

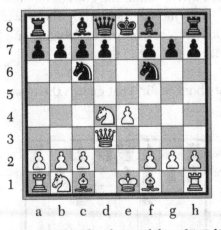

Diagram 193. After the possibility of 5. Qd3.

Teacher: You can guard the menaced e-pawn this way, but making this choice relies on the queen unnecessarily. At d3 the queen blocks in White's light-square bishop, which means it's unable to get to d3, c4, or b5 in the present situation. Moreover, the queen would now be overburdened with the defense of the d4 and e4 squares. As a rule, try not to use the queen in the opening, unless it's clearly desirable for the circumstances at hand. If possible, develop your lighter pieces first; then you're better prepared for the queen's participation.

Student: I have another idea. What about interposing the capture 5. Nxc6 first, and then dealing with the threat to e4?

Teacher: This is actually a strong continuation. White can start by playing 5. Nxc6 before satisfying the defensive needs of the e-pawn. Taking on c6 practically forces an exchange of knights. Otherwise, Black loses a piece and faces an additional attack on his queen, which would have no safe place to go. After 5 . . . bxc6 (diagram 195), where Black takes back toward the center to avoid an unpleasant trade of queens on d8, White can

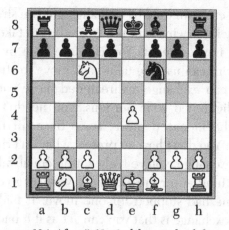

Diagram 194. After 5. Nxc6, delaying the defense of e4.

then secure his e-pawn. By exchanging knights on c6, White doesn't lose time. But he does make it easier to defend his center, for now the knight that used to be at d4 no longer has to be guarded. Such a decision illustrates two sides of an important chess principle: You can gain time by exchanging pieces, or you can lose it.

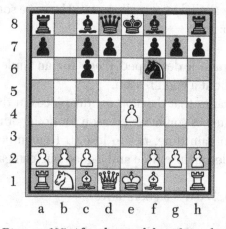

Diagram 195. After the possibility of 5 . . . bxc6.

Student: Could you explain that a little bit, please?

Teacher: You can gain time by exchanging if you stop the opponent in his tracks, leaving him no choice but to take back without positional improvement. You can lose time by exchanging if your opponent can use the take-back move to strengthen his game. If you can exchange a threatened piece without losing time, you've lightened your burdens. You needn't worry anymore about the menaced piece, since once off the board it ceases to exist. You don't have to protect what isn't there. And by virtue of the exchange, you've truly gotten equal value for it, so you've lost nothing. After the exchange, you can go on with your game as if time had stopped for one move. It hadn't, but the beauty of the exchange is that you can act as if it had.

Student: I thought a trade is just a trade, and you don't necessarily have to have a reason for making it.

Teacher: You have to have a reason for everything in this game. Otherwise, it's not chess. A trade ought to have a purpose, like anything else. If you decide on an exchange that allows your opponent to develop his pieces or improve his position, you have helped build his game at the expense of yours. Then you've gained no time at all, but actually lost it. Here are some standard rules of thumb:

- Don't trade a developed piece for an undeveloped one without a good reason.
- Avoid trades that develop enemy pieces in the transaction, unless you have a reason for doing otherwise.
- Trade to gain time, not to lose it. Remember that a bad trade can lose time and a good one can gain time.

Student: So 5. Nxc6 is a good move?

Teacher: It's not only good, it's a kind of chess tactic known as a *zwischenzug*.

Student: I *know* that's not French.

Teacher: It's a German term that means "in-between move." A *zwischenzug* is usually played in between a series of other moves without necessarily affecting them. It can be an unpleasant surprise, particularly if your *zwischenzug* poses an additional and unexpected threat to your opponent's game—for example, if it raises the specter of an uncomfortable check, which would stop the action in its tracks. In this case, 5. Nxc6 qualifies as an in-between move, but not a terribly frightening one.

Student: I've seen that White could play 5. Nxc6 quite satisfactorily, but I'm not going to make that move. Instead, I'm going to protect my e-pawn by **5. Nc3** (diagram 196), and develop a new piece toward the center.

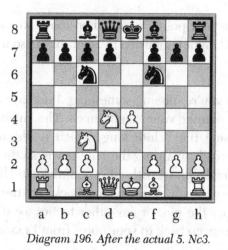

Diagram 196. After the actual 5. Nc3.

Teacher: Of course, we have to respond to opposing threats, but it doesn't seem that you have any. I will accordingly use this free move to continue my own plans. So I'm going to continue my development with **5 . . . Bb4** (diagram 197). Now, in addition to clearing the way for castling, what does this move threaten?

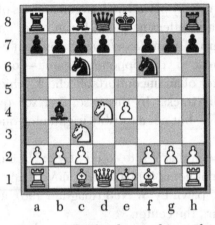

Diagram 197. After the actual 5 . . . Bb4.

Student: I see your point. Your bishop move attacks my knight on c3. But the knight is guarded by the b-pawn, so my position is all right.

Teacher: But you're missing something. I do have a threat. My bishop is now pinning your knight on c3. The knight can't move without exposing the White king, which is illegal. If it can't move, it's not really guarding the king-pawn, so the f6-knight is threatening to take on e4 without repercussions. The pin on the c3-knight prevents you from taking back. By the way, if you don't remember the pin, or any other tactics we may find ourselves discussing, go back to your notes from Lesson 2.

Student: Fortunately, I remember. But how does this relate to the position after **5 . . . Bb4**?

Teacher: After **5 . . . Bb4,** the bishop pins the knight to the king. The knight can't move no matter what because it would be against the rules. So this is known as an *absolute pin*. If the knight were free to move, then it would be only a *relative pin*, where White would have the choice of moving the knight on c3 and accepting the consequences. But there is no choice here because you're not allowed to expose your king to capture. Diagram 198, for example, shows a relative pin, with Black to move. Black may move the knight and expose his queen to capture, if he so chooses.

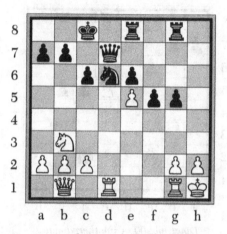

Diagram 198. A relative pin: Black's knight may move.

Student: Could you walk me through a sample variation from here?

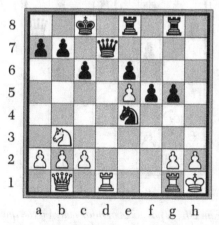

Diagram 199. After breaking the relative pin by 1 . . . Ne4.

Teacher: Let's say Black plays 1 . . . Ne4 (diagram 199). If the rook takes the queen, the knight gives a *smothered mate* at f2 (diagram 200). If instead the d1-rook moves to f1 to guard f2, 2. Rdf1, then Black mates in two moves: 2 . . . Ng3+ 3. hxg3 Qh7# (diagram 201).

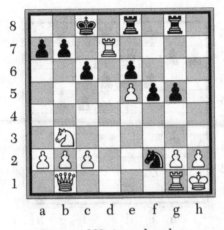

Diagram 200. A smothered mate.

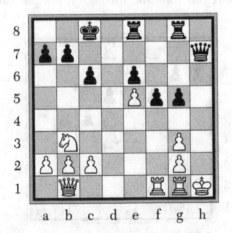

Diagram 201. A possible corridor mate by the queen.

Student: So a player can move pieces and pawns out of relative pins, if he can accept the consequences, and in an absolute pin units can't move off the line of the pin no matter what, right?

Teacher: Correct. Absolutely pinned units can't move off the line of the pin, even if threatened further. That's why it sometimes makes sense *not* to capture them right away. Bringing in additional forces may lead to the gain of material. In diagram 202, we see a situation where piling up on a pinned piece offers White a significant advantage. Instead of capturing Black's rook at b5 with his bishop at a4, winning only the exchange (a rook for a bishop), White should push his c-pawn, attacking the helpless rook. White will thereby be able to capture the rook for a mere pawn on the next free move. It's this threat to attack pinned pieces with lesser material that gives the tactic much of its strength.

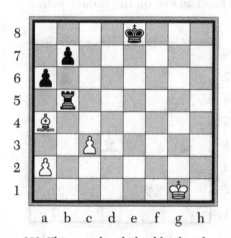

Diagram 202. The pinned rook shouldn't be taken, it should be attacked again.

Teacher: If you have the time, and circumstances allow you to do so, attack pinned pieces and pawns again and again. Pile up on them, if you can; or, as the saying goes, pin it and win it.

Student: So far in the game much of the discussion has focused on the development of knights and bishops. Both are minor pieces, but their powers are vastly different. Which is better?

Teacher: You know what I'm going to say, right?

Student: It depends.

Teacher: You got it. A bishop is usually better when: (1) the position is open and diagonal attacks from far away are possible; (2) there are potential targets or operations on both sides of the board; (3) facing a knight, which the bishop can corral on the side of the board, so that the knight can't move safely (see diagram 203); and (4) time-gaining or time-losing moves must be played, when the same key squares remain guarded by the bishop after it moves. One drawback with a knight is that it can't move and still keep an eye on the same squares.

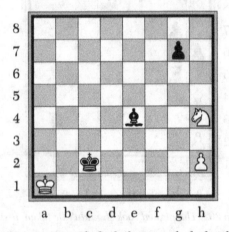

Diagram 203. Black's bishop corrals the knight.

Student: I guess if it's Black's turn, the knight is lost after 1 . . . g5. Let me turn it around: when is a knight preferable to a bishop?

Teacher: Knights get the nod over bishops when: (1) the position is blocked and the knight can jump over obstructions that impede a bishop; (2) the knight is anchored deep in the enemy position and can't be dislodged; and (3) squares of both colors must be guarded. The last condition obviously can't be satisfied by a bishop, which can guard only the color it travels on. In diagram 204, we see the knight dominating the bishop. No matter who moves, Black can play to win the c-pawn and eventually the game.

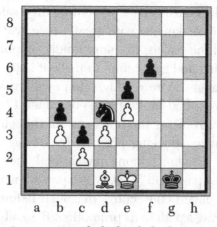

Diagram 204. Black's knight leads to a win.

Student: That's quite a knight you have there. But don't think you're off the hook yet. I hear a lot about the two bishops. Why are two bishops generally considered to be superior to a bishop and a knight or to two knights?

Teacher: Two bishops, often used as a technical term signifying a type of advantage, tend to be stronger than other minor-piece combinations because, when working in synchronization, they negate a single bishop's chief failing, the inability to guard squares of both colors. In cooperation, each bishop can stand sentinel for the other, allowing each to achieve fuller potential.

Student: I suppose two bishops can be particularly strong when they attack in the same direction.

Teacher: United bishops, also known as the *two bishops* or the *bishop pair,* tend to be stronger than other minor-piece combinations because they: (1) control the center more easily, either aligned in the same direction or crosswise from opposite sides of the board; (2) are effective long-distance attackers and therefore don't have to be close to their targets, as do knights; (3) restrict minor-piece movement better, especially by coralling knights along the board's edge, preventing their safe movement; (4) induce pawn weaknesses with greater ease, whether from far away or behind the pawns; (5) more fluidly support an invasion by their own king and gain tempi to make it happen; (6) create favorable exchanges more readily, often enabling simplification to good-bishop-vs.-bad-minor-piece endgames; (7) contend satisfactorily with advancing pawn masses, for though driven away, bishops remain in attacking position by staying on the same diagonals, still assailing enemy pawns and the squares over which they must pass; and (8) convoy a passed pawn splendidly, controlling in concert consecutive diagonals before the advancing pawn, clearing a path to its promotion. Basically, two bishops are wonderful, as we can see from diagram 205.

Student: Egad. I think I'm going to have to review that a few times. Funny thing is, I know that some players prefer having a combination of bishop and knight to either two bishops or two knights. Why is that?

Teacher: When they're feeling that way for logical reasons, it could be because the bishop and knight work very well in the situation at hand. A bishop-and-knight combination may be preferable when it's not clear where the position may lead, and it's unclear whether the resulting situations will favor a knight or a bishop. By keeping one of each, you're covered for any possibility.

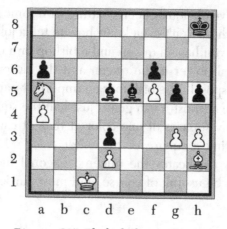

Diagram 205. Black's bishop pair is strong.

Student: Could you offer anything more about the qualities of knights?

Teacher: There is something nice about knights. By being able to guard both light and dark squares, the knight is suited for both offensive and defensive action. For example, it can attack squares of one color while occupying the other color, enabling it to confront an opposing bishop without the bishop being able to attack the knight. Moreover, by attacking and guarding squares a friendly bishop can't cover, a knight is able to help a player influence squares of both colors. The two pieces can work in beautiful harmony. Style is another factor. Some players have a bent for manipulating the bishop-and-knight combination, but this works only when the position permits such flexibility. Then there's sheer obduracy. Some players prefer particular circumstances, without regard to truth or merit, simply because they just do. Seek out such people and use their own thinking, or lack of it, against them.

Student: If bishops are generally superior to knights, why are a queen and a knight working together preferred to a queen and a bishop?

Teacher: You've obviously been chatting with some strong players, many of whom don't even know how to tell a joke. In either case, whether you have a queen and a bishop or a queen and a knight, the real power is the queen and the various attacking motifs at its disposal. The bishop is an imperfect partner for the queen because at most it can guard just half the squares on the board, and only squares of one color at that. It can't protect a queen occupying a square of the other color. Moreover, the bishop merely duplicates the queen's diagonal move. Admittedly, that can be useful, of course, and most particularly when it's needed.

Student: I get it. A knight, on the other hand, is capable of attacking all of the board's squares and can offer the queen twice as many support points as the bishop. The knight moves in a way the queen can't, and that's sure to add a vital extra dimension to the assault. If the knight can get near the target, it must be an excellent attack-mate for the queen, both as a supporter and because of its unique weaponry.

Teacher: Once again we see how circumstances can change everything. A bishop is generally slightly better than a knight, but in the above discussion the knight gets the edge over the bishop. What a world this chess is. It doesn't allow us to fall back on mindless platitudes or feckless placebos, and it punishes us for failing to look at what's actually happening. How fair is that?

Accumulating Advantages

PAWN PLAY AND WEAKNESSES

Teacher: Let's get back to our game. The knight at c3 is pinned to your king. What does this mean about the pawn on e4?

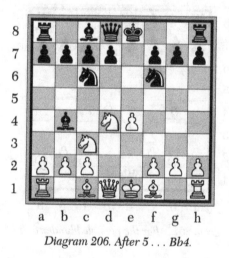

Diagram 206. After 5 . . . Bb4.

Student: That it's no longer guarded?

Teacher: That's right. Chess can be complicated—and beautiful. By pinning the knight, Black's dark-square bishop, the one on b4, is actually attacking the pawn on e4 by immobilizing the pawn's defender, the knight on c3. Bishops can assail squares of the other color by attacking pieces that guard those squares—in particular, knights. Close analysis of this position also demonstrates that players do not have to occupy or guard the center to gain control. They can also exercise influence over it by attacking or driving away enemy units that guard it. Affecting the center in this way can be just as vital as inhabiting or protecting it.

Student: How should White save his e-pawn?

Teacher: We've already reviewed the protective possibilities offered by moving the pawn to f3 and the queen to d3. The reasons they failed earlier still essentially hold now. Both moves are premature, and the pawn move is weakening. Let's consider another idea, 6. Bd3.

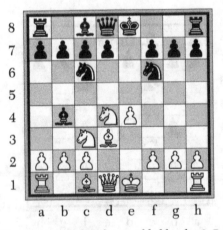

Diagram 207. After the possible blunder 6. Bd3?

Student: That seems like a reasonable move.

Teacher: On the surface, it may seem to work fine. It deals with the threat to the e4-pawn, and it develops a piece to prepare kingside castling. But there's one terrible drawback.

Student: What's that?

Teacher: It cuts the communication between White's queen and d4-knight, so that the knight is no longer protected. Black's c6-knight could take White's knight for free.

Student: Too bad. If only there were some way that White could develop his bishop to d3 without losing his knight.

Teacher: But there is. Any ideas?

Student: How about moving the knight somewhere, say to b5 or b3?

Teacher: Look again. Neither of those moves would immediately threaten Black, so he would be able to pursue his own plans. He could use the time to capture the pawn on e4 for nothing. White could expect the same result—losing a pawn for nothing—if before moving the bishop to d3, he were to expend a tempo instead by defending the knight with 6. Be3 (diagram 208). White's bishop would secure d4, but it would ignore e4. Again Black would just take the e4-pawn.

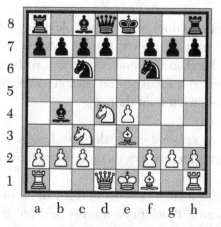

Diagram 208. After the possibility of 6. Be3.

Student: Okay. None of those work, but you implied there's a knight move that does work. What is it?

Teacher: The only knight move for White that gains time meaningfully is to capture Black's knight, **6. Nxc6** (diagram 209).

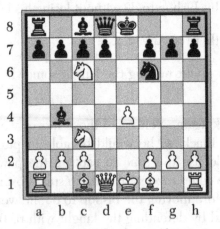

Diagram 209. After the actual 6. Nxc6.

Student: But that doesn't do much.

Teacher: Actually, it does. After Black plays the natural and virtually forced recapture on c6, say **6 . . . bxc6** (diagram 210), White can go ahead and defend his e-pawn without fear of losing his knight on d4, for it would no longer be on the board. How can you lose what's not there?

Student: If I'm remembering the last lesson right, this exchange represents an in-between move or *zwischenzug*.

Teacher: Yes, it's a *zwischenzug*, and it can be played without losing time because Black must use his next move to take back

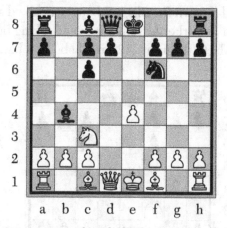

Diagram 210. After Black takes back, 6 . . . bxc6.

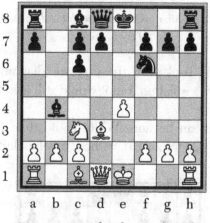

Diagram 211. After the actual 7. Bd3.

on c6. After Black does so, White has the freedom to go on with his game. He could then play **7. Bd3.**

Student: Hold on for a bit. I'd like to go back to the point where you recaptured with your b-pawn on c6 (diagram 210). That creates an isolated a-pawn for Black. I know we talked about a similar variation in an earlier lesson, but would taking back with the d-pawn, 6 . . . dxc6 (diagram 212), really be that bad here?

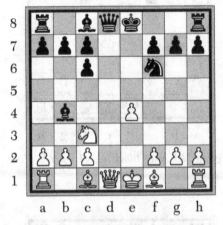

Diagram 212. After taking on c6 with the d-pawn instead of the b-pawn.

Teacher: Taking back with the d-pawn (diagram 212) would avoid the a-pawn's isolation, but it would still lead to a problem.

Student: You mean because White could then just guard his e-pawn, 7. Bd3 (diagram 213), without any hassle?

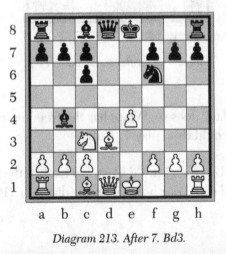

Diagram 213. After 7. Bd3.

Teacher: No, that would hardly be a problem for Black. But what would surely be a problem is the possibility of 7. Qxd8+ (diagram 214). After the forced 7 . . . Kxd8 (diagram 215), Black has then moved his king and lost the right to castle in the future.

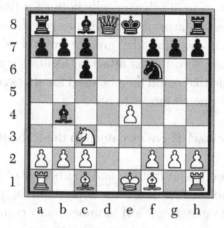

Diagram 214. After 7. Qxd8+, beginning a queen trade.

Student: Let me stop you right there and rephrase my question. Even though 6 . . . dxc6 7. Qxd8+ Kxd8 (diagram 215) denies Black the right to castle, doesn't it leave Black's pawn structure a little healthier?

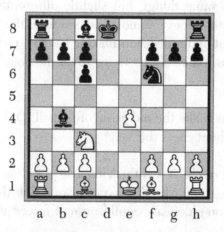

Diagram 215. After 7 . . . Kxd8, losing the right to castle.

Teacher: In a way, insofar as it keeps his queenside pawns together in one mass, on a7, b7, c7, and c6, so that they could conceivably defend each other. And it's true that taking toward the center, 6 . . . bxc6 (diagram 210), would isolate the a-pawn, so that no other Black pawn could guard it, if protection were needed. But even so, it's dynamically better for Black to accept this a7-weakness in favor of what he does get: the retained ability to castle on the kingside; greater control of the center, because he has more pawns attacking central squares; and a semi-open b-file that could then be used for attack, especially by Black's a8-rook once it moves to b8.

Student: Holy cow! There's so much to think about.

Teacher: Indeed. The trouble and the beauty of chess is that every reasonable move suggests a plethora of plausible responses, and it's easy to get lost in unnecessary complications.

Student: It seems to me that we're constantly comparing things, even very small things.

Teacher: We see which is better, and then we try to base our strategies on these comparisons. You've already seen how much chessplaying consists of weighing alternative possibilities that do essentially the same things, but slightly differently. We try to find the move that does the most and concedes the least. Practically 99 percent of our decision-making has to do with comparative evaluations. We're always trying to tilt the board's balance in our favor.

Student: Sounds like the old game of pinball. Did chessplayers always think about chess this way?

Teacher: Not really. It was the Viennese grandmaster Wilhelm Steinitz (1836–1900) who first hypothesized that the balance of power hinges on a delicate equilibrium of forces and elements.

To achieve an advantage in one of these elements, Steinitz said, players have to surrender another kind of advantage of about equal worth. You simply can't get something for nothing in a well-balanced chess game.

Student: Really? What about if you win a pawn?

Teacher: That's a good question. Because even if you win a pawn, it could easily cost you several moves in development. You might have to move your attacking piece into position, capture the enemy unit, and then move your own unit back to safety. In those three moves, your opponent might be able to build an attack with his probable initiative. Other than your opponent overlooking something and giving you material for nothing, you can't gain a material advantage without surrendering something. Usually, you have to cede a significant advantage in time, when time may be of greater importance than material.

Student: It sounds as if various individual advantages go into determining the larger, total-position advantage.

Teacher: Very true. Steinitz understood that the overall advantage is always dependent on a number of factors, both tangible and intangible. At any given moment, one may be more important than another. Advantages in material or pawn structure— the way the pawns are dispersed over the board, taking into account their weaknesses and strengths and how they create harmony or disharmony for the pieces—are tangible. Unless a major upheaval takes place, these factors are likely to remain unchanged throughout the course of a game. A lead in development, however, is transitory, or intangible. If you don't exploit it immediately, your advantage is likely to evaporate once your opponent completes his development.

Student: It seems that time is a critical advantage that can outweigh everything.

Teacher: Time, or more specifically initiative, is a key factor, especially in the opening, when the game can sometimes be decided in ten or fifteen moves. White tries to convert his first-move advantage into something concrete by maintaining the initiative, and Black attempts to equalize by taking the initiative away. In the fight for the initiative, players sometimes make serious concessions by accepting weaknesses and conceding space, or committing themselves to risky material sacrifices, such as opening gambits of pawns and even pieces.

Student: Okay, so how is a chess game won?

Teacher: This may seem absurd on the surface, but if both players are making their moves with discrimination, neither one should be able to win merely by making direct forcing moves. For everything that one side can do, the other side has a counterbalancing action to keep the game in equilibrium. Theoretically, the game should be drawn. Of course, one sits down to win at chess, not to draw.

Student: Actually, many players sit down not to lose.

Teacher: And some of these may have lost already. Playing not to lose can certainly be a viable strategy. Still, most of the time we're concerned with winning. To win, you must follow a course of action that increases your winning chances without incurring unacceptable risk. This is where Steinitz's strategy of *positional chess* comes in. Steinitz advocated playing for small advantages—apparently so small and insignificant that your opponent either doesn't see the threats or irreverently deems them irrelevant. None of these atom-sized advantages might mean very much at the time.

Student: Yet if I understand you correctly, once you accumulate enough of them they may add up to a definitive superiority.

Teacher: Indeed they may. If things have gone according to Hoyle, suddenly you'll have a concrete edge that translates to a powerful initiative. Your opponent, to break this initiative, must in turn surrender something. Usually, this turns out to be material. Possibly, after you capture the material, the game will seem to return to a state of equilibrium, where neither player has an immediate attacking advantage. But there should be one telling difference: You should now have extra material—and, in a sense, you've literally stolen it from your opponent because you never had to make legitimate sacrifices for it.

Student: Good, because I don't like making sacrifices of any kind. But where do weaknesses fit in?

Teacher: They can seem very small, but play your Steinitizian cards right and you might be able to build a mountain out of a molehill. Positional chess—Steinitz's brainchild—often focuses on weaknesses and their exploitation. In chess, however, there are really two kinds of weaknesses. One type involves points or sectors of the board that are tactically vulnerable because of particular and immediate circumstances. As such, they should not be evaluated as part of a long-term plan. Often they are based on temporary piece placement. Usually, you have to capitalize on such frailties at once to prevent your opponent from rectifying the problem by guarding the weak point or removing a threatened piece.

Student: What's the other type of weakness?

Teacher: The other type of weakness is structural. Structural weaknesses involve badly placed pawns. In some cases, the pawns can no longer guard certain squares, either because they've advanced too far or because they're unable to exercise their protective ability. They could, for example, be pinned. In other instances, the pawns themselves become nagging targets, difficult to defend. Because structural weaknesses tend to be of a lasting nature, they must be considered when formulating long-range plans.

Student: When people talk about weak pawns, don't they usually mean isolated pawns?

Teacher: Yes. The *isolated pawn* is basic to the problem of structural weakness. An isolated pawn is often a disadvantage because it can't be protected by other pawns and because the square immediately in front of it can be occupied by opposing pieces. Without a friendly pawn to the side to guard the occupied square, there's no guarantee that an obstructing enemy piece, one stationed in front of the isolated pawn under view, can be driven away. Pieces able to sit in front of isolated pawns are called *blockaders,* and the concept is usually referred to as the *blockade.*

Student: Could you show me a position with some different kinds of pawns in it, just so I can get a feel for what you're talking about?

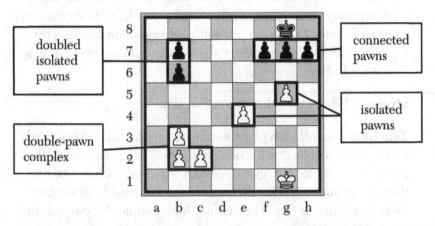

Diagram 216. *White has isolated pawns on e4 and g5; Black, on b6 and b7.*

Teacher: Consider diagram 216. It shows four isolated pawns: two for White, two for Black. White has isolated pawns at e4 and g5, Black, at b6 and b7. Black's isolated pawns are doubled on the b-file and are called *doubled isolated pawns*. White's doubled pawns on the b-file are not isolated because they have an adjacent partner on the c-file that, under the right circumstances, can defend either White b-pawn. Healthy pawns are represented by Black's three on the squares e7, f7, and g7. They are *connected pawns,* situated on adjacent files.

Student: Can we look at a blockade, too?

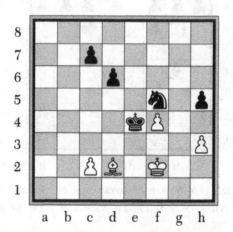

Diagram 217. Black's knight blockades the f-pawn.

Teacher: Take a look at the position of diagram 217. It illustrates how a blockading piece, here the knight, can sit securely on the square in front of an isolated pawn, here White's pawn on f4. To dislodge the knight from f5, White needs a pawn on either the e- or g-file. It's not going to happen.

Student: Can an isolated pawn ever be a good thing?

Teacher: There are times when an isolated pawn, or *isolani*, can offer compensation. In fact, some openings are designed to produce an isolated pawn center. A player might accept such a pawn—normally a handicap—if he gets more space, control of useful strongpoints, or the opportunity to hamper or cramp the enemy's position in the process.

Student: I hope we can get to talk a little more about pawn features as we move on.

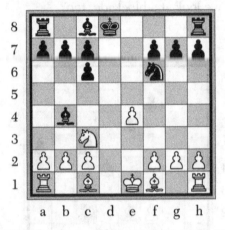

Diagram 218. After the possible variation 1. e4 e5 2. Nf3 Nc6 3. d4 exd4 4. Nxd4 Nf6 5. Nc3 Bb4 6. Nxc6 dxc6 7. Qxd8+ Kxd8.

Teacher: We can and shall, but let's get back to our earlier analysis, to the point at which the queens could be traded and Black's king would have to take back on d8 (diagram 218). If we imagine dividing the board in half between the queenside and the kingside, we notice that Black has four pawns on the queenside and White three—whereas White has four pawns on the kingside and Black three. On the queenside, Black has the extra pawn; on the kingside, it's White with the extra pawn. It turns out, however, that Black's doubled c-pawns reduce the value of Black's queenside pawn majority. White's three queenside pawns, with proper play, can hold back Black's four queenside pawns. Meanwhile, White's healthy kingside pawn majority should be able to eventually produce a *passed pawn*. In effect, it will be as if Black lost a pawn—without having actually lost one!

Student: I think I'm beginning to understand. Taking back toward the center, **6 . . . bxc6** (diagram 210), avoids this unfavorable imbalance, even when Black has to accept an isolated a-pawn. However, taking away from the center, 6 . . . dxc6 (diagram 212), avoids the weak a-pawn, but in effect creates a pawn imbalance that favors White, as if White has won a pawn because White will be able to create a passed pawn. Wow! By the way, what's a passed pawn?

Teacher: A pawn that can't be stopped by any enemy pawn from moving up the board to queen—it's literally passed the opposition's pawns. But after **6 . . . bxc6** (diagram 210), there's no way for White to create a passed e-pawn by force, because Black's d-pawn is able to control squares on the e-file that White's e-pawn must still pass over.

Student: You also mentioned that Black would be able to use the b-file for his rook after taking back with the b-pawn. Could you explain that further?

Teacher: Another advantage to taking toward the center (**6 . . . bxc6**—diagram 210) is that Black then gets an open b-file for his rook. At the right moment he can shift his rook to b8, either threatening to capture the White b-pawn, if it's no longer defended, or to force White to make a special effort to get his queenside bishop out. With Black's rook at b8, the c1-bishop would otherwise be unable to move without abandoning the b-pawn. The usual way to defend such a pawn, incidentally, is to push it one square, so that its neighboring pawns then guard it.

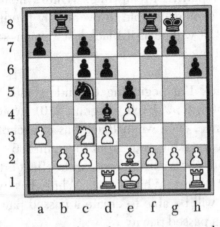

Diagram 219. Black's rook exerts pressure on the b-file.

Student: I see another problem for White with Black's rook at b8 (diagram 219). If White pushes his b-pawn to b3, instead of leaving it on b2, the squares a3 and c3 are weakened. Since they are no longer protected by a pawn, they are susceptible to Black's forces. In diagram 219, pushing the b-pawn loses White's knight to Black's bishop. Now that I think about it, it's remarkable how effective a rook can be from so far away.

Teacher: Bishops, rooks, and queens are long-range pieces. They can strike suddenly from a distance, but they must have avenues of attack, such as the b-file after Black takes back with **6 . . . bxc6** (diagrams 210 and 219). They seek open lines: ranks, files, and diagonals unobstructed by pawns of the same color. That's how you can control a line: by occupying it with a piece that can move along it freely.

Student: Is it important to secure control of open lines before your opponent does?

Teacher: I have a typically chessic answer for you.

Student: I bet it depends.

Teacher: Something like that. You should aim to control open lines before your opponent when doing so is useful. After capturing vital highways of attack, you should reinforce your conquest by occupying them with two or more pieces that move in the same way. Use a bishop and a queen to try and dominate a diagonal. Use either a rook and a queen or two rooks to commandeer ranks and files. In either case, diagonal or file, you will control these critical rows because the pieces that occupy them protect and support one another. The doubling of like forces in this manner, along the same row of squares, is called a *battery*.

Student: I have a feeling that I should try, wherever possible, to set up batteries and other forms of double attack.

Teacher: You bet. The effectiveness of this strategy is illustrated by doubled rooks—two rooks stationed on the same file or rank. One very devastating battery in chess is a pair of rooks doubled on the seventh rank, as White's rooks are in diagram 220, because the enemy often has a vulnerable row of pawns ripe for capture. As a rule, you should try to beat your opponent

Diagram 220. Black is in trouble.

to the punch, seizing important open lines as soon as you can and then controlling them as long as possible.

Student: Where are we now, in the grander scheme of things?

Teacher: Somewhere on Planet Earth, enjoying the study of this universal game called chess. We're starting to transition from the opening to the middlegame, where chess wizards often determine the game's outcome. For now, pay no attention to that man behind the curtain gearing toward an early endgame. There's more adventure to come before finally going home.

DOUBLED PAWNS, CASTLING, AND OPEN LINES

Teacher: Let's do a little adventuring. After Black's sixth move, White must once again defend his e-pawn. Could you please review our present chessic state of being?

Student: That depends.

Teacher: Excuse me?

Student: Just joking. Let's see. Although the knight at c3 is in position to guard my e-pawn, Black's bishop at b4 pins the knight to its king. As a result, my c3-knight can't move legally. So the pawn at e4 is hanging, which means it's attacked and un-protected. But I have an idea. I know we've already settled on **7. Bd3** (diagram 211) as being a good move, but could I take us back and suggest a different try? What do you think of 7. Bd2 instead of 7. Bd3? Doesn't 7. Bd2 break the pin on the knight, thus enabling the c3-knight to once again protect the pawn at e4?

Teacher: The move 7. Bd2 certainly ends the pin. Thereafter the knight may be able to move freely again. As usual, however, no move is without consequences, and not all of them are good

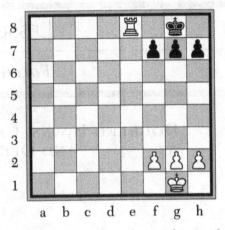

Diagram 221. If White were to play 7. Bd2 instead of 7. Bd3.

ones. Did you notice that Black's **5 . . . Bb4** wasn't just a pin? It was also a threat to capture the knight, which is another way to lessen White's control of e4. Black's **5 . . . Bb4** was designed to win the White king-pawn in one of two ways: by maintaining the pin or, if the pin were broken by White, simple removal of the c3-knight by capture.

Student: Okay, 7. Bd2 doesn't necessarily save the e-pawn because the knight on c3 could still be captured whenever Black thinks it's a good idea. But at least it's a developing move.

Teacher: Actually, it's not even a good developing move. It's too passive. A much more imposing post exists at g5, if White ever finds the time to move his queen-bishop there. Funny thing is, 7. Bd2 is not usually the best way to break the pin on the c3-knight in general, even when it works. Usually, castling kingside is more effective. Not only is White's king then out of the pin for good, White has also improved his overall position without relying on a purely defensive move. Castling also activates the king-rook.

Student: So why is it that so many people seem to play such moves as bishop to queen-2 as a matter of course?

Teacher: It's one of those knee-jerk responses, where one reacts mainly to avoid the acceptance of doubled pawns, as if that were the worst thing in the world. It's not. Even doubled pawns can sometimes be desirable, especially when their existence enables certain squares to be guarded. But even when they're not an attractive acquisition, wasting time to avoid them can often be far worse than accepting them in the first place. For example, consider diagram 222. It's Black's turn. It would be a mistake for Black's bishop to capture White's bishop on e3

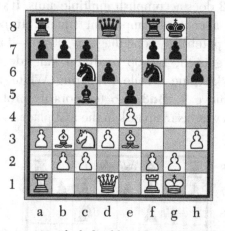

Diagram 222. Black shouldn't take White's e3-bishop.

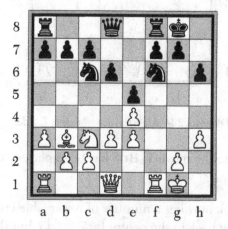

Diagram 223. The exchange on e3 has given White the advantage of the doubled pawns.

(diagram 223), for that would enable White to open the f-file by taking back with the f-pawn. Afterward, White's doubled e-pawns would guard important squares in the center. In effect, White would have the advantage of the doubled pawns.

Student: Okay, 7. Bd2 isn't the right move, nor can we break the pin by castling because the f1-bishop is still in the way.

Teacher: Precisely, which gives us the actual move: the naturally developing and simultaneously threat-meeting move **7. Bd3.** Playing **7. Bd3** does accomplish multiple aims. It's a sound development to a centrally important square. It positions the bishop along a potentially good diagonal, d3-h7—if it ever opens up—and that gets the bishop ready for kingside action, once Black castles kingside. While preparing White for kingside castling, the move **7. Bd3** also temporarily protects White's e-pawn, which was his main task in the first place.

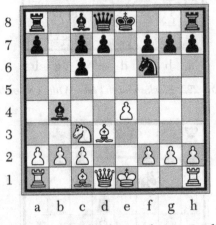

Diagram 224. After the actual move, 7. Bd3.

Student: Fine. The move **7. Bd3** has been played. What should Black do about it?

Teacher: Black now has a number of reasonable continuations. He could strike back in the center by 7 . . . d5, but this may be a little premature and therefore unduly risky. He could instead strengthen his position a bit, so that he could play d7-d5 shortly, by first castling kingside, 7 . . . 0-0. With his king out of the center, Black faces less risk if he decides to allow the center to eventually open up through pawn exchanges. Black could also abandon the idea of playing the queen-pawn two squares for now, playing it only one square instead, 7 . . . d6, in order to restrain White's e-pawn, but this is a comparatively inert reply. A curious try, which many players consider a good idea, is 7 . . . Bxc3+. Trading the dark-square bishop for White's knight at c3 seems attractive. After White takes back, 8. bxc3 (diagram 225), he's saddled with doubled isolated pawns, not that that's the end of the world.

Diagram 225. After a possible exchange of bishop for knight,
7 . . . Bxc3+ 8. bxc3.

Student: You mentioned doubled isolated pawns in the last lesson, right?

Teacher: In that case, you probably remember that isolated doubled pawns are doubled pawns that can't be defended by other pawns because there are no friendly pawns on adjacent files. If they're subject to attack, especially from along a half-open file in front of them, they can be quite difficult to support. Avoid them if you can.

Student: Doubled pawns? Isolated pawns? Doubled isolated pawns? Excuse me while I trip over my own tongue.

Teacher: It's not really as confusing as it sounds. It's true that when most people talk about pawn weaknesses, they usually start with the isolated pawn and doubled pawns. That's because these two types of pawn weaknesses commonly occur in most chess games and typical chess-play must cope with them. The question you posed was about doubled isolated pawns, a kind of combination of both, which is a weakness that's normally discussed after first considering the other two.

Student: All right. Allow me to step back a bit so we can get specific about the nuances. What do I need to know about doubled pawns?

Teacher: Doubled pawns are two pawns of the same color, also known as *friendly pawns*, occupying the same file. They always come about by capture, which takes the second pawn to the same file as the first one. Generally, they become weaker because they lose the ability to guard each other. The front doubled pawn even impedes the back one's movement. But they can have strengths, too, such as enabling key squares to be guarded, as in diagram 223, where the doubled White e3-pawn strengthens the square d4. Sometimes they also create a greater bulwark in front of the friendly king. But we'll talk more about their role as royal defenders when we get to the section on pawn majorities, coming up in a later lesson.

Student: Can you go into more detail about their weaknesses?

Teacher: Let's expand and summarize. Doubled pawns can be weak for several reasons: (1) as a group they tend to crawl along because the back doubled pawn is unable to move until the front one does, so they often obstruct the development of their own forces; (2) their movement can be frustrated by a single enemy pawn, either by blocking them on the same file or, from an adjacent file, by guarding a square they need to pass over; (3) the exchange producing them might also result in the creation of an isolated pawn; and (4) they might be isolated themselves. In that situation, neither can be defended by a pawn and one or both may be subject to direct piece attack as a result. But they're not weak if they can't be exploited, and what doesn't kill us makes us strong.

Student: You argue that there is an occasional advantage to be found in doubled pawns, as in the position of diagram 223, but this seems to directly contradict most ordinary chess advice. Could you put this to me again: When should I be willing to accept doubled pawns?

Teacher: You might be willing to accept doubled pawns to: (1) open lines for attack; (2) facilitate or expedite development; (3) add protection to key squares; (4) buttress a castled king's position; (5) create an escape square for the king; (6) save time if it would be wasted trying to avoid doubled pawns; (7) simplify the position; (8) win material; (9) avoid material loss; (10) make necessary captures or recaptures; and/or (11) when trying to avoid them would be dumb.

Student: I might as well ask, even if this doesn't necessarily relate to what we're looking at now: Are there other sorts of pawn weaknesses I ought to know something about?

Teacher: Sure. There are other types of pawn weaknesses worthy of your attention, such as backward pawns, tripled pawns, hanging pawns, and the isolated pawn pair. We're not going to examine them here, but in all such cases, the pawns are weak because they can be exploited tactically or because they are simply unable to guard certain squares. If they can't be exploited, however, they may not be so debilitatingly weak that you have to worry much about accepting them. In fact, forget about it. Have a snack or do something else for a while.

Student: So should I play to avoid weaknesses or accept them?

Teacher: You should always play to avoid weaknesses, but not to the extent that it messes up your game. Moreover, you should always be willing to accept weaknesses if in doing so you gain advantages that outweigh their drawbacks. The greater good should decide.

Student: One thing seems to be a constant in this game: To get something you have to give something.

Teacher: That's true. Your hope is that you obtain a better share of the bargain.

Student: I'd like to get back to the question I was starting to frame earlier. What's wrong with playing 7 . . . Bxc3+ 8. bxc3 (diagram 225)?

Teacher: Nothing really, but it could be viewed as being unnecessarily committal. Reason it out this way. Black's bishop may possibly be more important to him than White's c3-knight is to White, because Black's king-bishop could be particularly helpful in safeguarding the kingside, especially the approach square g5. As a rule, you shouldn't surrender bishops for knights early on without a definite reason. Creating doubled pawns at c2 and c3 is not a particularly good reason—not unless, as I've said, the doubled pawn weakness could then be exploited, and this doesn't seem to be particularly likely or relevant here. Besides, if Black meant to take the knight on c3 with his b4-bishop, it would be more sensible to do it after White's dark-square bishop had first been developed, say to g5. But since the bishop at c1 hasn't yet moved, it retains the option of shifting to a3 in one play after an unwise or premature exchange of bishop for knight on c3. It takes two moves to get to a3 from g5, but only one move from c1.

Student: Why would White want the option of posting his bishop on a3?

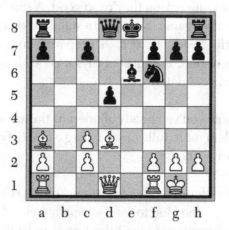

Diagram 226. White's a3-bishop prevents Black from castling kingside.

Teacher: Because from a3, White's bishop could wreak havoc, cutting across the board into the heart of the Black camp, as in diagram 226. Black would be unable to castle, for at a3 the bishop guards a square the king would have to pass over, namely f8. Black would then have to try to block the a3-bishop's diagonal, and this isn't always so easy. As a rule, it's generally desirable to prevent your opponent from castling, especially when the center is relatively open.

Student: So White is trying to castle early while simultaneously hoping to stop his opponent from doing the same.

Teacher: That's right. We could even take this a step further and say that if doing something in the opening is desirable for you, you should try to stop your opponent from achieving the same goal. If you're playing for the center, for example, it would be wise to try to prevent your opponent from also doing so.

Student: What about castling? Most good players seem to castle fairly early.

Teacher: That's one reason they're so good. A sure sign of chess naiveté, game after game, is to ignore standard theory by failing to castle. Castling early, or at least preparing to castle early so you retain the option, is almost always a good decision for two reasons—attack and defense.

Student: I know you've already alluded to this chessic fact, but could you explain more fully how castling can satisfy both defensive and offensive needs?

Teacher: The defensive side of your question is easy. Castling is an attempt to get the king to safety, usually behind a protective wall of unmoved pawns. One of the fastest ways to lose a chess game is to allow the center to open up with your king exposed in the middle of the board. Castling can be an attacking move too. It's usually the most convenient way to bring out the rooks; otherwise, they tend to be ineffective. Rooks may be posted profitably on:

- Open files, containing no pawns whatsoever.
- Half-open files, containing only enemy pawns.
- Files containing advanced pawns that may soon be exchanged.
- Files containing pawns you intend to advance.

Student: What's wrong with keeping a rook on a closed file?

Teacher: A rook cannot penetrate into enemy territory if the file on which it stands is obstructed by one of its own pawns—if it's on a closed file. Enemy pawns in a rook's path are another matter. Rather than obstructing movement, the enemy pawns tend to become targets for attack, which rooks can assail easily from a distance. A rook is not really hindered if its own pieces block the way either, because they usually can be moved off the file, clearing it for rookish action. This is not true for friendly pawns, however, which tend to be clunkier, often blocking their own supportive forces. To clear away obstructive friendly pawns, you have to exchange them for enemy pieces and/or pawns or allow them to be taken.

Student: Does castling help both rooks offensively, or just the one involved in castling?

Teacher: The effects of castling are often salubrious for both rooks, except in the smaller percentage of cases where this isn't true.

Student: I know, it depends.

Teacher: That's right. Still, it's true that castling always brings one rook closer to the center, and closer to its rook partner. Castling also unblocks the king's starting square, making it easier for the rooks to support each other directly.

Student: So it's important that the rooks be able to defend each other?

Teacher: Yes. This way they back each other up for both defense and attack. When rooks defend each other along the home rank, they are said to be *connected.* As a rule, you should aim to connect the rooks fairly early. Once the rooks have been connected, the opening's initial stage is generally over, and you're probably in a transitional phase between the later opening and the early middlegame. At that point, you better keep your eyes open.

Student: Could you explain more specifically why it seems that players usually castle kingside instead of queenside?

Teacher: They don't necessarily castle kingside because it's the best choice. Often they castle kingside because it's faster and simpler: There's one less piece to get out of the way. The real dilemma doesn't arise until you have the chance to castle either way. You should determine which side is best to castle on by analyzing the particular position under consideration. Don't resort to mindless rules of thumb, as if memorizing them confers true wisdom. It doesn't. To get at the truth, it might help to ask certain types of probing questions. For example, will the king be safer on the kingside or on the queenside? Which side has the best cover of protective pawns? It's usually safer, after all, to castle where the pawns have not been moved. Which side has the greatest concentration of opposing forces? Usually, you'll want to castle on the other side, away from the bigger army. On which side do you intend to attack? You'll mainly want to castle on the side away from where you expect to make line-opening pawn moves. There also may be other reasons to castle one way or the other, and these factors, regardless how subtle, might be paramount in making a choice.

Student: I know we went over this when we started our very first lesson. If I remember rightly, you said that I could still castle even if I had been checked earlier (see page 26).

Teacher: You remember rightly, all right. The right to castle is not forfeited, even if the king in question has been checked, as long as the check is ended in a way that keeps the necessary conditions for castling still intact. You may still castle after being checked as long as, in ending the check, the king doesn't move and castling is still legal. So if you've answered a previous check either by interposition or capture, and not by moving your king, you may still be able to castle and do great things.

Student: Is castling permitted if I move my king once and then move it back to its original square?

Teacher: No, you can't castle once you've moved the king, no matter what.

Student: Suppose it's not the king that's moved, but the rook involved in the castling act. Can I castle with a rook that's moved once and then moved back to its original square?

Teacher: The rook can't pull this either. The rules state clearly that neither the king nor the castling rook may have previously moved in the game. It doesn't matter if they wind up on their original squares after moving away and back. Fortunately, you start the game with two rooks, and if you haven't done something with the other one, you might be able to castle the other way.

Student: Can I castle and give check to the enemy king with the same move?

Teacher: Castling is usually a defensive move to get the king to safety. But since activating the rook is also offensive, you may be able to throw in an offensive check, or an even more offensive checkmate, as part of the castling move. You can start with either piece, although it's customary to touch the king first and then the rook. At one time the rules mandated moving the king before the rook. Moving the rook first was construed as a rook move and you weren't allowed to castle. Today the rules are more understanding, though some opponents aren't.

Student: Can I castle and capture on the same move?

Teacher: No. You capture by replacing an enemy unit with your own. When you castle, the king and rook move across unoccu-

pied intervening squares. It's against the rules to castle if any of
these squares are occupied. Since early castling is usually desirable, we can appreciate another reason to develop minor pieces
so quickly. The squares separating the king from one of the
rooks must be unoccupied to make castling possible, so minor
pieces must be developed just to create castling potential. That
potential can be crucial to survival. For example, if your king is
going to be threatened on the next move, it can be quite helpful
to have the option of castling. If two pieces still block the way,
however, it's impossible to protect yourself by castling immediately, and your king may wind up stuck in the center. This
explains why, in our little game, the move **7. Bd3** is particularly
desirable. It deals with the threat while preparing kingside
castling.

Student: It seems that players tend to be more concerned with
castling themselves than preventing their opponents from
castling. Shouldn't that be just as important?

Teacher: Absolutely. If an idea is good for you, it's good for you
to stop your opponent from using the same idea. Obviously, it
can be effective strategy to prevent your opponent from
castling. To this end:

- Try to keep the enemy king pinned down in the center.
- Try to hit the enemy king with a combined assault of
  all your pieces.
- Be willing to sacrifice some material in order to do
  this, if your chances seem reasonable.
- Once your opponent's king is confined to the center,
  don't relent. Keep hammering away to prevent your
  opponent from regrouping and organizing a defense.

Student: Are you going to castle now on your seventh move?

Teacher: You betcha. Black castles, **7 . . . 0-0** (diagram 227).

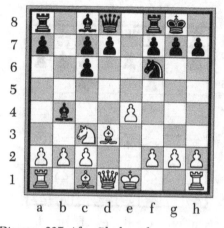

Diagram 227. After Black castles on move seven.

Student: So you feel you have the time to play a defensive move like castling?

Teacher: Don't forget—castling is hardly just a defensive move. Here, White must be careful. If he keeps his king centralized, Black may have enough time to harass actively along the e-file by shifting his rook to e8. When the e-file is at least half-open to the enemy's advantage, it's potentially dangerous to leave your king sitting on its original square at e1. Though White's e-pawn would screen the White king from Black's pressuring rook at e8, the threats against the then pinned e4-pawn might become quite serious. White might become overtaxed, trying to extricate his king to safe quarters while also securing his menaced e-pawn. There's an old Yiddish expression that goes "You can't dance at two weddings at the same time," and it applies nicely to chess. You may not be able to cope with contemporaneous threats. Look for double threats, on both attack and defense. Try to avoid situations where you'll be faced with dual responsibilities.

Student: Suppose I were now to attack your bishop by 8. a3 (diagram 228)? Would that be good?

Diagram 228. After the possibility of 8. a3?

Teacher: Not really, because it's an unnecessary waste of time that practically compels Black to help himself out. After 8. a3, Black willingly exchanges bishop for knight (8 . . . Bxc3 9. bxc3), which gains vital time. After White takes back on c3 (diagram 229), it would be Black's move, and he'd be free to go ahead with his own plans. You might also note that White's bishop can

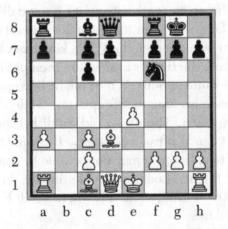

Diagram 229. In a side variation after White takes back, 9. bxc3.

no longer access the a3-square, because in this line White's own a-pawn is there.

Student: Instead of taking on c3, why doesn't Black just retreat his bishop to a5 (diagram 230), maintaining the pin?

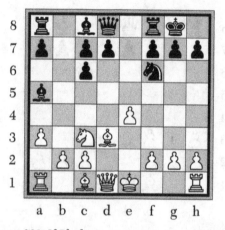

Diagram 230. If Black were to answer 8. a3 by 8 . . . Ba5.

Teacher: If, instead of taking on c3, Black's bishop retreats to a5, no time would be gained, for White would then have the freedom to play whatever relevant move he wanted. So much of exchanging has to do with time, trying to arrange it that the next free move is yours, not your opponent's. Black wouldn't retreat to a5 because taking on c3 is much stronger.

Student: What do you mean by *free move?*

Teacher: A move is free if you can continue with your own ideas, if you have the initiative. A move is not free if you must respond to your opponent's move in a way that doesn't allow you to pursue your own plans, if your opponent has the initiative.

Student: So after the imaginary 8. a3? Bxc3+ 9. bxc3 (diagram 229), how should Black continue?

Teacher: Black should continue operations against the e4-pawn. The slow but effective way would be to seize the e-file with 9 . . . Re8 (diagram 231). Black would be threatening the e-pawn twice, and White, only defending the e4-pawn once, would have to expend a tempo to protect it again.

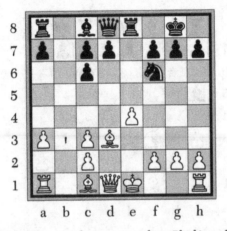

Diagram 231. Continuing the imaginary line: Black's rook threatens e4.

Student: So, should Black play 9 . . . Re8?

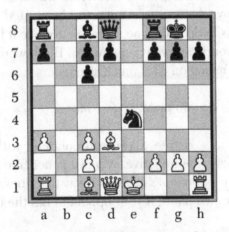

Diagram 232. Black just takes the e4-pawn: Why prepare to do what can be done at once?

Teacher: Not if he sees the better move, the immediate capture of the e-pawn with his knight, 9 . . . Nxe4!.

Student: Why can't I take your knight for free, 10. Bxe4 (diagram 233)?

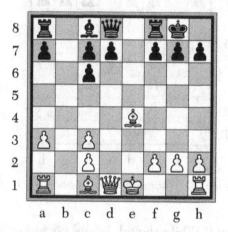

Diagram 233. If White were to take the knight, 10. Bxe4.

Teacher: After the obvious 10. Bxe4, Black can regain the piece by 10 . . . Re8 (diagram 234), pinning the bishop to the king.

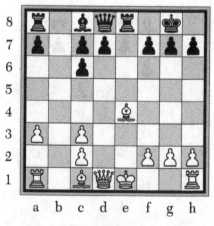

Diagram 234. Black pins the bishop.

Student: Why can't I just protect my bishop with 11. f3 (diagram 235)?

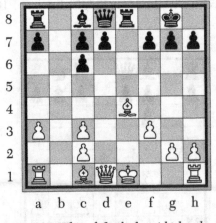

Diagram 235. White defends the e4-bishop by 11. f3.

Teacher: Even if White should defend his bishop with a pawn by 11. f3, Black merely attacks the helplessly pinned e4-unit with his own pawn (say 11 . . . f5—diagram 236), and in the next move recaptures it with his f-pawn.

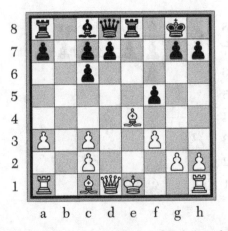

Diagram 236. Black attacks the pinned bishop with a pawn.

If White then moves out of the pin by the natural 12. 0-0, Black winds up a pawn ahead after 12 . . . fxe4 13. fxe4 Rxe4 (diagram 237). This variation reinforces important principles, and it demonstrates the classic difficulty triggered by unnecessary pawn moves.

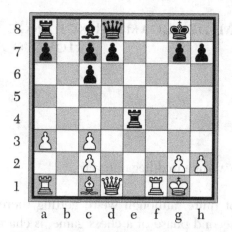

Diagram 237. After 12. 0-0 fxe4 13. fxe4 Rxe4, winning a pawn.

Student: It's interesting how this example illustrates the trouble you can get into if you waste a move, the way I considered doing with 8. a3 (diagram 228).

Teacher: You're right. The example also demonstrates the problems that can ensue from the delay of castling, especially after the other side has castled *and* is prepared for full-scale attacking operations against the stuck and centered king. And finally, the variation demonstrates the value of pins.

Student: Pins can be insidious.

Teacher: True enough. But these sly devices don't necessarily just happen. They're usually set up, and they often are the logical outcome of a carefully planned assault, which sometimes take the perpetrator a long way. In our own case, we'll have to move to the next lesson to appreciate just how far along a long way is.

Evaluating and Calculating

THE MIDDLEGAME, EXCHANGE VALUES, HOW TO ANALYZE

Student: Are we in a middlegame yet?

Teacher: Not quite, although we're getting there. The middlegame, or second phase of a chess game, is characterized by planning and implementation. The player's goal is to accumulate advantages that can be converted into something concrete and decisive. But the middlegame doesn't fit nicely into simple categories to facilitate study. Unlike openings, the starting point is seldom the same, and unlike endgames, the resulting positions are harder to classify and research, mainly because there tend to be numerous units on the board often placed in intricate situations.

Student: I know that time plays a crucial function in the opening. How important is it to the middlegame?

Teacher: To be sure, time is almost always a critical factor in any phase of the game. If you have a move or two on your opponent in a middlegame, you might be able to gain control of a file, occupy a key square, prevent your opponent's plan from being realized, or simply get your attack going first. These are meaningful advantages. Look for them. In those middlegames where time is a little less important, structural features may play a greater role, and getting the upper hand might be more a matter of avoiding weaknesses and maneuvering pieces to better squares, regardless of how many moves it takes.

Student: In the interests of saving time, let me suggest my next move. I think White should castle, **8. 0-0** (diagram 238). I'm just not certain what you're going to do in response to it. Would you play 8 . . . d6?

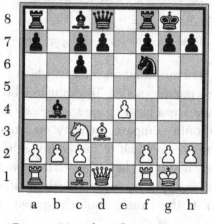

Diagram 238. After White castles, 8. 0-0.

Teacher: Black could continue here with 8 . . . d6 (diagram 239), opening the way for the queen-bishop and guarding e5. Though that advance would stop an immediate movement of the White e-pawn to e5, White would still have a spatial advantage in the center.

Student: Why is that?

Teacher: Generally, the side with the farthest advanced center pawn has a space edge. When neither side has a center pawn positioned farther ahead than the opposition, then we must con-

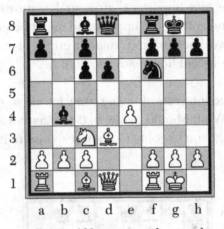

Diagram 239. White would have a central space edge after 8 . . . d6.

sider other facets of the situation, such as which side has better-placed and more mobile pieces. To evaluate who has the edge when neither side has a clear space supremacy based on pawn structure, we should compare territory controlled and influenced within the enemy's half of the board. Admittedly, this is not always so easy to do. But here the relative pawn placements, with the White king-pawn on its fourth rank vs. the Black queen-pawn on its third rank, confer a spatial superiority for White.

Student: What if Black chooses a different strategy? Suppose, instead of playing his d-pawn one square to d6, he moves it two squares to d5?

Teacher: If Black were to play **8 . . . d5,** it would be to swap d-pawn for e-pawn to get rid of the White center pawn altogether. Afterward, Black would have the only pawn in the center, and this might give him enough chances there to secure the draw.

Student: You mean Black is playing for a draw?

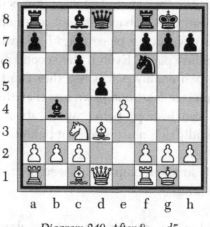

Diagram 240. After 8 . . . d5.

Teacher: Neither side is really playing for a draw. But since Black starts a move behind, he must first establish equality before he can obtain the advantage. You must first go through step one before reaching step two. Real fighters want to win regardless of the color with which they start the game. But let's not divagate too far here. Get back to what's happening in the center. Is the White king-pawn now safe?

Student: On the surface, Black is attacking the White e-pawn twice, once with his knight and once with his d-pawn. The White e-pawn, on the other hand, appears to be defended twice, by the c3-knight and d3-bishop. The e4-pawn is attacked twice, but defended twice, so it's probably safe for the moment. Black isn't threatening to win it.

Teacher: True, when like defenders are involved, a unit is adequately protected if the number of defenders equals the number of attackers. This is not necessarily so when unlike attackers and defenders are facing each other. For example, if two enemy pawns are threatening a friendly pawn defended *in toto* by a queen, rook, bishop, and knight, the friendly pawn is not adequately guarded. If either enemy pawn captures it, none of the friendly pieces can take it back without a serious sacrifice of material, because whichever piece takes back will be captured in turn by an enemy pawn. Even if the second enemy pawn is then taken, the two enemy pawns together can be worth only two pawns, which is at least one pawn less than the value of any piece—knights and bishops being worth about three pawns each. So the friendly side must come out behind.

Student: Why is so much emphasis placed on material? What's it got to do with strategy?

Teacher: Just about everything. In fact, it's almost always the key determinant in formulating a strategy. By first consulting the material situation, you immediately have a barometer that suggests where to go and what to do. I pointed out in an earlier lesson that if you're ahead in material, you should play to exchange pieces, hoping to head for an endgame, where the extra force will be decisive (see page 173). If you're behind in material, you should avoid exchanges, so that you steer clear of a simplifying endgame and maintain your chances to drum up counterplay.

Student: Do I just count up pieces and pawns, totaling their points to see who's ahead?

Teacher: You might want to avoid using the word *points*, because it gets away from the process of making comparisons, which is what chess thinking is about. Don't say a knight is worth three points. Say it's worth about three pawns. Furthermore, instead of totaling points, which doesn't tell you as much as you might think, you should compare and contrast—for calculation's sake, forgetting similarities and noting differences.

Student: You're not going to tell me that knights and bishops aren't worth three points each, are you?

Teacher: Actually, neither type of minor piece is worth exactly "three points," or more properly, exactly three pawns. In most situations, each is worth a little more than three pawns, more like three pawns and an incalculable fraction, with bishops tending to have a slight advantage in a majority of, though not all, positions.

Student: Are you telling me that I can't rely on the material values we've taken for granted since Lesson 2?

Teacher: No, of course you can. In fact, you have to. But as you become a more advanced player, you should also temper your calculations, realizing the values pointed out earlier are highly subject to the changing fortunes of the game. Not only does the relative worth of a piece tend to fluctuate slightly from position to position, but in extreme cases the change can be quite great. A pawn that reaches the back rank to become a new queen by force is surely more valuable than a feckless knight, removed from the main theater.

Student: I think I'm beginning to understand some things about Steinitz's positional chess theory, at least that it's a theory and that I have a ways to go to understand it.

Teacher: Even Steinitz would want you to rely on standard values to help determine the worthiness of most captures and exchanges.

Student: Could you go into how a calculation is actually made?

Teacher: Some ground rules first. Generally, unless exchanging brings you non-material compensation—for example, an attack against the enemy king—you'll want to get back at least as much material as you give up. So start evaluating an exchange of material by counting and comparing specific types of units for each side. Begin, for example, with the pawns. Then ascend up the scale in value, doing the same kind of calculating and comparing for each unit, going from minor pieces to rooks to queen(s). For this analysis, it's often convenient to group bishops and knights together under the broader category of minor pieces, so that having a force of two knights and one bishop means you have three minor pieces. It doesn't have to be done this way if you prefer comparing by specific piece, of course.

Student: Could you run through an unambiguous example?

Teacher: I'd be happy to. Let's take a look at diagram 241. Begin by counting the pawns for each side. Then compare. White has six pawns and Black has five. Since we're only concerned with noting differences, at this stage of the calculation you could say White is ahead by a pawn.

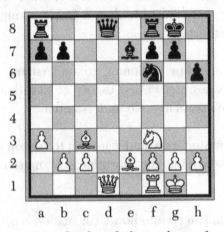

Diagram 241. White has a bishop and pawn for a rook.

Student: So far, that's just pawns. What about the rest of the stuff?

Teacher: Now you're ready for stage two, counting and comparing minor pieces, which are worth about three pawns each.

In diagram 241 White has three minor pieces (two bishops and one knight), while Black has two minor pieces (one bishop and one knight). So at this point of the calculation White has an extra bishop. Combine your first two calculating steps and you can conclude that White is ahead by a bishop and a pawn. But there's still more to calculate—the rooks and queens.

Student: Why can't I just say I'm ahead by four points?

Teacher: It lacks specificity. You should always try to state exactly what the differences are, because being precise tells you so much more.

Student: Okay. So what about the rooks?

Teacher: Here it's Black who has the edge, two rooks to one. So if we restate the situation of our calculation so far, White has a bishop and a pawn for a rook. Since both sides have a queen, they balance out and need not be factored into the calculation. And there's my point: there never was a need to total points. By specific comparison you can conclude that White has a bishop and a pawn for a rook. You could also say that Black is up a rook for a bishop and a pawn, or that White is down a bishop and a pawn for a rook. They all indicate so much more than saying that White is behind by a point—which could mean many things. Remember that the specific says so much more than the general, which can sometimes say nothing.

Student: What was so wrong about saying that Black is ahead by a point? That's what it seems to come to, after all.

Teacher: That remark alone doesn't really convey an accurate picture of the position. Being ahead by "a point" in value could mean different things.

Student: What do you mean?

Teacher: Think about it. If you claim you are ahead by a point you could be implying a number of possibilities. Like these:

- One side has an extra pawn.
- One side could have a bishop, the other two pawns.
- One side could have a rook, the other a knight and a pawn.
- One side could have a queen, the other a rook and a bishop.
- One side could have two rooks, the other a queen.

Student: It's true. They're all tantamount to the same difference, but they're all different.

Teacher: Each statement reflects circumstances where one side is ahead by about a pawn. Each is different, and each requires a different plan of action for both sides. To say that one is down by a single point to describe all of these situations is confusing and meaningless. It certainly would not help us assess accurately enough to formulate an intelligent plan of action.

Student: I get the point—or should I say, I get the pawn? If you want to avoid muddled reasoning in your own games, always express material differences in concrete, specific terms. State exactly how much material you have or are getting, and what your opponent has for it or is getting.

Teacher: Let me advise you about another habit you might want to avoid. Don't calculate by counting the units standing off the board, thinking you're basing your assessments on what's been captured. You can't rely on that because some of the captured units may not be there. They may have fallen off the board, or could even be in your opponent's possession. And if you're playing in a club or tournament, neighboring sets tend to mix with your own, further complicating rather than simplifying your task.

Student: It always seemed so much easier to look to the side. I never considered these potential problems.

Teacher: In addition to being impractical, it's also bad form to count the pieces sitting on the side. Do you look to the side of the board to find a brilliant combination, or to find your next move? When you're playing chess, the board is your universe. All your information should come from there and nowhere else. *Always* play the board—not the person or the side, unless winning and losing have no relevance to you.

Student: Speaking of which, after **8 . . . d5** (diagram 242), is Black threatening to win material?

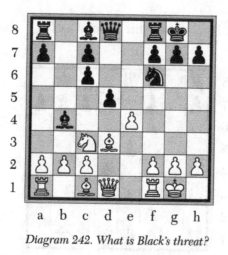

Diagram 242. What is Black's threat?

Teacher: Yes, not by capturing White's e-pawn right away, but by first reducing the number of defenders the pawn has through the exchange of b4-bishop for c3-knight. If given the opportunity—say White plays an irrelevant move such as 9. a3— Black will continue 9 . . . Bxc3 10. bxc3 dxe4 (also good is

10 . . . Nxe4), winning a pawn (diagram 243), because 11. Bxe4 would then lose the bishop to Black's knight at f6.

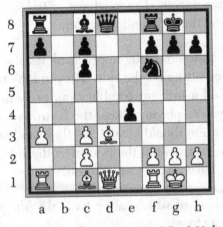

Diagram 243. After the variation 9. a3 Bxc3 10. bxc3 dxe4.

Student: Isn't 10 . . . Nxe4 just as good as 10 . . . dxe4?

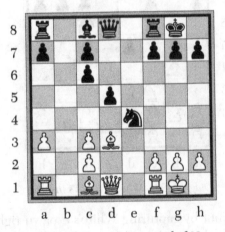

Diagram 244. If 10 . . . Nxe4 instead of 10 . . . dxe4.

Teacher: Pretty much. But one reason for playing 10 . . . dxe4, instead of 10 . . . Nxe4, is that it forces White's d3-bishop to move, allowing a favorable trade of queens from Black's perspective. In this line, a queen trade would be desirable unless White chooses a different tenth move that might radically change the circumstances. The point is that, if you're ahead in material, you'll want to trade as many pieces as soon as possible, especially the queen. This will tend to make your material advantage more important while diminishing the significance or possibility of opposing counterattacks.

Student: It almost seems that the bishop on b4 is attacking the e4-pawn more than it's attacking the c3-knight.

Teacher: That's a very insightful observation. The possible move 9 . . . Bxc3 emphasizes the subtle chessic fact that one can attack the center indirectly by removing something that guards it. Once again, as you point out, it's clear that a dark-square bishop can influence a light square.

Student: So how should White save his threatened e-pawn?

Teacher: He could advance his pawn, 9. e5 (diagram 245), which threatens Black's knight.

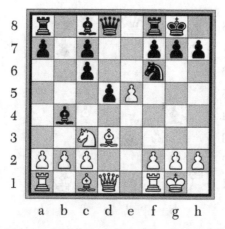

Diagram 245. After the possible advance 9. e5.

Student: Couldn't Black answer that by 9 . . . Ng4?

Diagram 246. After 9 . . . Ng4.

Teacher: Quite right. After 9 . . . Ng4, White's safest protection for his advanced pawn would be 10. Bf4. Of course, that move leads to the exchange of the pawn after 10 . . . f6 (diagram 247), leaving Black the only pawn in the center after the exchange. It also opens the f-file for Black's f8-rook, so that it could attack the White position.

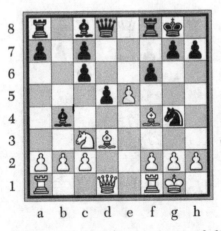

Diagram 247. After the variation 10. Bf4 f6.

Student: What about after 9. e5 Ng4 if White were to reply 10. f4 (diagram 248)?

Diagram 248. After 10. f4.

Teacher: That would surely guard the e5-pawn with a pawn, when pawn protection tends to be more secure. But it exposes the White king to attack along the a7-g1 diagonal. After 10 . . . Bc5+ 11. Kh1 Qh4 (diagram 249), White gets into serious trouble.

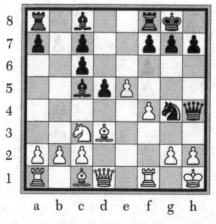

Diagram 249. After 10 . . . Bc5+ 11. Kh1 Qh4.

Student: But couldn't White defend himself with 12. h3 (diagram 250) to stop the mate?

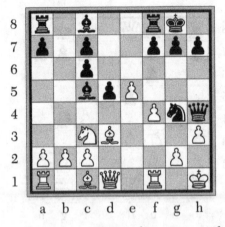

Diagram 250. After continuing the variation with 12. h3.

Teacher: It doesn't quite work. Among other things, Black has 12 . . . Qg3 (diagram 251), when the capture 13. hxg4 is crushed by 13 . . . Qh4# (diagram 252). That's checkmate (see page 35).

Student: This example reminds me that I wouldn't want to move my f-pawn, out of fear of getting my king in trouble.

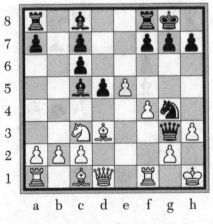

Diagram 251. After 12 . . . Qg3.

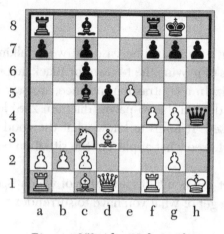

Diagram 252. After 13. hxg4 Qh4#.

Teacher: Beginners are often quite afraid to move their f-pawns early in the game. Possibly that's because most teachers and books try to discourage them from doing so. Their argument makes some sense, but sometimes such an advance can be necessary and even good. If you operate in a climate of fear, you'll wind up taking no risks at all, and possibly fritter away your opportunities to achieve anything distinctive or outstanding. In the world of chess, as in many other domains, it's not the mindless principles that intrigue us, but their exceptions. It's too bad that often we don't start to think until something doesn't make sense. At that point it may be too late.

Student: I'm still going to be careful about moving my f-pawn, though I won't shy away from doing so if it seems purposeful in the position before me.

Teacher: That's right. Be cautious, but don't be afraid to move the f-pawn if it significantly helps your attack without causing too much weakness. Moving the f-pawn may be unwise in the first few moves of the game, when development is crucial. But as many discussions in this book imply, changing circumstances can and should force you to modify principles whenever necessary.

Student: It all depends.

Teacher: That's right. In one case we were talking about the positive effects of moving the f-pawn for Black, to open the f-file for the f8-rook. In a contrasting instance, we saw how moving the f-pawn to defend the e5-pawn (diagram 248) left the a7-g1 diagonal exposed. It helps to know what the good and bad are like, and then to see what applies in the situation before you.

Student: I get the point. It's a matter of which is more significant: what you get or what you have to surrender to get it.

Teacher: This brings us back to White's ninth move and how he should defend against the threat to his e-pawn.

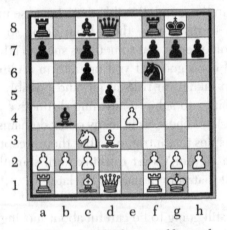

Diagram 253. How should White avoid losing the e-pawn?

Student: Couldn't White add protection to his e-pawn either by 9. f3, 9. Qf3, or 9. Re1?

Teacher: Yes, not that any of them are spectacular. But have you considered not defending the pawn at all? Rather than defend it or push it, why not exchange it for equal value? Then you'd never have to guard it again because it wouldn't be on the board. Think of the toil White would save.

Student: You mean, just play **9. exd5** (diagram 254), losing the pawn?

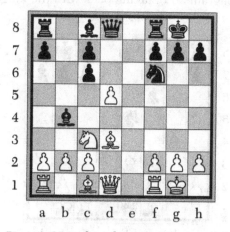

Diagram 254. After taking Black's pawn on d5.

Teacher: That's not losing the pawn. That's exchanging the pawn for equal value, which can be as good as defending, while saving a lot of trouble. By exchanging in this manner, **9. exd5,** very likely followed by **9 . . . cxd5,** White gains time because Black had to expend a move to take back. After Black takes back, it's White who has the next free move. If White had defended his e-pawn instead of exchanging it, as we considered, then Black would have the next free move.

Student: A free move is one in which a player doesn't have to respond in a particular way, or possibly at all, right?

Teacher: Exactly. Although White's exchange eliminates Black's doubled c-pawns, they were never a serious drawback anyway. White would have had to wait some time before trying to exploit them, and at this point, gaining the initiative is more significant. Also, **9. exd5** is an answer to Black's threat of winning a pawn. Good decision.

Student: Should Black, instead of replying **9 . . . cxd5**, play 9 . . . Nxd5 (diagram 255), taking back with the knight?

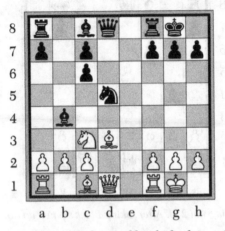

Diagram 255. After the possible take-back 9 . . . Nxd5.

Teacher: Taking back with the c6-pawn makes more sense, for it would allow Black to get rid of his doubled pawns without too much trouble, as a natural course of play. Why get unnecessarily fancy when a perfectly good move would do?

Student: I'd like to try to analyze the new position myself. Let's see: (1) It's White's move, and he still has the initiative; (2) Black has the only pawn in the center, thus a better chance to control the region; (3) White might be able to complete his development sooner; (4) White's pieces seem to be bearing down on the Black kingside. I'd say, especially since White has the initiative, that he stands slightly better here.

Teacher: Not a bad analysis. While we're on the subject, let's define the subject. *Analysis* is the process of determining by

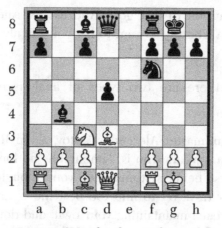

Diagram 256. After the actual 9 . . . cxd5.

careful examination the best moves in a variation or position. The ability to analyze is an essential tool in a chessplayer's arsenal. The art of problem-solving itself involves two types of reasoning: specific calculation and general judgment. Chessplayers use specific calculation to consider particular moves and variations, evaluating them, weighing their strengths, weaknesses, and consequences. They make general judgments to decide which types of moves or plans, rather than what specific ones, they wish to consider.

Student: In many cases I think I'd rather just play the move that seems right, without too much analysis.

Teacher: In many places you should go with your intuition, but not before you've tried to analyze. You should rely on intuition mainly when analysis doesn't seem to be working. Anyhow, the real purpose of analysis is this: Until you know precisely where you stand, you can't decide what your best course of action should be. So first you analyze the situation, and then you choose a plan that is consistent with it. In other words, as with any problem-solving situation, you determine what is given, decide what your goal is, and then develop a plan of action that seems to bring you to that goal. And as I've said, if analysis doesn't get you where you want to be, you can always fall back on intuition.

Student: So there are two types of analysis: specific and general.

Teacher: Grandmaster Alexander Kotov, a top Russian chess teacher for many years who is, lamentably, no longer with us, used to suggest being systematic in your thought processes. When it's your turn, try to find the best move, answering the opponent's threats, maintaining your own, and doing whatever the exigencies of the position require. When it's your opponent's turn and he's doing the thinking, use your time to make general plans, considering the strategy and ideas that might be worth trying if chances should later materialize.

Student: How should you go about conducting a general analysis?

Teacher: The process for eliciting information can be more important than the elements of the process. When trying to analyze generally, ask probing questions that help you construct a picture of the position, particularly in terms of strengths and weaknesses, possible attacks, piece placements, and so on. This technique, known as the analytic method or the Socratic method, is the basis of problem-solving and can be traced back thousands of years to the Greek philosophers and thinkers.

Student: So I should ask myself internalized questions to help understand things better. But what kinds of questions?

Teacher: It depends a little on whose move it is. If it's your move, you ask one group of questions. If it's your opponent's move, you might ask a different group of questions.

Student: Can you show me what you mean?

Teacher: Sure. For example, if it's your turn, you might ask questions such as this:

- Does my opponent's last move threaten me in any way?

If it does, this should lead automatically to the next question, or a similar one:

- What can I do about it?

When you have answered this question satisfactorily, you'll have found your next move. The next question(s) to ask might be:

- Has my opponent responded adequately to the threat contained in my previous move?
- If not, can I now execute my threat to good effect?
- If not, why not?

And so on. You need not ask only these questions, nor do you have to phrase them this way. But your questions should direct your attention to what's important. If they're appropriate for the immediate situation, they will more or less suggest the answer or at least a way to get at it. In this sense they serve the same purpose as principles. They do no more and no less than activate and direct the thinking process.

Student: What about when it's my opponent's move?

Teacher: In those situations, when you're not as pressed to find a particular answer to your opponent's last move and your mind is freer to wander about, you might turn to other factors. You could ask yourself questions like these:

- Have I successfully completed my development?
- Does my position contain any weak points?

- If so, what can I do to strengthen them?
- What targets should I be focusing on in my opponent's camp?
- How should I go about assailing them?

Student: I think I see, therefore I exist to play chess. On my turn, I should try to be specific. I should try to get down to business and deal with what's happening. On my opponent's turn, I can explore possibilities in a way I couldn't do as well on my own turn, when I'm trying to figure out my next move.

Teacher: That's right. Clearly, your questions form a mixture of the specific and the abstract. Usually, the specific pertain to immediate concerns; the abstract to long-range possibilities and future plans. Both types of questions are useful and necessary in any analysis. You should try to incorporate them into your thinking at once. This technique takes practice. Use it and eventually you should find yourself improving your overall gameplay. And if it doesn't eventually lead to mastery of the most challenging and entertaining game ever invented, it should at least goad you into asking questions, none of which can be posed or answered until we get to Lesson 13.

STRATEGY AND TACTICS, THE IMPORTANCE OF MATERIAL, AVOIDING ERRORS

Student: We're beyond the beginning and not yet at the ending. Is there a way to define what it is that a middlegame demands?

Teacher: The middlegame requires both step-by-step implementation and future planning, so strategy and tactics must go hand-in-hand. These two terms are virtual opposites, but they are also counterparts, which is why chessplayers may confuse them. Don't forget what we learned in Lesson 2: A strategy is a plan, and usually long-term. Sometimes a strategy is confined to a particular phase—opening, middlegame, or endgame—and sometimes it overlaps from one phase to the other. Less often, a specific strategy may dominate throughout an entire game. But strategies can go with the wind, and a player must adapt to the vicissitudes of move-to-move combat.

Student: If I remember correctly, you told me that tactics tend to be short-term, immediate, specific, and concrete. Is there a neat way to put the difference between strategy and tactics so that I can remember it?

Teacher: How about this: You could say that strategy is what you plan to do, while tactics are how you'll do it.

Student: Is one of the two easier to study than the other?

Teacher: Since tactical operations play a role throughout a game, it's easier to study them because you tend to get more practice seeing them work for—or against—you. You get lots of opportunities to seek out forks, pins, and skewers. But strategy requires the ability to see the big picture, so most of us need experience to understand the larger chessic context. Since strategy simply takes longer to learn, newcomers naturally focus on tactics rather early in their apprenticeship. As students consider these little nuggets of specific tactical truth, one after the other, they correspondingly develop a feeling for strategic understanding as well. Over a period of time, they come to assimilate and appreciate how and when to apply strategy.

Student: I guess we should get back to the game. What should White play now?

Teacher: How about **10. Bg5**?

Student: Why?

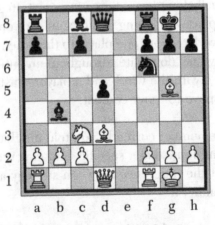

Diagram 257. After 10. Bg5.

Teacher: For one thing, this move attacks and pins the f6-knight. But it's not really the knight that White has focused on. This doesn't mean that White won't pile up on the pinned f6-knight if given the opportunity. But White's main concern is the Black d-pawn. White would like to remove some of its protection. Once again, with **10. Bg5** (diagram 257), we see that a dark-square bishop can indirectly attack a light square by threatening to capture the piece that guards that square. So the bishop attacks f6 directly and therefore d5 indirectly.

Student: Could Black now make a pesky bishop move of his own, 10 . . . Bg4 (diagram 258)?

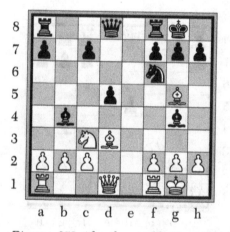

Diagram 258. After the possible 10 . . . Bg4.

Teacher: You've obviously noticed that 10 . . . Bg4 is potentially annoying, issuing as it does a direct attack to the White queen. Moreover, the bishop is protected by the knight at f6, so White can't win the bishop by 11. Qxg4 because of 11 . . . Nxg4.

Student: Wait a second. Couldn't White then continue by taking Black's queen, 12. Bxd8?

Teacher: Yes, but Black would take the bishop back and the overall result would be a set of trades, queen for queen and light-square bishop for dark-square bishop, as echoed in some aspects of a subsequent variation to be seen shortly. Nevertheless, it's true that Black's g4-bishop's protection isn't really so solid in diagram 258. White could win a piece by playing a *zwischenzug*. As you know, such a stratagem is also called an in-between move. The idea is that instead of White dealing with the attack to his queen, he could delay saving his queen for a move, stopping to first capture the piece that defends the g4-bishop.

Student: That means playing 11. Bxf6 (diagram 259).

Diagram 259. A winning zwischenzug.

Teacher: Correct. At this point, White would be ahead by a knight. Black hopes this is only a temporary advantage, but White knows it's a permanent one. White recognizes that his queen remains attacked, but he also realizes that Black's queen is now equally menaced.

Student: Couldn't Black just take the White queen, 11 . . . Bxd1 (diagram 260)?

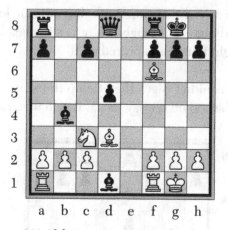

Diagram 260. If the variation continued with 11 . . . Bxd1.

Teacher: Yes, but it wouldn't be getting the White queen for free, because Black's own queen would go via 12. Bxd8 (diagram 261). It doesn't help Black to capture White's queen if he in turn loses his own queen.

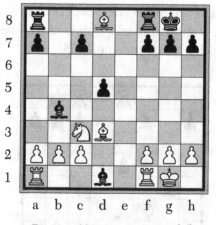

Diagram 261. Queens are traded.

Student: So it's a trade of queens. What's so bad about that?

Teacher: You're right. Neither side has won or lost a queen. They've traded queens, though White is still ahead by a minor piece, the knight that was captured on f6.

Student: But couldn't Black then tie up the score, so to speak, by taking the bishop on d8, say 12 . . . Raxd8 (diagram 262)?

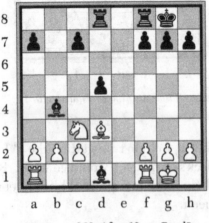

Diagram 262. After 12 . . . Raxd8.

Teacher: Right again, but White would once again go ahead by a piece when he captures Black's bishop at d1, taking back with the queen-rook, 13. Raxd1 (diagram 263).

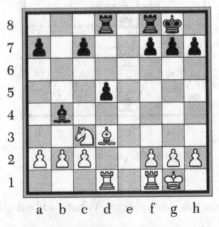

Diagram 263. White winds up a piece ahead.

Student: Okay, but I think we're missing something in this discussion. Can we go back to the position where the knight was captured on f6 (diagram 259)? Instead of now taking White's queen, 11 . . . Bxd1 (diagram 260), why doesn't Black simply take back the bishop on f6, 11 . . . Qxf6 (diagram 264), so that his queen never gets taken at all?

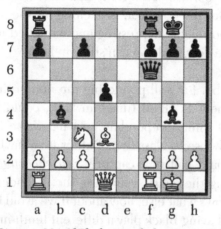

Diagram 264. If Black instead plays 11 . . . Qxf6.

Teacher: Yes, that's possible too. But then White has the time to save his own queen, which he could do most intelligently by capturing the bishop on g4 for free, 12. Qxg4 (diagram 265).

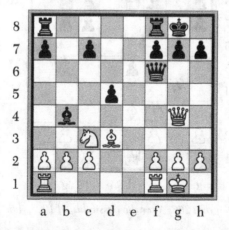

Diagram 265. White still winds up ahead by a piece.

Student: You're right. White's won a piece with, I hope I'm pronouncing this right, a *zwischenzug?*

Teacher: Right. White's *zwischenzug,* or in-between move, illustrates a broader class of tactic, that of *removing the defender* or *removing the guard,* and both of those are also called *undermining.* It's these unexpected turns that can make a chess game so interesting for the observer, so exciting for the winning tactician, and so thoroughly depressing and wretched for the losing player. But lose now, and you can still win later.

Student: Maybe. I'm still pondering the notion that a particular move, namely 11. Bxf6 (diagram 259), could be called so many different things, depending on what we've read about it and how we choose to classify it. Rather than having to decide whether I should call it a capture, *zwischenzug,* in-between move, removing the guard, removing the defender, undermining, or who knows what else, how about if we avoid having to call it anything by having Black play a different tenth move? Instead of 10 . . . Bg4 (diagram 258), what about 10 . . . h6 (diagram 266), attacking the g5-bishop?

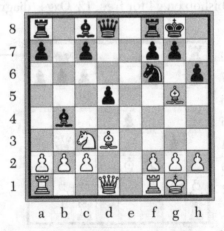

Diagram 266. After the possibility of 10 . . . h6.

Teacher: It's possible that Black, in playing the move 10 . . . h6, might be thinking that White would try to maintain the pin, retreating the dark-square bishop back one square, 11. Bh4.

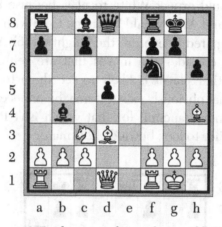

Diagram 267. After responding with a possible 11. Bh4.

Student: But Black could then break the pin with the pawn-block 11 . . . g5, compelling White to retreat the bishop further, 12. Bg3 (diagram 268).

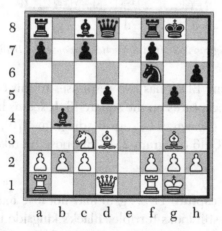

Diagram 268. After the pin is broken by 11 . . . g5.

Teacher: But White doesn't have to fall in with Black's plans. Real chessplayers don't tend to cooperate with their opponents. Instead of retreating the bishop to h4, White could take the knight on f6, 11. Bxf6 (diagram 269). In fact, this is the move that Black should expect White to play, because it's the most direct and natural. Why would White go to g5 with his bishop if he weren't prepared to capture the knight on f6? As a rule you should always consider the moves that are self-evident first, because the other player is likely to see them too. Once you understand what obviously exists, it may be unnecessary to look for anything more fanciful, for that which isn't likely ever to exist. Why bother to look beyond checkmate?

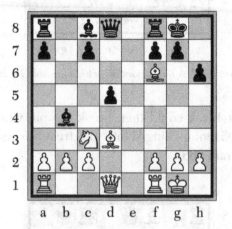

Diagram 269. After the better response, 11. Bxf6.

Student: I think Black has two responses to this capture, both of which are recaptures on the square f6. It seems he could take back with his g-pawn, 11 . . . gxf6 (diagram 270), or with his queen, 11 . . . Qxf6 (diagram 281). Suppose he takes back with his g-pawn.

Teacher: The capture 11 . . . gxf6 may not lose material on the surface, but it still looks terrible. Black's kingside is thoroughly ripped open, and White's direct 12. Qh5 (diagram 271), simulta-

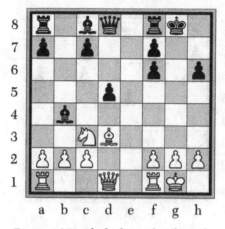

Diagram 270. Black's kingside is busted up.

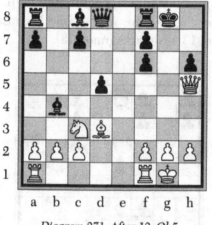

Diagram 271. After 12. Qh5.

neously attacking the h-pawn and the d-pawn, which is also attacked by the c3-knight, appears sufficient to gain an advantage.

Student: But couldn't Black save himself with a *zwischenzug*, 12 . . . Bxc3 (diagram 272), removing a d5-threatener, before having to guard h6?

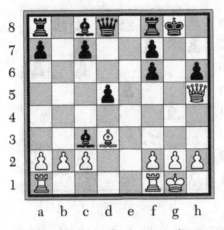

Diagram 272. After Black tries his own *zwischenzug*, 12 . . . Bxc3.

Teacher: He most definitely could. But then White has a counter *zwischenzug*, a more serious one because it threatens immediate mate, 13. Qxh6 (diagram 273).

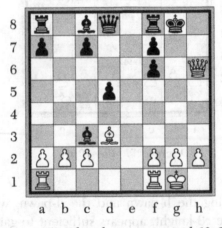

Diagram 273. White threatens mate with 13. Qxh6.

Student: That's no problem. Black could stop the mate by interposing his f-pawn, 13 . . . f5 (diagram 274).

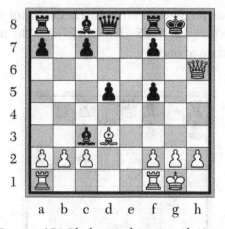

Diagram 274. Black stops the mate with 13 . . . f5.

Teacher: True enough. But then White just takes back the bishop hanging on c3 (diagram 275), and he's a pawn ahead, with a much better position because of Black's battered king-side.

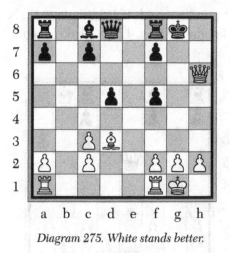

Diagram 275. White stands better.

Student: So after 11. Bxf6 gxf6, White should just play 12. Qh5 (diagram 271), with a winning game.

Teacher: He could do that—that is, 12. Qh5. But what's wrong with the immediate 12. Nxd5 (diagram 276)? Why prepare to do what you could do at once?

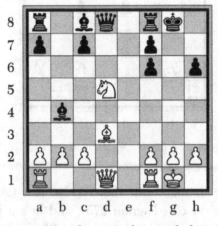

Diagram 276. After 12. Nxd5 instead of 12. Qh5.

Student: Wait a millisecond. If White plays 12. Nxd5, couldn't Black win the knight for free, 12 . . . Qxd5 (diagram 277)?

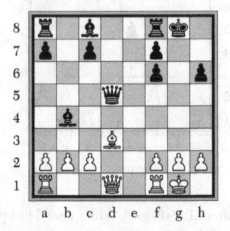

Diagram 277. After the possible response 12 . . . Qxd5.

Teacher: Not exactly. After 12 . . . Qxd5, look at the alignment of White and Black pieces on the d-file. If White's bishop were not on d3, White's queen would be able to take Black's queen for nothing.

Student: Are you suggesting that the White bishop move out of the way, to a square like e2, so that White's queen would then be in position to take Black's?

Teacher: No, withdrawing the bishop to e2 would be too slow. It would then be Black's move, not White's, and Black would have the time to save his queen, say by moving it away, protecting it, or trading it for White's queen. The trick is to make a bishop move that prevents Black from responding to save his queen. In a sense, White has to move and freeze the action, and 13. Be2 (diagram 278) doesn't do that.

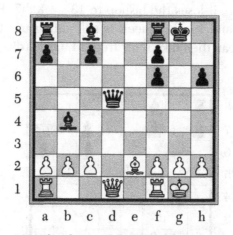

Diagram 278. After the possibility of 13. Be2, which is too slow.

Student: But there's really only one type of move that can stop everything in its tracks. That's a check. Wait another small time

segment, please. I think I have it! White could play 13. Bh7+
(diagram 279)!

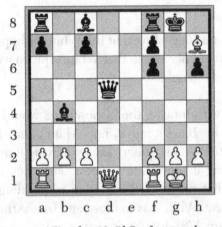

Diagram 279. After 13. Bh7+, freezing the action.

Student: Sure, it loses the bishop to 13 . . . Kxh7. But then it's
White's turn and Black's queen is still sitting out there like a
dead duck. I can then take it for free, 14. Qxd5 (diagram 280).

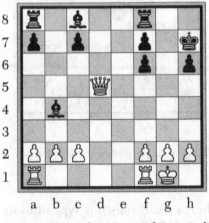

Diagram 280. After 13 . . . Kxh7 14. Qxd5.

Teacher: Very, very good. Note that when White checks, 13. Bh7+ (diagram 279), he unleashes a discovered attack uncovering an attacking line to the opposing queen by moving away an intervening piece, the bishop. For further reinforcement, you might want to go back to Lesson 2, when we first talked about this tactical idea.

Student: So if Black dares to take White's knight at d5 with his queen, he will pay a massive price for neglecting to check out plausible time-gaining checks. You're right. White, as we have seen, doesn't have to prepare to take on d5 by first moving his queen to h5. He can just take the d5-pawn without setting up any additional support. The support is already there in the form of a hidden tactic, a discovery.

Teacher: So the first lesson here has taught you not to prepare the unnecessary. There's something else to be learned about the process we used to come to the right decision. We did that by understanding what the problem was and then asking questions about the problem. When we realized that the d3-bishop was in the way, preventing White's queen from taking Black's, we asked something like: How can I get the bishop out of the way with a gain of time so that I can capture the queen? The question practically gave the answer away. So we see that a large part of analysis has to do with asking leading questions—questions that practically give us the next move, or at least point the way. The most precise formulation of a question practically contains its answer.

Student: Do good players always verbalize thoughts to themselves this way?

Teacher: Sometimes they don't articulate the thoughts necessarily in words, but a lot of this has to do with practical understanding. They've gone through similar operations so often that much can be achieved almost intuitively, without having to spell things out so deliberately. But you'd be surprised at how often thoughts are distinctly and clearly expressed, step by step, in some of their internal analytic monologues, even at advanced degrees of skill. Nevertheless, when they were at your introductory level, most of them did go through these somewhat mechanical processes until they acquired sufficient experience to do virtually the same things without much apparent thought at all.

Student: Let me ask another general question, if I may. How can I increase my tactical ability?

Teacher: To increase your ability to find tactics, and to heighten your awareness of them, you might, for example, nurture the habit of scouring the board for useful connections between pieces and squares. To help you in this quest, you might try asking directive and relevant questions, such as: Are there any enemy pieces on the same lines as my pieces? Are there two or more enemy pieces on the same rank, file, or diagonal? If not, do several of the opponent's pieces connect to the same square? Can my queen move to a square that connects to several enemy units?

Student: It seems that certain tactics are more likely to occur in certain corresponding positions.

Teacher: Great observation. For that reason you should always be looking for patterns and thinking in terms of schemes and analogies. Notice how certain tactics seem to occur with the same pieces, or under the same type of situations, or out of the same openings. And when the tactics are not presently a factor in the position, think: Is there some way I can play to set up pertinent tactics in the future? Can I do so without giving away my intentions?

Student: You mean I shouldn't announce to my opponent what I intend to do?

Teacher: Not if you can help it. But let me return to your earlier question. Once you've learned a tactical idea, or any useful chess concept for that matter, file it away for the next game. Maybe you'll be able to use it again at some other time and in some other place. Get into the habit of asking yourself: Does this situation remind me of anything I've ever seen before? If it does, then you can pursue your analysis further, to see what useful information you can recall—information that might help you navigate through chessically deep and muddy waters.

Student: Okay. I'm convinced. I won't play 11 . . . gxf6 (diagram 270). How about if I were to play the recapture 11 . . . Qxf6 (diagram 281)? Would that be any better?

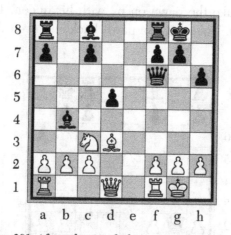

Diagram 281. After taking with the queen instead, 11 . . . Qxf6.

Teacher: That would avoid the busting up of Black's kingside pawn structure. But it leaves d5 totally undefended. White could simply capture the d-pawn for free (diagram 282). Not only that, from d5 the knight would also be threatening the Black queen, b4-bishop, and c7-pawn, a triple fork.

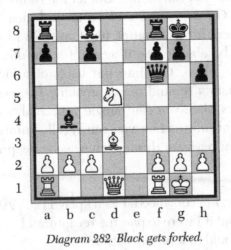

Diagram 282. Black gets forked.

Student: I have an answer to that. After 12. Nxd5 (diagram 282), Black could take the pawn on b2 with his queen, 12 . . . Qxb2 (diagram 283). This gets the pawn back and even defends the b4-bishop.

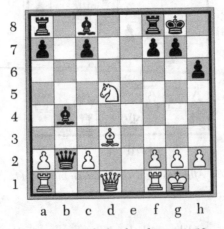

Diagram 283. After Black takes the pawn, 12 . . . Qxb2.

Teacher: Yes, but you've overlooked something. After 12 . . . Qxb2 (diagram 283), White has the lethal attack 13. Rb1 (diagram 284). This not only threatens Black's queen, it also threatens what's behind the queen on the b-file, the b4-bishop. After the queen moves to safety, White's d5-knight would be able to capture the b4-bishop for free.

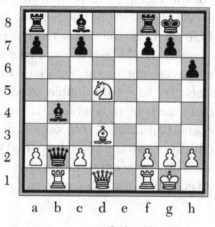

Diagram 284. Black is skewered.

Student: My goodness. That's a skewer. The rook attacks the queen and forces it to move to safety, exposing a unit behind the queen to capture.

Teacher: The skewer wins a piece and, as you probably remember from our earlier discussion, once White is a piece ahead, he's ready for a systematic set of exchanges. He thereby hopes to reduce counterplay and leave his opponent nothing in the way of resourceful resistance. The extra piece will eventually decide the outcome. Either it will enable White to develop a winning mating attack, or it will win more material, increasing White's overall advantage. Material makes material.

Student: To me it seems that many players hope to get through a game taking but never giving, even when giving leads to greater taking.

Teacher: One of the most difficult things in chess is to keep all your material. It's not really possible to get through a game without any of your forces being captured. All you can hope for is that the results of the exchange favor you. Maybe you'll have opportunities to take things for nothing. If so, look for these desserts and gobble them. If waiting for these oversights is too passive for you—and it should be—you can take a more active stance. Use your pieces, not pawns, to attack the opponent's undefended targets. Try to set up double attacks, threatening two or more enemy units simultaneously. If you keep up the pressure, issuing constant attacks, your opponent is eventually bound to miss a threat or two and you'll be poised to come away with material gain. This may seem simplistic, but it's exactly how most chess games go between average players. Just watch. Even better, just do.

Student: I know we've talked about this a lot, but could you just go over one more time what to do once a material advantage has been gained?

Teacher: Once you've obtained a material advantage, you should exchange pieces, thereby emphasizing your advantage while reducing the enemy's potential for counterplay. Exchanges impair your opponent's capacity to resist. Your goal should be to eliminate all the opponent's pieces, forcing a very clear and simple endgame, one in which you have total control. Don't be afraid to trade queen for queen, rook for rook, and minor piece for minor piece. When trading minor pieces, aim to swap bishops for bishops and knights for knights, avoiding endings of knight versus bishop, or bishop versus knight, where your remaining minor piece may be less effective. As a rule, avoid disturbances that could lead to imbalance and throw you off your game.

Student: And clarify this again, too: Should I trade all my forces, pawns included?

Teacher: You have to be careful here. The trading-down policy doesn't pertain to pawns. You prefer to win pawns, not trade them. As you trade pieces, the defender's ability to guard the pawns decreases, and you might get them for nothing.

Student: Is there a problem with trading too many pawns?

Teacher: You bet. Exchanging too many pawns, particularly in minor-piece endings, could give your opponent surprising opportunities to draw. For example, the ending of minor piece and pawn versus minor piece is drawn if the defender sacrifices the piece for the pawn. After the sacrifice, the attacker doesn't have sufficient mating material.

Student: Could you show me an example?

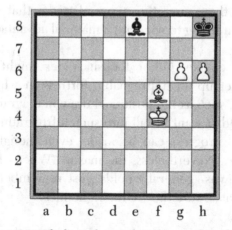

Diagram 285. Black can force a draw by sacrificing his bishop for the g-pawn.

Teacher: It is Black's move in diagram 285. By sacrificing his bishop, 1 . . . Bxg6 2. Bxg6 (diagram 286), the position becomes drawn, with White unable to queen his pawn by force.

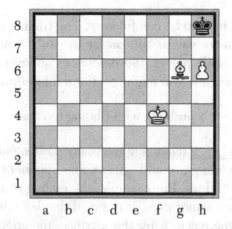

Diagram 286. A positional draw, White being unable to promote the pawn by force.

Student: Are there any other types of trades that might pose problems when trying to win with a material advantage?

Teacher: Of course. Other foolish trades might allow the defender to set up an impregnable fortress in which passive defense holds, such as the positional draw in diagrams 285 and 286. You wouldn't want to fall into such a frustrating situation, where no real progress can be made, even though you have superior forces. Nevertheless, the maxim "When ahead, trade pieces, not pawns" generally holds. Just remember, if you do swap pieces, make sure they're the right ones.

Student: What are the most serious dangers to a player who has gained a material advantage?

Teacher: Besides what we've just discussed, the chief dangers tend to be psychological and positional, and like Tweedledum and Tweedledee, they go together. It's natural for a player to relax or get complacent after gaining material, thinking the game's already won. But when the opponent resists, the win can easily slip away. Extra material doesn't guarantee a win. You still have to make it work for you.

Student: In what way might it not work for me?

Teacher: One problem in winning material is that your forces can become separated from the main theater and unable to fight off enemy invaders. Be especially careful not to stretch your army to win a questionable pawn if it leaves certain key pieces, like the queen, out of position for defense. Think of what happened to Napoleon in Russia. Then get back to chess.

Student: Are there any things I could do to minimize the possibility of failures?

Teacher: You could do several things. Try to avoid a psychological letdown and stay alert. Cope with disarray in your forces by: (1) consolidating; (2) warding off potential threats; (3) activating key forces; (4) simplifying ruthlessly; and (5) maintaining your focus. Trade enough pieces, within reason, and your opponent will have nothing left to do. But you still shouldn't relax—not until you get the win. And remember, once you're ahead, be careful about trading too many pawns. With a material advantage, it's easier to win more material. Concentrate on using any advantage. Play down your disadvantages. Always play to win. Always. Okay, that's my Vince Lombardi pep talk for now.

Student: I'm not sure if we're discussing the endgame or football, so maybe we should just get back to our game. How about

if Black avoids all we've just looked at and defends his d-pawn
instead with 10 . . . c6 (diagram 287)?

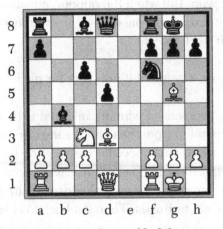

Diagram 287. After the possible defense 10 . . . c6.

Teacher: This is solid defense, ending all immediate threats
against the d-pawn. Its only drawbacks are that the move doesn't
develop a new piece, and in some cases it will lose a tempo if
Black should later move his pawn to c5 where, along with the
d-pawn, it would control a block of squares along White's fourth
rank.

Student: Should Black think about defending the d-pawn in
some other way? What about protecting it with 10 . . . Be6 (diagram 288)?

Teacher: The bishop move develops a new piece and also adequately secures the d-pawn. Sometimes, though, the bishop is a
better defensive piece at g6, where it cuts the White light-
square bishop's d3-h7 diagonal. To get to g6, Black must find
the time and safety to play Bg4 and then Bh5 and then Bg6.

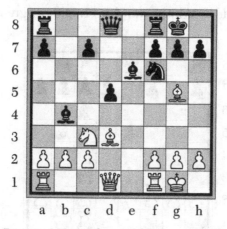

Diagram 288. Another possible d-pawn defense,
10 . . . Be6.

But we've seen that 10 . . . Bg4 (diagram 258) loses a piece because of White's pin on Black's knight at f6. To retain this possible maneuver of shifting the bishop to g6, Black now plays **10 . . . Be7** (diagram 289), breaking the pin.

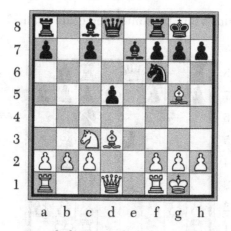

Diagram 289. Black retreats the bishop and breaks the pin,
10 . . . Be7.

Student: Couldn't White now play 11. Qf3 (diagram 290)?

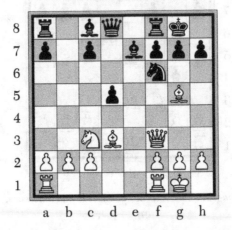

Diagram 290. After the possible continuation 11. Qf3.

Teacher: This development of the queen to f3 would clear the center files for White's rooks. The queen-rook might then be moved to d1 and the king-rook to e1. But Black should be able to exploit White's queenly development by the simple 11 . . . Bg4 (diagram 291), and the queen would have to waste a move to get to safety.

Student: Could White try something other than 11. Qf3?

Diagram 291. Now it's okay to attack White's queen, 11 . . . Bg4.

Teacher: Sure. One legitimate possibility is 11. Re1, seizing the open file. But that's not what White winds up doing. Instead he plays **11. Bxf6** (diagram 292).

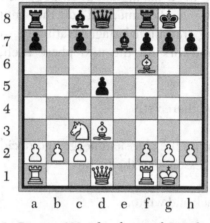

Diagram 292. After the actual 11 Bxf6.

Student: Should Black then take back with the king-knight pawn, 11 . . . gxf6?

Teacher: No, that wouldn't make too much sense, for the king-side then becomes disrupted and broken, as we've discussed in a related variation (diagram 270). It would be much better to take back with the bishop, **11 . . . Bxf6** (diagram 293).

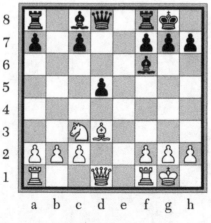

Diagram 293. After taking back, 11 . . . Bxf6.

Student: Things are starting to get interesting. I wonder where we're going to go from here.

Teacher: We've been talking about strategy and tactics, their importance to the middlegame, and how they continue to apply to the oncoming transitional stage. Naturally, we've also had to lay the groundwork for the next phase itself, namely, the endgame.

Student: Are we there yet?

Teacher: Count up the chessic mileage and decide for yourself during our next lesson. Got the picture?

Student: In black and white.

ENDGAME PRINCIPLES, CENTRALIZATION, THE ACTIVE KING, AND PAWN PROMOTION

Student: I've checked out the position and I think an endgame is in sight. Do chessplayers need to adjust their thinking during the last stages of a game?

Teacher: Endgames are a little different from openings and middlegames. Time is still critical, except that in this last phase material is no longer its enemy. The two begin to merge into a concluding strategy, which may yet require a tactical turn. The same ideas are always there. We're just not used to looking for them in different settings.

Student: How is the endgame different from the earlier stages?

Teacher: The endgame features simplification to exploit tangible and positional superiority. The inferior side meanwhile tries to complicate the issue, keeping the position alive to stave off ignominious defeat. Endgames are distinguishable from openings and middlegames in at least several of the following ways: (1) fewer pieces are on the board (often the queens have been exchanged); (2) the kings are more active; (3) calculations can be more precise; (4) the relative values of the units change (pawns become more important and minor pieces less important);

(5) material advantages are emphasized; and (6) it's often desirable not to move because of *zugzwang* or the opposition.

Student: Hold on. *Zugzwang?* What's that?

Teacher: *Zugzwang* is a German word meaning something like "compulsion to move." In the endgame you can find yourself in *zugzwang* when any move you make worsens your position. The rules of chess dictate that you have no choice but to move when it's your turn. Given that fact, a clever opponent may actually be able to create circumstances that make all your choices bad ones—and you have no choice but to make one, either.

Student: That's a scary thought. Here's another one: I don't actually know when an endgame begins. Is there a way to tell?

Teacher: You can usually call it an endgame after the queens are traded and it's safe enough for the kings to become active. But the opening shouldn't necessarily be separated from the endgame. In many ways, the final phase is actually the logical outcome of everything that comes earlier, beginning with the opening. Formations created in the first few moves of a contest can last right down to the end of a game, many moves later. This is especially true with regard to pawn structure, inasmuch as every pawn move leaves an indelible mark on the overall position. Thus, the consequences of structural problems in the opening tend to be real and lasting.

Student: But aren't certain factors important throughout an entire game, not just in particular phases?

Teacher: Absolutely. Time, for example, is important from beginning to end. In the opening, an advantage in time means that one can control the flow of play. In the middlegame, time can be used to implement your own plans before the opponent gets to play his. In the endgame, having an extra move or two can translate, among other things, to queening first, moving your

king in time to catch a dangerous pawn, or getting more dominant piece positions and placements. You may also use extra time
to seize control of a line or square, or take out time to make *luft*.

Student: Sounds like another German word. What does it
mean?

Teacher: You're right, *luft* is another German term. It means
"breathing space." In chess it specifically refers to the act of creating an escape hatch for the castled king. Which reminds me
that I should warn you. Just because you're ahead in some way
doesn't mean you can afford to coast along. Your opponent isn't
going to let you. Most will snarl on like cornered chess rats. So
you shouldn't quit planning, analyzing, and fighting unless you
want to quit the game. As far as what you're fighting for, some
factors can apply over the course of a game, when and if the situation dictates. As we've seen, time is almost always significant.
The same is largely true for the center: We generally need to try
to keep it foremost in our thoughts.

Student: Why might it still be important to play for the center
in the endgame?

Teacher: The principle of centralization is vital throughout a
game, just like the element of time. True, in the opening you
should try to develop to the middle and guard the central
squares. But even in the endgame, centralizing the king can be
paramount. Once established in the center, the king is more
ready to attack and defend key squares while monitoring activi-
ties across the board.

Student: So you're implying that pieces in general should head
for the center in the endgame too, as in the opening?

Teacher: Most pieces, though not necessarily rooks, should be
centralized in the ending, simply because from the center they
radiate in all directions and are better prepared to do business

anywhere. Queen endings, for instance, can be dominated by a centralized queen, whose power from the center is so great it can thwart its enemy counterpart, denying it access to good squares and a good time. Frustrating your opponent can be excellent strategy. It could result in your opponent resorting to unsound and risky play, and in an ending with queens a careless mistake is often fatal.

Student: Could you say a little more about queen placement in the endgame?

Teacher: In the endgame, where your queen faces off against its rival, you'll want to centralize your own queen as a dominant principle. In the center, your queen impairs the opposing queen's function, whether in attack or defense, by guarding many of the squares the enemy queen would like to use.

Student: But in the opening, it would be virtually impossible to keep your queen stationed in the center.

Teacher: That's true. In the earlier phases, it's too tricky to maintain your queen in the center. You may be able to get it there, but keeping it there could be a problem. Generally, the enemy is able to attack a centralized queen with minor pieces or pawns, forcing a withdrawal. To save the queen, you'll wind up losing time, space, and maybe even the queen. In the endgame, however, the opponent often doesn't have the firepower or ability to drive away a centrally based queen as easily.

Student: All right, let's get back to our game. What's the position?

Teacher: Black has just taken back on f6 with his bishop (diagram 293).

Student: I think one thing we've been looking at is something like 12. Qh5. Is that what we should play?

Teacher: No, let's try a different tack and simply capture the d-pawn outright, **12. Nxd5!**.

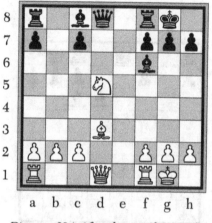

Diagram 294. After the actual 12. Nxd5!.

Student: I think I get the point. As we've already more or less considered, if Black's queen takes back, 12 . . . Qxd5 (diagram 295), White wins the queen with 13. Bxh7+, discovering an attack from White's queen to Black's.

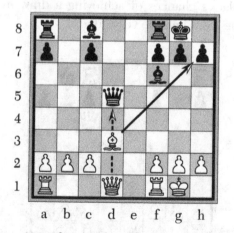

Diagram 295. White now has a discovery on Black's queen,
13. Bxh7+.

Teacher: Very good. Black will have to accept the idea that he's dropped a pawn and play on from there. He can at this point, for example, complete his development with 12 . . . Be6 (diagram 296).

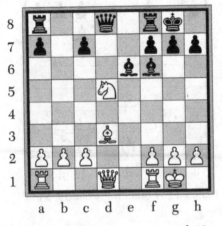

Diagram 296. If Black were to go on with 12 . . . Be6.

Student: Then what?

Teacher: White would simplify further, 13. Nxf6+ Qxf6 (diagram 297). Black's chances of achieving a draw in the pawn-down endgame would not be very good.

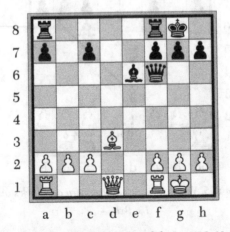

Diagram 297. After the further simplification 13. Nxf6+ Qxf6.

Student: I guess it depends on the pawn's value in the ensuing endgame. But how is it that an extra pawn usually wins, and how is the win typically executed?

Teacher: Having an extra pawn doesn't necessarily mean very much in the opening, when time, development, and the initiative supersede. An extra pawn stars in the endgame, when it has a real chance to forge ahead and become a new queen. Not surprisingly, endgame theory often relies on converting an extra pawn into a win. Once a pawn becomes a new queen, checkmate can't be too far away. According to theory, an advancing pawn may force the losing side to sacrifice material to stop it, most likely a knight or a bishop. With the extra piece it has won for its pawn, the superior side will probably be able to win additional enemy pawns as well, which will likely threaten to queen. Sooner or later, the superior side will either force mate or increase its material advantage so greatly that mate becomes imminent.

Student: Just to be overly sure—when I'm ahead I should trade pieces, right?

Teacher: That's right, and you've heard me say that, I'm sure, for the umpteenth time. The way to a winning technique is fairly direct. The stronger side should systematically try to exchange pieces, minor piece for minor piece, rook for rook, and queen for queen. As we've already pointed out, however, he must be chary about trading pawns. If he swaps too many, the inferior side may see an opportunity to give up a minor piece for the final pawn. With no pawns left, it's impossible to make a new queen—or even an old one. Meanwhile, the extra minor piece itself, without the presence of pawns, may not lead to a forced win. Pawns can become a lot more important that you'd imagine, and mostly during an endgame.

Student: So the main reason to trade pieces is to emphasize the difference in the ratio of forces?

Teacher: Yes, but there's something else. A further benefit of systematic exchanges is that they virtually reduce all counterplay. One generally needs material to create attacking chances, and the less you have, the harder it becomes to get back in the game. So not only should we trade when ahead, we should also trade to avoid complications, for they may lead us to losing our way. If we lose our way, we'll possibly lose control, and that's when we can kiss the game good-bye.

Student: Since it's good to trade when ahead, obviously it's bad to trade when behind. I love corollaries, but they don't always love me.

Teacher: Yes, you should try to avoid trades when behind, but you always have to base your decision on what's really happening on the board, not on abstractions and generalities.

Student: I remember. It all depends. But since endgames usually have less on the board, I presume they're a little simpler to play than the other phases.

Teacher: Not really. Because there's less on the board it's often harder to find specific places to begin your analysis. Of the three phases, the endgame tends to be the least understood and worst played. Indeed, one of the marks of a really strong player is the ability to convert endgame advantages consistently into victories.

Student: I realize that endgames can vary tremendously, but what are their most common characteristics?

Teacher: I think we can at least say the following: (1) Usually, less material is on the board and the queen is gone; (2) Advantages in pieces and pawns in the endgame tend to be decisive, whereas in the opening and the middlegame material superiority can be countered by other factors, such as initiative and king safety; (3) Pawns in the endgame assume greater importance because they may threaten to become new queens by reaching the eighth rank; (4) The most distinctive feature of the endgame is probably that the king can be active without fear of stumbling into a sudden mate, unlike the opening or the middlegame, since there generally aren't enough enemy men left to pose serious threats; (5) Many endgames pit king and pawns against king and pawns. Victory may hinge on the ability of one king to outmaneuver its opposing counterpart. The king can be a strong piece. Use it.

Student: Why would a player want to aim for a draw?

Teacher: All players draw at times. It's better than losing, right? There are many reasons to strive for a draw when the opportunity arises. You may be feeling ill or too tired to tackle the position. You'd want to achieve a draw if your position were obviously failing. You may choose to draw in a tournament because you're short of time or to insure your standing. A draw can even lock up first place in a tight race. And there may be any number of personal reasons to steer the game toward a draw—although doing so is often no easier than playing for a win.

Student: So what does Black do after **12. Nxd5!** (diagram 294)?

Teacher: Naturally, Black snatches his pawn back, **12 ... Bxb2** (diagram 298).

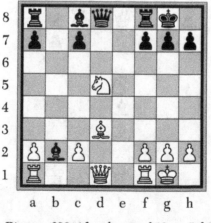

Diagram 298. After the actual 12 ... Bxb2.

Student: With only one safe square for White's attacked rook, I suppose he should play it over a square, **13. Rb1** (diagram 299), menacing the bishop.

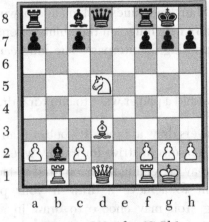

Diagram 299. After 13. Rb1.

Teacher: Unfortunately, Black is still unable to safely capture the knight at d5 with his queen because of the discovery Bxh7+. So he's going to have to move his bishop to safety. Where would you move it to?

Student: The c3-square is guarded by the knight, so this move is clearly unacceptable. Black could retreat his bishop back

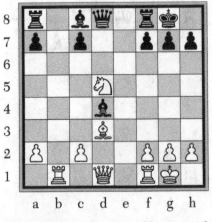

Diagram 300. After a possible 13 . . . Bd4.

where it came from, to f6, I guess. What about moving it to d4, 13 . . . Bd4 (diagram 300)?

Teacher: That fails too, to a similar discovery, 14. Bxh7+. After 14 . . . Kxh7, White gets back the piece with 15. Qxd4 (diagram 301).

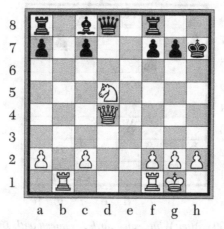

Diagram 301. After 14. Bxh7+ Kxh7 15. Qxd4.

Student: Hold on for a second. After 15. Qxd4, can't Black attack the pinned knight by 15 . . . c6 (diagram 302), and if it moves, Black's queen then takes White's?

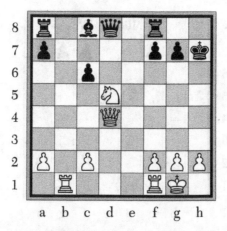

Diagram 302. If Black tries to exploit the pin with 15 . . . c6.

Teacher: It may seem that Black, with 15 . . . c6, can attack White's knight, since it's pinned to its queen by the Black queen. But White can get his queen out of the pin with a gain of time by 16. Qd3+ (diagram 303). After Black gets out of check, White can move his knight to safety.

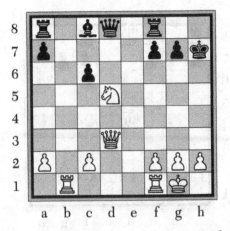

Diagram 303. After White safeguards his queen with 16. Qd3+, ending the pin with a gain of time.

Student: Okay, maybe 13 . . . Bd4 doesn't succeed. But what about 13 . . . Be5 (diagram 304) instead?

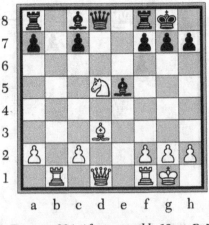

Diagram 304. After a possible 13 . . . Be5.

Teacher: The defense 13 . . . Be5 (diagram 304) also flops, a simple winning line being 14. Bxh7+! Kxh7 15. Qh5+ Kg8 16. Qxe5 (diagram 305), and White has gained another pawn.

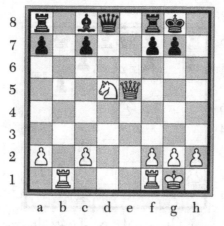

Diagram 305. After the line 13 . . . Be5 14. Bxh7+ Kxh7
15. Qh5+ Kg8 16. Qxe5.

Student: Couldn't Black then try 16 . . . Re8 (diagram 306)?

Teacher: That would bring the rook to an open file with a gain of time, since it attacks the White queen. But White has the

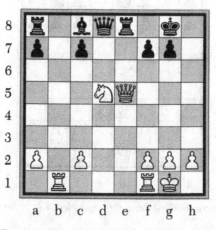

Diagram 306. Continuing the line, 16 . . . Re8.

escape 17. Qh5, still keeping his knight protected. The further annoyance 17 . . . g6 doesn't disrupt the knight's defense either, for White still has 18. Qf3 (diagram 307), when the queen is free of Black threats and still covers the knight.

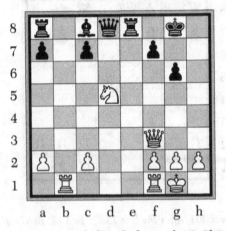

Diagram 307. After concluding the line with 17. Qh5 g6 18. Qf3.

Student: Okay, but I'm not prepared to give up on this so easily. What about moving the bishop the other direction, 13 . . . Ba3 (diagram 308)?

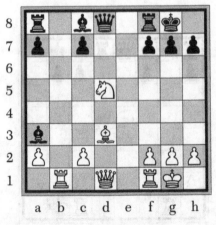

Diagram 308. After a different idea, 13 . . . Ba3.

Teacher: At a3 the bishop doesn't contribute to the kingside defense, and may fall victim to an insidious veiled threat if White plays a timely Qf3. In the right circumstances, if the White queen moves to f3 it would menace two potential discoveries: one to the Black bishop at a3, by moving the bishop at d3, and the other to the Black rook at a8, by shifting the knight at d5. Always remember, when looking for possible tactics, to note which pieces line up on the same rank, file, or diagonal.

Student: Chess is geometrical.

Teacher: Indeed, as geometrical as any flat surface with figurines can be, whether played on oak with finely crafted wooden pieces, a computer screen with special graphics, or in the head with only a head. Shall we move on ahead by going back to our game?

Approaching the Goal

THE PASSED PAWN AND PAWN MAJORITIES

Student: Do you remember where we were supposed to start this lesson?

Teacher: I remember where I was supposed to, I think. Back to our game. So, then, Black elects to retreat the bishop, **13 . . . Bf6** (diagram 309). Now it's time to evaluate.

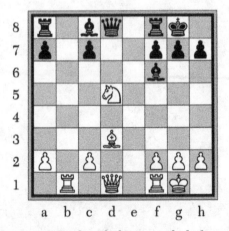

Diagram 309. After Black retreats the bishop to f6.

Student: It seems to me that White has the overall advantage, though I'm not entirely sure why.

Teacher: Let's analyze the situation: (1) White is better developed; (2) Black must yet develop his queen-bishop; (3) White's rook occupies the open b-file; (4) Black's queen-rook doesn't yet have a safe move, thanks to White controlling the b-file; (5) White's knight is tactically infuriating from d5; (6) White has the next free move and a decent initiative. So I agree with you. White stands better.

Student: It's White's turn. What do you think of 14. Qf3 (diagram 310)?

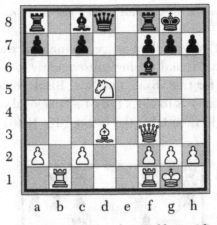

Diagram 310. After the possible 14. Qf3.

Teacher: This move does threaten a discovery on the a8-rook, as well as smashing up Black's kingside by 15. Nxf6+. Black could try to cope with the threat by developing the queen-bishop, 14 ... Be6, so that Black's major pieces are connected along his home rank.

Student: Suppose White plays to set up a different discovery, and decides on playing 14. Be4 (diagram 311)?

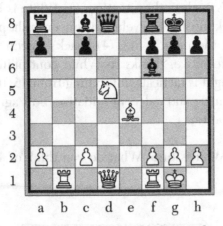

Diagram 311. After another possible fourteenth move, B4.

Teacher: That, too, would menace winning the exchange, starting with 15. Nxf6+, and hoping subsequently to be able to take the rook at a8 for free, Bxa8. One way Black could try to avert losing the exchange is to block the e4-a8 diagonal with 14 . . . c6. If White's knight then takes the bishop, 15. Nxf6+, Black could

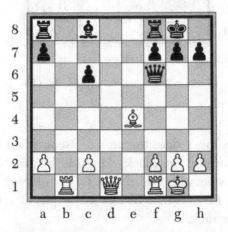

Diagram 312. After the possible continuation 14 . . . c6 15. Nxf6+ Qxf6.

take back with the queen, 15 . . . Qxf6 (diagram 312), guarding the pawn at c6 to boot.

Student: Let's go with **14. Qh5** (diagram 313). I have a feeling about it.

Diagram 313. After the actual 14. Qh5, threatening mate at h7.

Teacher: That threatens mate at h7. Black could stop the mate by moving the king-rook pawn one square, 14 . . . h6 (diagram 314).

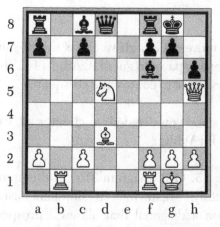

Diagram 314. After the possible defense 14 . . . h6.

Student: I think Black should play **14 . . . g6** (diagram 315). It ends the mate threat and gains time by driving away the queen. I'd go with it if I were Black. What do you think about that?

Diagram 315. After the actual defense, 14 . . . g6.

Teacher: Okay, it's your instructional funeral. The move **14 . . . g6** does attack White's queen, and as a rule, you should drive off enemy pieces whenever you can do so without incurring problems. But in shooing away her ladyship, Black weakens f6. Do you see why?

Student: The move **14 . . . g6** weakens the f6-square because there's no longer any pawn to guard it. After 14 . . . h6, Black's f7-pawn still allows Black to control the g6-square.

Teacher: But since you decided on g6 after all, can you find a strong counter for White?

Student: I like **15. Qf3** (diagram 316). It threatens the bishop at f6 immediately. Meanwhile, it simultaneously places the White queen on a diagonal that allows a prospective discovered attack to the rook at a8. All White would then have to do is move the d5-knight with a gain of time, and the rook at a8 would be toast.

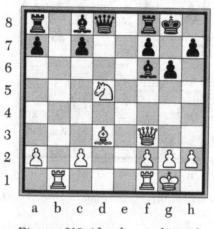

Diagram 316. After the actual 15. Qf3.

Teacher: Very good answer. Black seems to have two choices: he can defend the bishop with his king, 15 . . . Kg7 (diagram 317), or get it to safety by repositioning the attacked bishop (15 . . . Bg7). Retreating the bishop would generally be the more reliable defense. You don't want to rely too much on the king as a defensive piece if there are perfectly plausible options. This doesn't mean that the king should never be used as a defender. The king is a chessic paradox: vulnerable but potentially quite powerful, since it's able to guard all the squares surrounding it. As a fighting tool, the king is probably slightly stronger than either a bishop or a knight, worth something like four pawns in native ability, though with no exchange value at all.

Student: Obviously, given that it's against the rules to take it or to allow it to be taken.

Teacher: You bet. Sometimes really young beginners forget that little fact, though.

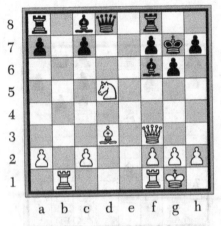

Diagram 317. After the alternate defense 15 . . . Kg7.

Student: You've convinced me once again. Let's make Black play **15 . . . Bg7** (diagram 318), but without being sadistic.

Teacher: You've persuaded me. Withdrawing the bishop to g7 also restores control over the two previously weakened squares, f6 and h6. A piece doesn't guard the square it occupies, which means it can't protect itself. Strangely enough, a piece can't guard the square it's on until it's no longer on it. When the

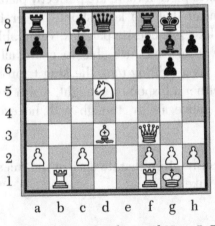

Diagram 318. After the actual 15 . . . Bg7.

bishop sat on f6, f6 wasn't so safe. When the bishop moves off f6, suddenly f6 is strengthened.

Student: I suppose White should still be looking for a way to uncover an attack to a8.

Teacher: If the knight is moved to e3 or f4, for example, Black cannot save the a8-rook by moving it, for b8 is guarded by White's well-placed rook at b1, currently dominating the open b-file. Black can nonetheless save the a8-rook by finally moving his light-square bishop, clearing the home rank, "connecting" the queen and rook, so that the queen then defends the rook.

Student: If I had White, and apparently sometimes I do, I might now ask which discovery is the most effective.

Teacher: That's asking an intelligent question. Black might indeed be wondering if White could move the knight with a gain of time. That is, could it be moved to give a threat while also posing an additional threat to the rook from White's queen? If so, White would then have issued two threats, and Black might be unable to guard against both.

Student: What about 16. Nf6+ (diagram 319)?

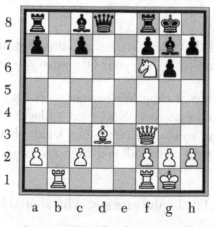

Diagram 319. After the try 16. Nf6+.

Teacher: This does gain time because it forces Black to save his king. After he does so, say by 16 . . . Qxf6, developing a new piece, White can go ahead with his other threat and capture the rook with 17. Qxa8 (diagram 320).

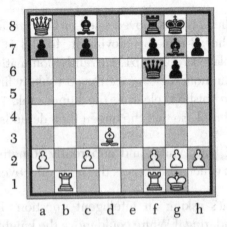

Diagram 320. After the conceivable continuation 16 . . . Qxf6 17. Qxa8.

Student: It certainly seems like a reasonable decision.

Teacher: It is. But a better idea for White is to move the knight and capture something in the process, even if it leaves the knight in a position to be captured. If Black takes the knight, he still loses his a8-rook, and also anything the knight captures in the process.

Student: I like that idea. You're not directing me to suggest **16. Nxc7** (diagram 321), are you? Of course you are.

Teacher: Your idea is clear. White snares a pawn while issuing a double attack to the a8-rook. Now even if Black's bishop cleared off the back row, so that Black's queen suddenly defended the rook, White's knight could still take the rook, gaining at least the exchange.

Student: Okay. I'll play the wise guy. What should Black do now?

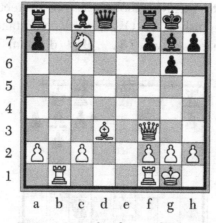

Diagram 321. After the actual 16. Nxc7.

Teacher: One defensive approach is to clear the back rank with a gain of time. If the bishop at c8 could menacingly enter the play, Black might be able to use the time to save the a8-rook. As you've probably analyzed, 16 . . . Qxc7 would win the knight but drop the rook to 17. Qxa8 (diagram 322).

Diagram 322. After the possible continuation 16 . . . Qxc7 17. Qxa8.

Student: I guess I see how Black could gain the time needed to guard his a8-rook. He could create his own threat, moving the c8-bishop to g4, even though it's not protected. Then, if White takes the bishop, 17. Qxg4, Black could take the knight, 17 . . . Qxc7. So let's go with **16 . . . Bg4** (diagram 323). I like it.

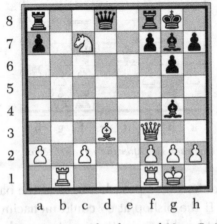

Diagram 323. After the actual 16 . . . Bg4.

Teacher: I like that you like it. But White doesn't have to take the bishop on g4. He could instead capture the a8-rook with his queen, **17. Qxa8** (diagram 324), since it's protected by the c7-knight.

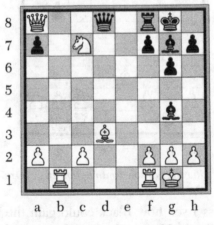

Diagram 324. After the actual 17. Qxa8.

Student: It seems that Black really now has two choices: he can take White's c7-knight, uncovering an attack to White's queen from his f8-rook in the process, or he can take the queen with his own, knowing he would still be able to capture the knight a move later. I'm a little worried about the intervention of White's queen. I prefer playing **17 . . . Qxa8** (diagram 325).

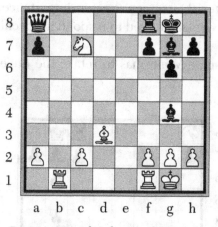

Diagram 325. After the actual 17 . . . Qxa8.

Teacher: I think it's wonderful the way you've gotten into the spirit of things: playing White *or* Black to aid the flow of the discourse. Let's look at the way you've chosen for Black to respond. There are two ways to play defense. You can play passively, taking no chances and, like many beginners, trying to guard everything, trading down to avoid attacks against you. Or, like experienced and solid players, you can play actively, combining defense with counterattack. The latter is riskier but more apt to succeed. The best defense tends to be a good offense. Black's most practical course of action was to play 17 . . . Qxc7, retaining his queen so as to be able to launch counterattacks. To get back in the game Black is going to need every resource he can find. The capture **17 . . . Qxa8** (diagram 325) plays into White's hands. It leads into a cut-and-dried endgame that is quite safe but also, in the end, quite hopeless.

Student: I'm remembering what I've forgotten. When behind in material, you should try to avoid exchanges, and especially of queens. I just planned for Black to voluntarily trade queens in the face of the appropriate strategic policy.

Teacher: That's right. Such transactions only kill counterplay and steer the game closer to a situation where the advantage of additional material assumes greater importance. White and Black are now virtually forced to respond in specific ways.

Student: I assume White has to retake the queen, **18. Nxa8** (diagram 326).

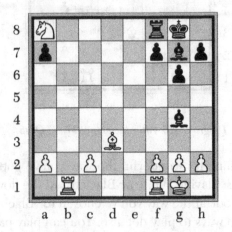

Diagram 326. After the actual 18. Nxa8.

Teacher: And Black has to take back, **18 . . . Rxa8** (diagram 327), before the knight gets a chance to run away. Why don't you try to evaluate the position again?

Student: Materially, Black has four pawns, while White has five. So far, White is ahead by a pawn in our calculation. Not counting the kings, both sides have three pieces, but White has two rooks and a bishop whereas Black has two bishops and a rook.

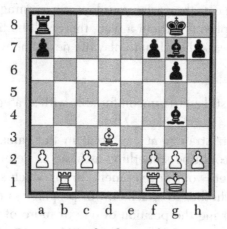

Diagram 327. After the actual 18 . . . Rxa8.

Since one rook and bishop balance out for each side, we don't have to factor them into our calculation, and the remaining difference is that Black has a bishop for a rook.

Teacher: Good job. This means that Black is down the so-called exchange. Take into account White's extra pawn, and the exact equation reads unhappily for Black: White is up a rook and a pawn for a bishop.

Student: It's White's move, and he's got to find a way to convert his material superiority into a winning game. What should he do?

Teacher: Chess is, above all, a logical game. Things happen on the board as they are made to happen, not as chance or fate would have it. Organization and consistency are almost always rewarded. It may be difficult at first, but you must strive in every game to form a series of feasible plans and to implement them faithfully and economically. Often a bad strategy is better than none at all. If you lose because of a bad one, you can review afterward to see where you went wrong and how to improve next time. You can always use your loss as a learning experience. But if you've played without a plan, there will be little to learn from your defeat other than to play the next time with a plan of some kind.

Student: I'm still a little uncomfortable with strategizing.

Teacher: Your strategy at any point in the game needn't be elaborate. It could be something as basic as determining how best to complete your development, or on which side to castle and why, or whether to attack now or prepare your assault further by improving the position of one or more of your pieces. But whatever you design for your immediate chessic future, try to play in accordance with it. Make sure to have an objective in mind and conform your play to its requirements *and* the changing conditions on the board.

Student: I never know when to stay with a plan or when to change it.

Teacher: The ideal is to think ahead but to be flexible at the same time: You might have to modify your design. After all, if your planned objective is to do one thing, and suddenly your opponent alters the character of the position, allowing you to do something else that's more suitable, your situation should be supple enough so that you can switch gears appropriately. Don't be afraid to change your mind if you see a better idea or suddenly realize that you've committed yourself to the wrong campaign. At the same time, be sure there are justifiable reasons for changing your mind. If you want to win, don't change on a whim.

1. **Stay with a plan, unless you suddenly shouldn't.**
2. **No plan is set in stone.**
3. **Even a bad plan can be better than no plan at all.**

4. **Small plans can lead to big results.**
5. **Be willing to change your plan if you can see through your opponent's.**

Student: But I'm not yet able to look far ahead.

Teacher: You needn't strive to look very far ahead at first. A move or two will usually suffice to get you going until you get better at it. In fact, in most cases, we're just looking ahead a tad to see the consequences of our moves and how we're going to respond. As I mentioned during an earlier lesson, you should try to see at least three half moves ahead. A half move is a move for White or Black; a full move is a move for both White and Black together. This means, in considering your next move, you should also try to consider your opponent's likely reply, as well as your best response to that. Here's the rule of the three: *Try to see your move, then your opponent's move, then your move.*

Student: Now, let's talk turkey.

Teacher: In addition to being up the exchange, White also has an extra pawn. Specifically, it's a passed pawn at c2. The further the contest heads toward a nuts-and-bolts endgame, the more important this passed pawn will become.

Student: Could you go over that passed pawn stuff again?

Teacher: A *passed pawn* is a pawn that's free to move up the board toward promotion without an enemy pawn being able to stop its movement—that is, no enemy pawn can block it or guard a square in its path. A passed pawn is generally advantageous because it can produce a new queen. A pawn becomes passed when it actually passes beyond the capturing ability of the enemy pawns that might stop its advance, or when those enemy pawns are exchanged off or lured away. Passed pawns can be (1) ordinary, (2) outside, (3) protected, (4) connected, or (5) split.

Student: What is an outside passed pawn?

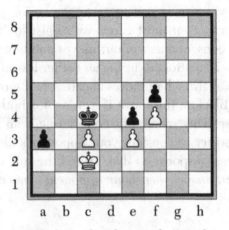

Diagram 328. Black wins by advancing his outside passed pawn.

Teacher: I thought you might ask that. An *outside passed pawn* is one that's positioned away from the main theater of pawns, free to move toward promotion. Threatening to become a new queen, it's typically used to decoy the enemy king to one side of the board, allowing the friendly king to invade on the other wing. The term often applies to endgames when each side has a passed pawn. The pawn "outside," or farthest away, confers advantage. It can often be sacrificed for greater gain elsewhere. So in diagram 328, Black to play wins by advancing his outside passed pawn, 1 . . . a2. White deals with that, 2. Kb2 a1/Q+ 3. Kxa1, but then Black eats White's own passed pawn, 3 . . . Kxc3 (diagram 329), and soon gobbles the remaining White pawns. He'll queen one of his own pawns shortly thereafter.

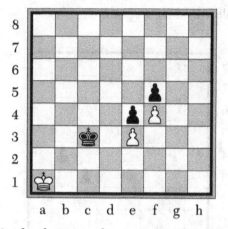

Diagram 329. After the winning line 1 ... a2 2. Kb2 a1/Q+ 3. Kxa1 Kxc3.

Student: I can see how from the position of diagram 329 Black's king is then going to clean out White's remaining pawns. What about a *protected passed pawn*? What's that?

Teacher: I thought you might ask that, too. Also known as a *supported passed pawn,* this is a passed pawn guarded by another pawn. A piece, whether knight, bishop, rook, or queen, can't capture the protected passed pawn without surrendering material, for it could then be recaptured by the protecting pawn.

Student: What's so good about it?

Teacher: The chief advantage of a protected passed pawn is that it frees friendly pieces from defensive chores and encourages them to pursue attack. They don't have to be tied down defending what's already solidly guarded by another pawn. In king-and-pawn endings particularly, a protected passed pawn restricts the defending king to a localized area. If the king wanders too far, say by capturing the back pawn—that is, the one that guards the lead passed pawn—the king might not be able to return in time to catch the lead pawn before it queens.

Student: Could you show an example?

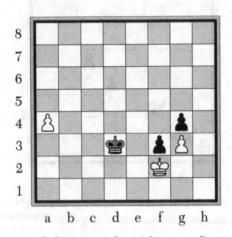

Diagram 330. Black's protected passed pawn at f3 insures the win.

Teacher: Consider diagram 330. It's Black's turn, though Black wins no matter who moves. The winning technique is simple: Black's king moves over to the a-pawn, wins it, and then comes back to the kingside to assist his own pawns in eventually producing a new queen. We're not going to run through all the reasonable variations, but I'm going to show you a sample one to provide you with a feel for what I'm talking about. I'm also going to give the moves without commentary. Just trust me when I say that both sides are making good moves. There are quite a number of them, but this way you can get some practice playing longer variations out on a board. As a test, see if what you play winds up looking exactly like diagram 331. Make sure to play out this test variation on your analysis board, not on your actual game board: 1 . . . Kc4 2. Ke3 Kb4 3. a5 Kxa5 4. Kf2 Kb4 5. Ke3 Kc3 6. Kf2 Kd3 7. Kf1 f2 8. Kxf2 Kd2 9. Kf1 Ke3 10. Kg2 Ke2 11. Kg1 Kf3 12. Kh2 Kf2 13. Kh1 Kxg3 14. Kg1 Kh3 15. Kh1 g3 16. Kg1 g2 17. Kf2 Kh2 18. Ke2 g1/Q (diagram 331). Note that at move 4 the White king was unable to attack Black's g-pawn with 4. Kf4 because that would have allowed the Black f-pawn to queen in two moves.

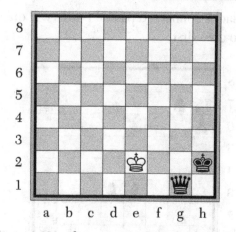

Diagram 331. After a test variation of eighteen moves ending in promotion.

Student: I'll save the test for later, if you don't mind, because something else is on my mind just now. Can you explain connected passed pawns?

Teacher: *Connected passed pawns*, also called *united passed pawns*, are two pawns on adjacent files that are both passed, so no enemy pawn can block them or guard squares in their path. Such pawns are free to advance toward promotion, assuming no enemy pieces can hinder them. They are particularly resilient if attacked, for they can defend each other: Whichever pawn advances is guarded by the pawn remaining a square behind.

Student: These sound really cool.

Teacher: You bet. Connected passed pawns can be extremely strong. When two of them occupy their sixth rank and confront a lone enemy rook, for example, unless there are immediate saving tactics or the defending king is close enough to lend a hand, the pawns are unstoppable. Attacked along the rank, either pawn can advance, threatening to make a new queen and effectively preventing the capture of the other. In diagram 332, at least one of Black's connected passed pawns will queen for sure, no matter who goes first.

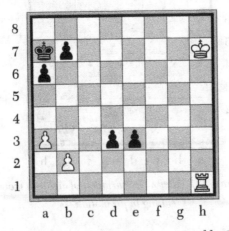

Diagram 332. Black's center pawns are unstoppable. One of them will queen for sure.

Student: Could you show another test variation for me to play out later? You don't have to explain all the side moves.

Teacher: Sure. This time, let's have White go first. A possible line for your analysis board might go: 1. Rh3 e2 2. Re3 d2 3. Rxe2 d1/Q (diagram 333), and Black's queen and pawn will eventually beat White's plain old rook.

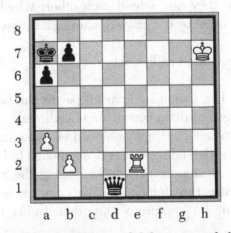

Diagram 333. After White's rook fails to cope with the pawns.

Student: It's amazing how helpless the rook was against those particular connected pawns. I might as well finish out your list. What are split passed pawns?

Teacher: *Split passed pawns* are two passed pawns of the same color, separated from each other by at least one file. Neither split pawn can be defended by a pawn and therefore both might be vulnerable to piece attack. In guarding them, friendly pieces may be forced to assume passive, defensive roles, losing scope and flagging into general inactivity.

Student: Are split pawns always a liability?

Teacher: Sometimes split pawns are more a weapon than a weakness, especially in pure pawn endings that do not include the presence of queens, rooks, bishops, or knights on the board. If both pawns are passed, and also within the enemy king's ambit, they can defend themselves by timely advances. As the opposing king attacks one of the pawns, the other can advance. If the attacked pawn is then captured, the other pawn advances unstoppably toward promotion. Diagram 334 provides an example.

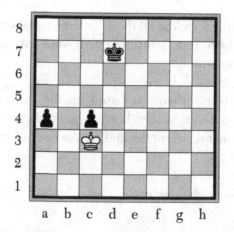

Diagram 334. Black to move: The split pawns can safeguard each other after 1 . . . a3.

Student: So those are split pawns. Why can't White's king simply capture the c-pawn and then catch Black's a-pawn?

Teacher: Because it's not White's move to start with. After Black continues with the push 1 . . . a3, White's king can't take the c-pawn and still get back in time to catch the a-pawn. A concluding line might go: 2. Kc2 Kc6 3. Kb1 c3 4. Ka2 c2 5. Kxa3 c1/Q+ (diagram 335).

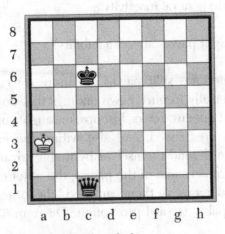

Diagram 335. After Black's c-pawn promotes.

Student: Okay. I'll look at all those specific variations later. But for now, could you just furnish me with some kind of endgame overview or something?

Teacher: Endgame theory is based on the conversion of an extra pawn into a win. Surely there are other factors that apply, such as basic mates, strengths and weaknesses of pieces, time, and so on.

Student: In some endgames we start off ahead by more than a pawn.

Teacher: Of course, in numerous theoretical and practical endgames, one side may have a material advantage greater than a single pawn. But the core of endgame theory has to be the methods and techniques for creating a passed pawn and advancing it to the promotion square, either to make a new queen or to force the defender into sacrificing a piece to stop the promotion. The extra piece should lead to a quick mate, win more enemy material, or help promote yet another pawn that will lead to mate. And if it doesn't result in any of this, well, there's always next game.

Student: Somewhere I've heard that unmoved pawns are considered strong in the endgame. Why is that?

Teacher: First of all, that's not always true. But sometimes unmoved pawns are easier to defend and, having remained on their original squares, have created no pawn weaknesses. But the chief value of an unmoved pawn is that it's still capable of moving either one or two squares, which can be a critical option at the right moment. On occasion, it can be desirable to take longer to do something, so that the other side must then respond in a way that commits to a losing strategy. By having to make a move, the other player loses because he must reveal his intentions or because he must move away from his true objective. In our game, White has a pawn majority on the queenside.

Student: Slow down, please. Could you once again say something about the pawn majority?

Teacher: As the name implies, a *pawn majority* is a numerically superior group of pawns. You have a pawn majority if, over any consecutive group of files, you have more pawns than your opponent does.

Student: Could you give an example?

Teacher: For instance, in diagram 336, White has a healthy queenside pawn majority. With sound play it can produce a passed pawn on the d-file. Meanwhile, Black's kingside pawn majority is unable to produce a passed pawn because of the doubled f-pawns. So it's as if White's up a pawn, even though in actuality he's not.

Student: When is a pawn majority considered healthy?

Teacher: A pawn majority is healthy if it consists of no doubled or backward pawns and can therefore produce a passed pawn. If one of the pawns in your majority is doubled, the value of your pawn majority is lessened because a single enemy pawn may be able to hold back your doubleton, which then functions as if it were one pawn. If your opponent has a healthy majority elsewhere on the board, even though the position might be materially even, you could be, in effect, a pawn down.

Student: Let's say I wind up with a passed pawn as a result of correctly advancing my pawn majority. Then what?

Teacher: Once a healthy pawn majority produces a passed pawn, the pawn should be advanced, or prepared for advance,

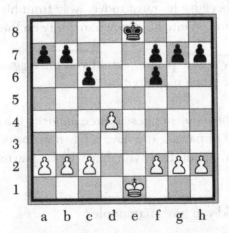

Diagram 336. White's queenside pawn majority is healthy. Black's kingside pawn majority is ineffective.

with the eventual threat of promoting. This is possible because no enemy pawn can block the passed pawn's advance or guard a square over which it must pass. Since no enemy pawn can stop your passed pawn, the enemy pieces will have to do the job, which forces them to assume defensive roles. This should increase the power and possibilities of your own pieces, which may be able to pursue their own plans unimpeded. If only kings and pawns remain, a passed pawn can signify an even greater advantage. It can be used to lure away the enemy king, so that other important individual pawns or groups of pawns might become totally indefensible to your marauding king. Such a passed pawn is known as a *decoy*.

Student: A decoy. I like that. So how should one best mobilize a pawn majority?

Teacher: Start the mobilization by advancing the unopposed pawn first, a technique classified as Capablanca's Rule, after José Raúl Capablanca, the third champion of the world (1921–27). He emphasized this principle in several of his books. The *unopposed pawn*, also known as the *candidate passed pawn* or even simply the *candidate*, has no enemy pawn occupying its file.

Student: Could you show me a concrete example?

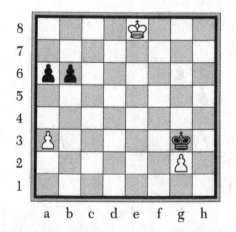

Diagram 337. Black wins by advancing the unopposed pawn first, 1 . . . b5.

Teacher: Black wins in diagram 337 by advancing the b-pawn first, 1 . . . b5, adhering to Capablanca's Rule. A possible conclusion might then be: 2. Kd7 a5 3. Kc6 b4 4. axb4 axb4 5. Kc6 b3 6. Kc5 b2 7. Kc4 b1/Q (diagram 338), and surely Black will win.

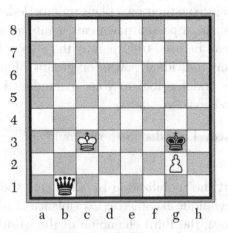

Diagram 338. After Black has made a queen.

Student: Would it be unwise for Black to instead push the a-pawn first, 1 . . . a5 (diagram 339)?

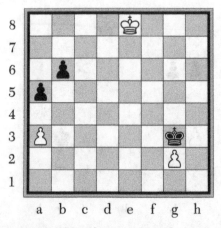

Diagram 339. After the erroneous advance 1 . . . a5.

Teacher: Absolutely. After 1 . . . a5, White can stop Black in his tracks with 2. a4 (diagram 340), and Black's queenside pawns aren't going anywhere in particular after that.

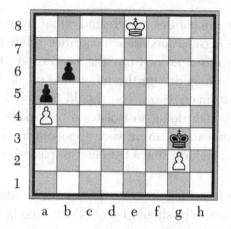

Diagram 340. After 1 . . . a5 2. a4, stopping Black's queenside pawns.

Student: What about if Black then sacrifices his b-pawn to create a passed pawn? Could you provide me with a sample variation to check out later?

Teacher: Sure. One possible conclusion might then be: 2 . . . b5 3. axb5 a4 4. b6 a3 5. b7 a2 6. b8/Q+ (diagram 341). Can you handle it from there?

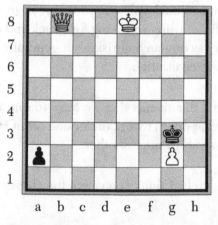

Diagram 341. After White queens with check.

Student: I sure hope so! Since we've been talking about pawn majorities, is there anything I should know concerning how they usually arise?

Teacher: Pawn majorities are created either by exchanging or by sacrifice. Kingside/queenside majorities often result when one player captures away from the center, which may give the opponent a majority on the other side of the board. This explains why, in many cases, you should take back toward the center even though doing so isolates a rook-pawn. Capturing toward the center may prevent your opponent from obtaining a workable pawn majority and a treacherous passed pawn.

Student: One last thing, for now: The endgame seems to rely a lot on king usage. Why should I seclude my king in the opening but activate it in the endgame?

Teacher: Okay. I'm happy to go over this again in greater detail. In the opening, you usually have to castle to get your king behind a wall of pawns, just for safety. If not, your king might be subjected to a fierce assault from numerous enemy attackers, since the center is likely to be open or may suddenly become so. But in the endgame, many of the enemy pieces—especially the queen—have been exchanged off the board, and the chance that a quick mating attack will sink your king is greatly reduced. Thus the benefits of using your king for attack and defense tend to outweigh the accompanying risk, so it generally makes sense to bring it back to civilization.

Student: I guess this means that we have to question absolute thinking, that what doesn't work under one set of circumstances might work admirably under another.

Teacher: Absolutely. I think you've got the chessic picture.

Student: That depends.

Teacher: On what?

Student: Our final lesson, of course.

All Good Things Come to an End

THE SEVENTH RANK, INVASION, AND SIMPLIFICATION

Teacher: I know I've mentioned this before, but it never hurts to repeat a principle, so long as you don't become enslaved to it. The correct strategy when ahead in material is to trade off pieces, accentuating your advantage and making it harder for the enemy to offset your extra force. It's also important to take note of what the difference in force really is.

Student: If you should have an advantage, as White does in this game, of a rook and a pawn for a minor piece, how should you generally proceed?

Teacher: You should use any greater mobility you may have gained to attack and force your opponent to play defensively. Keep up the pressure, eke out as much as you can from the position, and at the right moment, if you can't really make further progress, be willing to sacrifice your rook for the minor piece to simplify to a winning endgame. The trade-down usually works if in the process you win a pawn, which can then be made into a new queen.

Student: Here, White is already up a pawn.

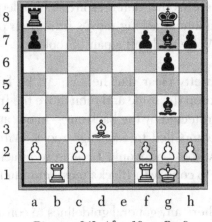

Diagram 342. After 18 . . . Rxa8.

Teacher: Exactly. So winning another pawn would put him up two pawns, and two is much greater than one. To best feel the effects of being up the exchange, it would make sense to exchange a pair of rooks, leaving Black only his bishops. White's remaining rook would then have no counterbalancing force.

Student: Other than the possibility of driving away Black's light-square bishop by a move like h3, what are the targets White should be shooting for?

Teacher: Possible attack points include a7 and f7. Now White can hit the a-pawn only with his rooks. Conceivably, he can do so from along the a-file, the seventh rank, or a combination of both. The f-pawn can be attacked by both rooks along the seventh rank. The f7-square can also be approached by White's bishop along the a2-f7 diagonal, most likely from c4. Black can defend the a-pawn with his rook, as long as it's not driven away, say by Be4, or traded off, and by the dark-square bishop from d4. The f-pawn can be guarded by the king, the rook from f8, and the bishop from e6.

Student: So it seems that defenses are so far adequate, but is it possible to combine attacking moves from both plans into one scheme? Can White trade off a pair of rooks?

Teacher: It's pretty clear that he can. All he has to do is to double his rooks on the b-file and then move the front one up to b8, where it's protected by the back one—in our analysis, on b1. Black is then compelled to exchange rooks. With White then having the only rook, he would be able to attack more freely without having to cope with Black's most important defender.

Student: Are there any general guidelines to consider?

Teacher: A number come to mind with regard to the rooks. White already has a rook on the open b-file, uncontested, which means that White controls the b-file. After occupying an open file, the next thing a rook should endeavor to do is reach its seventh rank. The seventh rank, the next-to-last rank on the board from either player's perspective, is a terrific place for a rook.

Student: I'm a little confused. In algebraic notation, the seventh rank is the second row in from Black's side of the board. Here, you seem to be using the term differently.

Teacher: We're not doing notation. We're talking about perspective. True, when a white rook moves to its seventh rank, we're referring to the rank on which the black pawns begin the game. When a black rook moves to its seventh rank, however, we mean the rank on which the white pawns start. The meaning in this case depends on the relevant perspective, and has nothing to do with the use of the number seven in algebraic notation. By occupying the seventh rank with a rook you can confine the enemy king to the board's edge and simultaneously blitz a row of several pawns because all the unmoved pawns remain on that rank. Many games are decided by such an incursion. Sometimes, in order to dominate an open line, or to insure the invasion, one has to double rooks, which strictly speaking is not necessary here, though we have discussed that possibility.

Student: Remind me, please. What are doubled rooks?

Teacher: *Doubled rooks* refers to a situation in which a player's rooks line up on the same row, so they defend and support each other. Whether in attack or defense, on a rank or file, such a battery presents the possessor with rich tactical possibilities.

Student: I think you mentioned batteries earlier, but I've forgotten what you said about them.

Teacher: A battery is a double force, with two friendly pieces of like power attacking in unison along the same rank, file, or diagonal. Rank or file batteries consist of two rooks, two queens on rare occasions, or a rook and a queen, with either piece being first in line. Diagonal batteries sport a bishop and a queen or two queens, which can only come about after a pawn is promoted to an extra queen. A battery is two-ended, in that threats can emanate in either direction along the line of attack, and either piece may capture with its partner's support. Either way, it can be assault and battery.

Student: Let's say my rook occupies the seventh rank. How can I intensify the pressure?

Teacher: Double your rooks on the seventh rank! If one is good, two must be twice as good. Two rooks on the seventh is almost always a winning advantage, since it then becomes easier to gain material by supported capture. Moreover, if the opposition's king is confined to its home rank, it's also easier to deliver checkmate. The secret here is to play flexibly, so that White can somehow achieve all ends of the plan, or at least retain all the options. So what do you want White to play?

Student: I'm going to play **19. Rb7** (diagram 343).

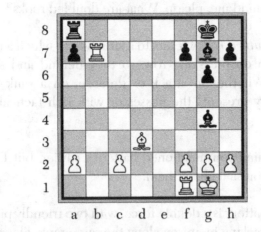

Diagram 343. After 19. Rb7, seizing the seventh rank.

Teacher: A nice decision. White has established a beachhead with this incursion into the heart of the Black terrain. He now is presenting Black with several serious threats. One is to double rooks on the b-file by playing Rfb1, preparing to exchange rooks. Another is to attack f7 again with 20. Bc4, which only results in further trades after 20 . . . Be6 21. Bxe6 fxe6. After the light-square bishops are exchanged, the seventh rank is even more exposed and vulnerable.

Student: Maybe, in anticipation of White's planned bishop redeployment to c4, Black should play **19 . . . Be6** (diagram 344), seizing the a2-g8 diagonal before White does.

Teacher: Let's go with it. Black plays **19 . . . Be6.** This defends the f-pawn and also prevents White's bishop from assuming a

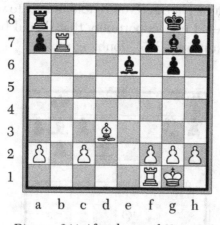

Diagram 344. After the actual 19 . . . Be6.

commanding post at c4. Moreover, it seems to counterattack by targeting the White a-pawn. White could save this pawn by moving it out of attack, but that would cost him time. If he's going to execute his plan efficiently, he really shouldn't be making unnecessary pawn moves. For reasons that will soon become clear, the a-pawn is immune anyway. To take it would leave Black open to a trap.

Student: The term *trap* has a more specific chess meaning, doesn't it?

Teacher: Yes, it does, as we discussed earlier. If you're lured into a line of play that seems to be good but really isn't, you have fallen for a trap (see page 56). The most familiar traps occur in the opening when unsuspecting opponents capture easily attained material. Take the material and, if it's a trap, you'll find that capturing boomerangs against you. Although the present situation no longer involves the opening, there's a booby trap waiting for Black. Let's see if you can find it. What move would you like to suggest?

Student: I've got a plan, and you've told me not to veer from my plan unless I see a new opportunity that should be seized. I'll play **20. Rfb1** (diagram 345), doubling rooks.

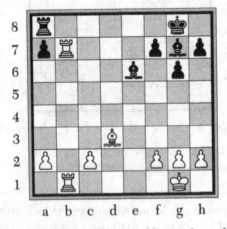

Diagram 345. After 20. Rfb1, doubling rooks on the b-file.

Teacher: Good move, which we shall analyze shortly. But first, consider this. If Black wanted to, he could now avoid an imme-

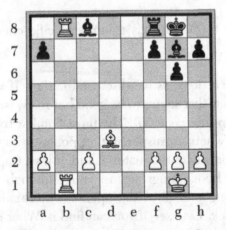

Diagram 346. After the possible line 20 . . . Rf8 21. Rb8 Bc8.

diate trade of rooks by playing 20 . . . Rf8. If White were then to continue 21. Rb8, as per his plan, Black could interpose his bishop at c8 (diagram 346).

Student: Would this delay matters for very long?

Teacher: Not really. White would soon be able to double rooks on the eighth rank or, if necessary, use the open king- or queen-files to penetrate the Black position. Sooner or later, Black would have to make further concessions, or lose more material, or a combination of both. The end result would be the same: Black would lose, but only if White were to find the right, or essentially right, moves.

Student: I shouldn't assume, of course, that my opponent is going to find the right moves.

Teacher: Actually, good players always assume their opponents are going to find the right moves. This way, they're always covered for any contingency. Even a bad player can play a good move, if only by accident. That doesn't mean you can't hope for your opponent to make a mistake. You just can't bet the ranch on it. There are times when you should play with hope, and that's when you're losing "hopelessly." If in a losing position you can muster the courage and wherewithal to fight on, you might be rewarded—if not in the game at hand, later on, in a subsequent game, by virtue of the experience acquired in playing out difficult positions, even those you might have lost. Russian world champion Alexander Alekhine once said that to win against him you had to beat him three times: "Once in the opening, once in the middlegame, and once in the end-game." Perhaps the final word on this should be that of grand-master Saviely Tartakover (1887–1956). The Russian-born writer and teacher once said: "No one ever won a game by re-signing."

Student: Black might as well then try **20 . . . Bxa2** (diagram 347), gobbling the offered a-pawn. The capture also attacks White's rook at b1.

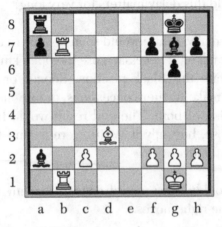

Diagram 347. After the actual capture 20 . . . Bxa2.

Teacher: But White doesn't have to break his flow and respond to the threat, mainly because his own threat comes first. White can continue as planned with **21. Rb8+** (diagram 348).

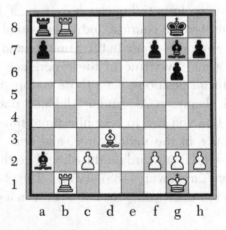

Diagram 348. White continues as planned, 21. Rb8+.

Student: I'm not certain that Black has to take White's b8-rook. Maybe he could instead try 21 . . . Bf8. If White then captures Black's rook, 22. Rxa8, then Black's light-square bishop can capture White's other rook, 22 . . . Bxb1 (diagram 349).

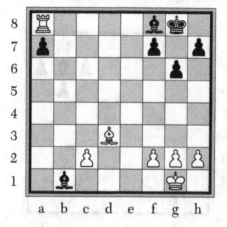

Diagram 349. After the possible line 21 . . . Bf8 22. Rxa8 Bxb1.

Teacher: Fine, but then push your analysis a step further. In this imaginary line, after Black takes the rook at b1, White's rook captures the queen-rook pawn, 23. Rxa7 (diagram 350), with a nasty threat to trap the b1-bishop by Ra1.

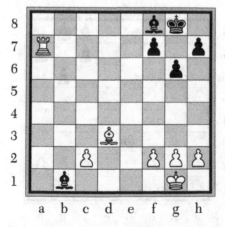

Diagram 350. After the continuation 23. Rxa7.

Student: That seems like good thinking, but even rational thought sometimes can't overcome the forces of nature. I see your threat in this line, to play Ra1, trapping my b1-bishop. But I can stop you from safely playing your rook back to a1 by guarding that square with 23 . . . Bg7 (diagram 351).

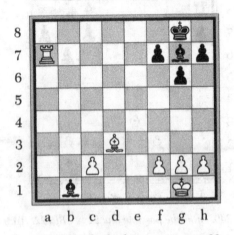

Diagram 351. After the further continuation 23 . . . Bg7.

Teacher: But it doesn't work, because with 24. Ra8+, White can force the dark-square bishop back to where it was, 24 . . . Bf8, so that a1 would no longer be guarded. At that point, White goes

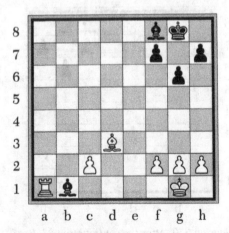

Diagram 352. After 24. Ra8+ Bf8 25. Ra1, and Black's bishop gets trapped after all.

ahead with his idea, **25. Ra1** (diagram 352), as if Black hadn't done anything, and traps the b1-bishop after all.

Student: Very persuasive. So let's assume Black does take White's b8-rook immediately, **21 . . . Rxb8** (diagram 353).

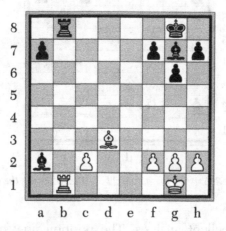

Diagram 353. After the actual 21 . . . Rxb8.

Teacher: And let's further assume that White takes back, **22. Rxb8+** (diagram 354).

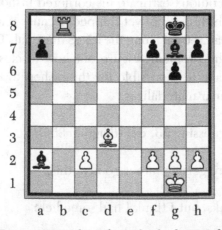

Diagram 354. After White takes back, 22. Rxb8+.

Student: I think it's clear that here Black has only one legal move. He has to play **22 . . . Bf8** (diagram 355).

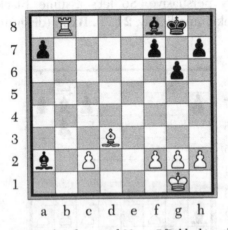

Diagram 355. After the actual 22 . . . Bf8, blocking the check.

Teacher: Excellent analysis. The position now poses a final problem. White is still up the exchange, but he lost back his extra pawn when Black's light-square bishop captured on a2. The difficulty with so many captures like Bxa2 is they often lead to the bishop being trapped. One famous example occurred during the first game of the Fischer-Spassky match in 1972, when Fischer couldn't extricate his cornered bishop satisfactorily. Here, the bishop is not yet trapped because if attacked, say by 23. Rb2, it can retreat along the a2-g8 diagonal. This suggests a solution to the problem: Figure out how to close the a2-g8 diagonal, to make it impossible for the bishop to retreat. One move in particular materializes.

Student: I'm guessing **23. c4!** (diagram 356).

Teacher: You're getting rather good at this.

Student: Thanks, but I think I had some help.

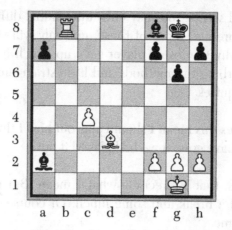

*Diagram 356. After the actual 23. c4!, trapping Black's
light-square bishop.*

Teacher: There is now no way that Black can extricate his
bishop safely. White will capture it in two moves, beginning with
24. Rb2. See how the well-placed rook currently prevents the
dark-square bishop from assisting in a possible defense of the
key b2-square by pinning the dark-square bishop to the king.
Ahead by practically a whole rook after this, White should have
little trouble bringing home victory, assuming he employs the
principles as well as you have apparently learned them.

Student: Does this mean that we reach a consensus? Does
Black resign?

Teacher: Why don't we simply agree that White wins and Black
loses—for instructional purposes?

Student: I'm still wondering something, though. How can I get
better at playing the endgame without having to study too much?

Teacher: There is no royal road to learning. But a good way to
improve your technique is to play out positions in which players
have already resigned, trying to imagine how the play would go

from the final setup. You may encounter initial difficulties, but as you do more and more of these, not only will you begin to understand why the losing player gave up, you'll naturally find yourself absorbing the methods and little stratagems that good technique requires.

Student: Does this mean I should play out how I think our little game would have gone if we had played it out?

Teacher: Yes, that is precisely what I mean. But do it after I leave. I need a break and some lunch. Of course, you're welcome to join me.

Student: It depends.

Teacher: On what?

Student: The restaurant.

EPILOGUE

Chess = mc²

Chess has amused kings and monks, court ladies and noble knights, lovers and enemies. It has become the pastime of mere tots whose feet are yet to reach the ground and wizened wizards whose eyes see the wisdom of the ages. Over the centuries, the universal game has earned aficionados in every country. Look into a time—any time in the last 1,500 years—and you'll find a chessiac there.

Great champions have brought the game more attention in recent decades. Modern technology has helped chess reach a larger public by making it more accessible and entertaining. What can we expect from the future? More of the same, only more so.

Before Bobby Fischer's meteoric rise, chess was often dismissed as an eccentric intellectual pursuit. That changed in 1972, when the brash American wrested the world championship from Boris Spassky in Reykjavík, Iceland. The media dramatized the event for a global audience. Back in the United States, chess suddenly became proof that Americans could beat the Russians at their own game. Immediately after Fischer's win, sales of books and chess sets doubled, clubs could hardly handle the number of new members applying, and sponsors discovered that chess was worthy of endorsement.

Computers gave the discipline another jump-start. Algorithmic chess began as far back as 1950, when applied mathematician Claude E. Shannon proposed the search and evaluation strategies that computers still use to generate moves. But it took decades to develop really powerful chess programs. In the 1980s, players could finally test their ideas in competition against machines, learning from the electronics on the desk about the pieces on the board.

By the turn of the last century, everyone with access to the right software could play against stellar opposition. Students without entrée to a chess master or a chess club no longer had to depend on tomes filled with numbers, charts, and diagrams. Suddenly, they could learn on screen, not by drudgery, but by the productive use of leisure time. Learning while playing electronically, players could begin to pave their own road to chess success with a click of a mouse.

Nowadays, we face the tantalizing possibility that the next world champion could be someone introduced to chess anywhere, from hamlet to metropolis. He or she could start by playing right at home or in a small school library, with access to an intelligent apparatus and the game's boundless horizon.

Artificially intelligent devices may also have helped improve the ratio of male to female players. Increasingly, women are contributing to the development and appreciation of the game worldwide. We can attribute this transformation partly to conscious egalitarian efforts. But it can't be denied that computers make it easy to study and practice in a gender-free environment. The computer deals in data. It conveys information disinterestedly. It doesn't care who you are.

These days we wage chess war with computers that can identify and recognize patterns, calculate faster, and adjust plans far more quickly than any human mind ever could. Some fear all that mechanical genius. Has the arrival of computerized chessplayers meant the inevitable departure of human ones? Surely not. And where would they go, anyway?

But while computers have altered the way students can

acquire chess knowledge, they haven't entirely changed where or how players play. Chessters still look for casual contests in the park. They still gather in the living room to set up the board. They still flock to chess clubs after work or on weekends. And they still enter tournaments in their spare time. The computer doesn't stop any of that. It just multiplies the raw power of chess exponentially. Why should such an obvious increase in opportunity lead to a decrease in actual participation?

The sport has flourished in recent years due to the determined efforts of charismatic champions like Garry Kasparov and Vladimir Kramnik. They have used computers to promote chess—not just the computer version but the game itself, however it's played. When he took on IBM's Deep Blue in 1997, Kasparov knew he was playing to a long-standing and historical interest in combat on any front between humans and machines. When Kramnik confronted Deep Fritz in 2002, he knew he was carrying the same trusty standard into the cutting edge of brain-battle.

Grandmaster against Machiavellian machine? That's the stuff of science fiction books and films, the *2001* series all over again. The two K's vs. the two metal minds made chess a totally compelling story. They accomplished what Fischer's match against Spassky had two decades earlier, and surely what Dr. Schach's match against Cyber Creature will two centuries later.

Computer programs catapulted chess to remote Andromeda when the Internet arrived. Today, devotees with or near a Web connection can luxuriate in a 24/7 right of entry to what will certainly become an interplanetary game. As we approach 2004, over half a million chess match-ups occur daily on the Internet route. Wherever it leads, who wouldn't want to take such a fascinating and revealing journey?

A plethora of Internet sites now offer seminars, interactive lessons, analyses, literature, and even special tricks to fool people into thinking they're not playing a machine. These days you don't have to wait weeks for the results of important tournaments. You can follow games on the Internet as they're happening. Theory is evolving as a consequence. When a grandmaster now tries a new opening over the Internet, players can get instant feedback, thanks to the system's lightning evaluations. Onlookers can predict the likely outcome long before the grandmaster sees his next move.

The Internet is a perfect venue for developing self-confidence, too. The Net shields players from personal conflict and the emotional tensions of tournament travail. Users grow intrepid, willing to take chances. They speculate, and the game profits. Chess has become more tactical, more creative.

Chess relies on transformational thinking, analytical drive, and the intuitive good sense to work out the way things really work. It's the multipurpose, all-meaning game. Chess is part of us and part of what we do, no matter who we are or how we structure our lives.

So join the universe. Now that you've learned the fundamentals and promise of chess, you can play the one game with potential enough to bring us all together, human and nonhuman. To get going, just set up a set, or click it on. Better yet, have an entity do it for you.

APPENDIX 1

Glossary

Advantage. Any superiority.

Analysis. An examination and assessment of moves and position.

Attack. A potential capture; loosely, to threaten. If you are in line to capture, that's an attack. If you are in line to capture with advantage, that's a threat.

Basic Mates. Four different checkmates brought about by a team of pieces against the lone enemy king. They are king and queen vs. king; king and rook vs. king; king and two bishops vs. king; and king, bishop, and knight vs. king.

Battery. A tactical force; two friendly pieces attacking in unison along the same line, such as a queen and a bishop on a diagonal; or a queen and a rook or two rooks along a file or a rank.

Bishop. The piece that moves only on diagonals. Each side has two of them: a light-square bishop and a dark-square bishop.

Black. The player who moves second at the start; initially, the defender; the darker-colored pieces.

Blunder. A serious mistake, typically one that changes the evaluation of the position.

Calculation. Analyzing specific sequences of moves, as opposed to general judgments.

Castle. To move the king and rook on the same turn, usually to safeguard the king and activate the rook.

Center. The middle four squares and surrounding area.

Checkmate. The end of the game, when the king would be captured next move.

Combination. A forced sequence of moves, usually involving sacrifice, leading at least to a clear improvement in position if not a win.

Counterattack. An attack mounted by the defender; to do so.

Defender. Player or unit under attack; Black at the start.

Defense. A protection or response to attack; Black's opening.

Develop. To move a piece to a better place or improve its scope by moving impeding pawns out of the way.

Development. Preparing pieces for action by either transferring them to better squares or moving pawn obstacles out of the way.

Diagonal. A slanted row of same-colored squares.

Discovered Attack. A type of tactic; another term for discovery.

Discovery. A type of tactic, moving a unit to unveil another unit's line of attack; also called discovered attack.

Double Attack. Any multiple attack with potentially serious consequences. Most tactics involve double attacks or threats.

Double Check. A type of tactic, a discovery in which both the moving and stationary attackers give check.

Draw. A game where neither player wins. The most common way to draw is by agreement. Other ways include stalemate, threefold repetition, perpetual check, the 50-move rule, and insufficient mating material.

Elements. Features of the position that can be evaluated to determine which side stands better. Mainly time, space, material, pawn structure, and king safety.

Endgame. The third and final phase of a chess game, revolving around pawn promotion.

Ending. Another word for endgame. Endgame is used more to describe the phase; ending is used more to refer to specific positions and situations in the endgame.

En Passant. A French term meaning "in passing." It's a rule of the game that signifies a particular type of pawn capture; also used to describe that type of capture.

En Prise. A French term meaning "in take." It refers to a situation where a unit can be captured for free; also, the actual capture itself.

Exchange. Equal trade; also, difference in value between a rook and minor piece.

Exchange Values. The relative values of the pieces.

File. A vertical row of squares.

Force. The element of material; also, to control the opponent's moves.

Fork. A type of tactic where one unit attacks two or more enemy units simultaneously; also, to give such a tactic.

Fundamentals. Moves, rules, and basic principles.

Gambit. A voluntary sacrifice in the opening, usually of a pawn.

Grandmaster. The highest official title.

Illegal. Against the rules.

Illegal Move. A move that can't be played. It violates the rules and must be replayed.

Initiative. The ability to attack and control the play.

King. The piece both sides are trying to trap and capture. It moves one square in any direction.

Knight. The piece that moves like a capital L. It moves in any direction.

Legal. Referring to a permissible move or position.

Legal Move. A move that can be played.

Line. Any rank, file, or diagonal; also, a sequence of moves.

Lose. To get checkmated, resign, forfeit on time, or be disqualified.

Lost Game. A game that should lose even with best play.

Major Piece. A queen or a rook.

Maneuver. Repositioning of a piece.

Master. An unofficial title for a strong player.

Match. A set of games between the same players or teams.

Mate. Short for checkmate.

Material. An element; the pieces and pawns collectively or individually.

Middlegame. The second phase of a chess game.

Minor Pieces. Bishops and knights.

Mobility. The freedom and ability to move.

Move. A turn for either side.

Open File. A file with no pawns on it.

Opening. The beginning phase of a chess game.

Open Line. A rank, file, or diagonal unobstructed by pawns.

Pawn. The weakest and most numerous unit; a symbol for helplessness. It moves one square straight ahead, but has a two-square option on its first move. It captures one square diagonally ahead.

Pawn-Grabbing. Taking pawns riskily.

Pawn Structure. An element; all aspects of pawn placement and dynamics.

Piece. Either a king, a queen, a rook, a bishop, or a knight, but not a pawn.

Pin. A type of line tactic in which a friendly piece attacks a shielding enemy unit that can't move without exposing another enemy unit or important square.

Plan. A general course of action; a strategy.

Positional. Concerned with small points and long-term effects.

Positional Advantage. Any non-material advantage.

Positional Chess. A style of play that aims to accumulate small but safe advantages, first advocated and developed by Wilhelm Steinitz.

Principle. A general truth, guideline, or piece of advice.

Promotion. Changing a pawn into a new piece.

Queen. The most powerful piece, able to move in any straight line.

Queening. Promoting a pawn to a queen.

Rank. A horizontal row of squares.

Removing the Defender. A type of tactic; the same as removing the guard.

Removing the Guard. A type of tactic in which an enemy unit's defender is removed by capture, leaving it inadequately protected; also called removing the defender and undermining.

Resign. To give up before being checkmated.

Rook. The piece that moves horizontally or vertically.

Sac. Short for sacrifice.

Sacrifice. A voluntary surrender of material.

Simplify. To avoid complications and trade pieces.

Skewer. A type of line tactic where a friendly unit attacks an enemy unit, forcing it off line so that another enemy unit or important square can be captured or exploited.

Space. The element concerned with territory and mobility.

Stalemate. A game drawn when the player to move is not checkmated but has no legal move.

Strategy. General thinking; opposite of tactics.

Tactics. Specific threats; opposite of strategy.

Tempo. Move as a unit of time.

Threat. Move that must be heeded.

Threaten. To attack in a serious way.

Time. The element concerned with the initiative.

Tournament. A contest in which a number of players compete.

Trade. An exchange of equal material; also, to make such a transaction.

Trap. A tricky way to win; also, to snare a piece.

Trapped Piece. A piece that can't get to safety and is in danger of being won.

Undermining. A broad type of tactic. It involves either removing a unit's defender, driving the defender of the unit away, or rendering it incapable of fulfilling its function.

Unit. Any piece or pawn.

Variation. Any sequence of moves.

Visualization. The ability to see possible moves in one's head.

Weakness. Usually, a hard-to-guard pawn or square.

White. The player who moves first at the start; initially, the attacker; the lighter-colored pieces.

Winning. Having an advantage that should win.

Won Game. A game that should be won with best play.

X-ray Attack. A type of line tactic in which a friendly unit joins up with another friendly unit by attacking beyond and through enemy unit along the same line.

Zwischenzug. A German word meaning "in-between move." It refers to an unexpected move inserted within a sequence that affects the initially assumed consequences.

Zugzwang. A German word meaning, roughly, "compulsion to move." It refers to a situation where the player must move and worsen his situation.

Alekhine's Defense	1. e4 Nf6
Benko Gambit	1. d4 Nf6 2. c4 c5 3. d5 b5
Benoni Defense	1. d4 Nf6 2. c4 c5 3. d5
Bird's Opening	1. f4
Budapest Defense	1. d4 Nf6 2. c4 e5
Caro-Kann Defense	1. e4 c6
Catalan Opening	1. d4 Nf6 2. c4 e6 3. g3 d5
Center Counter Defense	1. e4 d5
Center Game	1. e4 e5 2. d4 exd4 3. Qxd4
Dutch Defense	1. d4 f5
English Opening	1. c4
Four Knights Opening	1. e4 e5 2. Nf3 Nc6 3. Nc3 Nf6
French Defense	1. e4 e6
Giuoco Piano	1. e4 e5 2. Nf3 Nc6 3. Bc4 Bc5

Grüenfeld Defense	1. d4 Nf6 2. c4 g6 3. Nc3 d5
King's Gambit	1. e4 e5 2. f4
King's Indian Attack	1. Nf3 2. g3 3. Bg2 4. d3
King's Indian Defense	1. d4 Nf6 2. c4 g6 3. Nc3 Bg7 4. e4 d6
Larsen's Opening	1. b3
Modern Defense	1. e4 g6
Nimzo-Indian Defense	1. d4 Nf6 2. c4 e6 3. Nc3 Bb4
Orangutan Opening	1. b4
Petrov's Defense	1. e4 e5 2. Nf3 Nf6
Philidor's Defense	1. e4 e5 2. Nf3 d6
Pirc Defense	1. e4 d6
Queen's Gambit	1. d4 d5 2. c4
Queen's Indian Defense	1. d4 Nf6 2. c4 e6 3. Nf3 b6
Reti's Opening	1. Nf3
Ruy Lopez	1. e4 e5 2. Nf3 Nc6 3. Bb5
Scotch Game	1. e4 e5 2. Nf3 Nc6 3. d4
Sicilian Defense	1. e4 c5
Slav Defense	1. d4 d5 2. c4 c6
Two Knights Defense	1. e4 e5 2. Nf3 Nc6 3. Bc4 Nf6
Vienna Game	1. e4 e5 2. Nc3

Do an advanced search using the words chess, play and tournaments, and your results will be staggering. In early 2003, around 50,000 hits turn up. Rather than kill a forest listing them all here, I chose ten top sites for good mention. These sites also include links to related sites (and their links will lead you to others) for opportunities to play, study, read, or just chat about chess.

For Play

www.chessclub.com—Internet Chess Club (ICC)
www.freechess.org—Free Internet Chess Server (FICS)
www.iecg.org—International E-mail Chess Group (IECC)
www.iccf.com—International Correspondence Chess Federation (ICCF)

For News and Commentary

www.chesscenter.com/twic/twic.htm—The Week in Chess
www.chesscafe.com—The Chess Café
www.chessbase.com—Chessbase Net
www.bcmchess.co.uk/news/events.html

For Everything

Including anything from archived games to today's tournament schedules, on-line lectures, products, and more.

www.uschess.org
www.LetsPlayChess.com
www.chessworld.net

APPENDIX 4

World Champions

Wilhelm Steinitz, Austria 1886–1894
Emanuel Lasker, Germany 1894–1921
José Raúl Capablanca, Cuba 1921–1927
Alexander Alekhine, Russia 1927–1935, 1937–1946
Max Euwe, Netherlands 1935–1937
Mikhail Botvinnik, Soviet Union 1948–1957, 1958–1960, 1961–1963
Vasily Smyslov, Soviet Union 1957–1958
Mikhail Tal, Soviet Union 1960–1961
Tigran Petrosian, Soviet Union 1963–1969
Boris Spassky, Soviet Union 1969–1972
Bobby Fischer, United States of America 1972–1975
Anatoly Karpov, Soviet Union 1975–1985
Garry Kasparov, Russia 1985–2000
Vladimir Kramnik, Russia 2000–2003

4000 B.C.	Earliest board games known at Ur in Iraq
1500 B.C.	Egyptian game of *senat* developed
300 B.C.	First 8 x 8 board
500 A.D.	Chess probably created in Indus Valley
600 A.D.	*Chataranga* appears in Persia
625–640 A.D.	First reference to chess in literature
660 A.D.	Arabs assimilate chess
850 A.D.	First Arabic writings on chess
1008 A.D.	First European reference to chess
1062 A.D.	Earliest Italian reference to chess
1066 A.D.	Chess introduced into Britain
1100 A.D.	The board becomes checkered
About 1400 A.D.	The counselor is feminized into the queen, making the weakest piece the strongest
1474 A.D.	First book ever published in English is a chess book: Caxton's *Game and Playe of the Chesse*
1497 A.D.	Luis Ramirez de Lucena publishes *Repeticion de Amores y Arte de Axedres*
1550 A.D.	First chess clubs organized in Italy
1575 A.D.	World's first chess tournament in Madrid
1748 A.D.	François-André Danican Philidor publishes *L'analyze des Echêcs*
1769 A.D.	Chess automaton "The Turk" appears
1786 A.D.	Benjamin Franklin publishes *The Morals of Chess*
1813 A.D.	First newspaper column on chess
1851 A.D.	First international chess tournament, won by Adolf Anderssen, a German mathematician

1858 A.D.	Paul Morphy wins the most famous chess game of all time at the Paris Opera
1866 A.D.	Wilhelm Steinitz of Austria declares himself world champion
1886 A.D.	First official world championship won by Steinitz in New York
1925 A.D.	Aron Nimzowitch publishes *My System*
1927 A.D.	Alexander Alekhine dethrones José Raúl Capablanca in Buenos Aires in 34 games, the first truly great and modern chess match
1938 A.D.	The A.V.R.O. tournament is held in Holland, possibly the strongest such event ever
1946 A.D.	Alekhine dies with the title, the only champion ever to do so
1948 A.D.	Mikhail Botvinnik of the Soviet Union takes Alekhine's title in a special tournament
1950 A.D.	The first computer chess algorithms are developed by mathematician Claude Shannon
1956 A.D.	Thirteen-year-old Bobby Fischer of Brooklyn plays the game of the century at the Marshall Chess Club
1969 A.D.	Fischer publishes *My Sixty Memorable Games*
1972 A.D.	Fischer defeats Boris Spassky in Reykjavík, Iceland, in the single greatest chess spectacle of all time
1975 A.D.	Anatoly Karpov of the Soviet Union is named world champion when Fischer fails to defend his title
1985 A.D.	Garry Kasparov of Russia beats Karpov to become world champion
1992 A.D.	First chess site on the Web: Internet Chess Server (ICS)
1993 A.D.	The movie *Searching for Bobby Fischer* is released, greatly popularizing the game throughout the United States
1997 A.D.	Kasparov loses a landmark six-game match to IBM's Deep Blue computer
2000 A.D.	Vladimir Kramnik of Russia defeats Kasparov to become the fourteenth world chess champion
2002 A.D.	Kramnik and the commercial chess program Deep Fritz tie an eight-game match
2003 A.D.	Kasparov draws a match with Deep Junior

Like a chess player, he cared more for the process than the result.
> **Fyodor Dostoevsky**

I think one reason why chess appeals so much to musicians is that playing it is like composing.
> **Mischa Elman,** violinist

Life is a kind of chess.
> **Ben Franklin**

Chess is the touchstone of the intellect.
> **Johann Wolfgang von Goethe**

I played Dr. Franklin at chess, and was equal to him at the game.
> **Thomas Jefferson**

Chess is a cure for headaches.
> **John Maynard Keynes**

A person of integrity does not take a dive for any reason whatever. Do your homework during the evening and play chess with friends.
> **Ann Landers,** replying to a teenager who wanted to appease his
> father by losing to him at chess (February 1964)

Whoever moves his hand and does not draw back is a great man.
> **Chinese proverb,** inscription on chessboards

So long as it [mathematics] remains pure, it is a game, like solving chess problems.

> **Bertrand Russell,** *The Art of Philosophizing*

It's the fairest of all games.

> **Isaac Bashevis Singer,** responding to a question about chess

Spock: A very interesting game, this poker.
Kirk: It does have its advantages over chess.

> *Star Trek,* "The Corbomite Maneuver"

Chess is the game that reflects the most honor on human wit.

> **Voltaire**

Chess in the Movies

2001: A Space Odyssey
Blade Runner
Blazing Saddles
Casablanca
From Russia with Love
Harry Potter and the Sorcerer's Stone
Monkey Business
The Seventh Seal
The Thing (1982)
The Thomas Crown Affair (1968)

Movies about Chess

Black and White Like Day and Night
Chess Fever
Dangerous Moves
Fresh
Searching for Bobby Fischer
The Chess Players
The Great Chess Movie
The Luzhin Defense
The Mighty Pawns
The Tournament

Chess in Classic Literature

Allen, Woody	"The Gossage-Vardebedian Papers"
Beckett, Samuel	*Endgame; Murphy*
Borges, Jorge Luis	"The Game of Chess"
Burroughs, Edgar Rice	*The Chessmen of Mars*
Carroll, Lewis	*Through the Looking-Glass*
Clarke, Arthur C.	*2001: A Space Odyssey*
Doyle, Arthur Conan	"The Adventure of the Musgrave Ritual"
Eliot, T. S.	"A Game of Chess" (in "The Waste Land")
Faulkner, William	"Knight's Gambit"
Fleming, Ian	*From Russia with Love*
García Márquez, Gabriel	*Love in the Time of Cholera*
Joyce, James	*Portrait of the Artist as a Young Man*
Kawabata, Yasunari	*The Master of Go*
Nabokov, Vladimir	*The Defense*
Orwell, George	*1984*
Poe, Edgar Allan	"Maelzel's Chess-Player"
Pound, Ezra	"The Game of Chess"
Tolstoy, Leo	*War and Peace*
Vonnegut, Kurt	*All the King's Horses*
Zweig, Stefan	"The Royal Game"

The Most Famous Chess Game of All Time

The following contest is the most famous one in chess history, even though it was a casual game played on the friendliest of terms. It was played in September of 1858 at the Paris opera, between acts of The Barber of Seville. *White was Paul Morphy and Black consisted of a team of two players, the Duke of Brunswick and Count Isouard, who consulted and advised each other throughout.*

	White	**Black**	**Comment**
1W.	e2-e4	. . .	A king-pawn opening.
1B.	. . .	e7-e5	A double king-pawn defense.
2W.	Ng1-f3	. . .	Attacking Black's e-pawn.
2B.	. . .	d7-d6	Philidor's Defense.
3W.	d2-d4	. . .	Threatening the e5-pawn again.
3B.	. . .	Bc8-g4	Pinning the f3-knight.
4W.	d4xe5	. . .	Essentially forcing Black's response.
4B.	. . .	Bg4xf3	Reducing the threat to e5.
5W.	Qd1xf3	. . .	Taking back by developing.
5B.	. . .	d6xe5	Re-establishing material equality.
6W.	Bf1-c4	. . .	Threatening mate at f7 with the queen.
6B.	. . .	Ng8-f6	Shielding f7 from the queen.
7W.	Qf3-b3	. . .	Giving a double attack to f7 and b7.
7B.	. . .	Qd8-e7	At least guarding f7.
8W.	Nb1-c3	. . .	Developing and stopping a queen check at b4.
8B.	. . .	c7-c6	Guarding b7 with his queen.
9W.	Bc1-g5	. . .	Developing and pinning the f6-knight.
9B.	. . .	b7-b5	Hoping to end the threat to b7.

10W.	Nc3xb5	...	A knight sac to keep the initiative.
10B.	...	c6xb5	Taking the knight to win material.
11W.	Bxb5+	...	Taking with the least valuable unit.
11B.	...	Nbd7	Blocking the check, but self-pinning his knight.
12W.	0-0-0	...	Castling queenside to pressure the d7-knight.
12B.	...	Ra8-d8	Adding protection to the pinned d7-knight.
13W.	Rd1xd7	...	Taking with the rook to keep the pin.
13B.	...	Rd8xd7	Taking back to avoid material loss.
14W.	Rh1-d1	...	Piling up on the pinned d7-rook with a new piece.
14B.	...	Qe7-e6	Offering a queen trade and unpinning the f6-knight.
15W.	Bb5xd7+	...	Taking the rook and clearing the b-file for use.
15B.	...	Nf6xd7	Taking back and guarding b8.
16W.	Qb3-b8+!	...	The most famous move in the history of chess.
16B.	...	Nd7xb8	A forced capture, but exposing the d-file.
17W.	Rd1-d8#	(1-0)	Black is checkmated.

Black is way ahead in material but it doesn't matter. He's checkmated. White developed and used all his pieces. In the end, only two remain: the dark-square bishop at g5 and the rook at d8. They give the mate. That's perfect economy of means and aesthetically most pleasing. A truly great teaching game. No wonder it's so remembered and so loved.

BIBLIOGRAPHY

Bell, Robert Charles. **Discovering Old Board Games.** Shire Publications Ltd., 1973.

Davidson, Henry A. **A Short History of Chess.** David McKay Company, 1981.

Hooper, David, and Kenneth Whyld. **The Oxford Companion to Chess.** Oxford University Press, 1992.

Murray, Harold J.R.A. **A History of Chess** (1913). Oxford University Press, 1978/Benjamin, 1985.

Pandolfini, Bruce. **Let's Play Chess.** Fireside, 1986.

———. **Principles of the New Chess.** Fireside, 1986.

———, (ed.). **The Best of Chess Life and Review,** vols. 1 and 2. Fireside, 1988.

———. **Pandolfini's Chess Complete.** Fireside, 1992.

ACKNOWLEDGMENTS

In writing this book, I had valuable help from members of the Carolina Chess Academy: I would like to acknowledge American Master Matthew Noble and Professor Ralf Thiede for creating the chess diagrams. Ralf also prepared the manuscript for submission. I am especially grateful to editorial consultant Dr. Barbara Thiede for her dedicated fine-tuning and creative energy; they made the book complete. We also had a chessic test reader, the Thiede's son Erik, who had a knack for asking the very questions I did not realize I had left open.